onlus 80p

G000245676

THE CANALS OF
EASTERN ENGLAND

THE CANALS OF THE BRITISH ISLES

EDITED BY CHARLES HADFIELD

THE CANALS OF
EASTERN ENGLAND

by

John Boyes
and Ronald Russell

WITH PLATES AND MAPS

David & Charles

Newton Abbot London North Pomfret (Vt) Vancouver

ISBN 0 7153 7415 X

Library of Congress Catalog Card Number: 77-89388

© JOHN BOYES and RONALD RUSSELL 1977
All rights reserved. No part of this publication may be repro-
duced, stored in a retrieval system, or transmitted, in any form
or by any means, electronic, mechanical, photocopying, recording or otherwise, without the prior permission of David &
Charles (Publishers) Limited

Printed in Great Britain by
Redwood Burn Limited, Trowbridge & Esher
for David & Charles (Publishers) Limited
Brunel House Newton Abbot Devon

Published in the United States of America
by David & Charles Inc
North Pomfret Vermont 05053 USA

Published in Canada
by Douglas David & Charles Limited
1875 Welch Street North Vancouver BC

CONTENTS

LIST OF ILLUSTRATIONS

PLATES

TEXT ILLUSTRATIONS AND MAPS

CHAPTER 1

Introduction

++◆++++++++++++++++++++++++++++++++++++

THE geographical concept of Eastern England can be defined according to the requirements of the subject. For the purposes of this book an arbitrary decision was made that the area to be included would be bounded by the Humber estuary in the north, the North Sea on the east, and the Thames estuary in the south, while the western boundary would be a line northwards from the Thames leaving the Lee valley to the east, and then continuing to the east of the line of the Grand Union Canal and its branches, to the east of the Grantham and Oakham Canals, and touching the Trent only at Torksey so that the Trent itself would be excluded, but the Fossdyke included. This area therefore covers the whole of the old counties of Essex, Suffolk, Norfolk, Huntingdon, Cambridgeshire, almost all Lincolnshire, and parts of Hertfordshire, Bedfordshire, and Northamptonshire, those parts of England not covered in previous volumes in the 'Canals of the British Isles' series. Ronald Russell has written Chapters VI, VII, VIII and IX, John Boyes the remainder.

While accepting the broad definition of the area the purist might well cavil at the title of the book in relation to its content. *The Canals of Eastern England* was used in conformity with the titles of the other volumes in the series. Yet, while it may be argued that there are very few true canals in Eastern England, the way its canalized river navigations and their traffic developed was analogous to canal systems elsewhere in the country. To change the title for the last volume of the series therefore seemed to offer no great advantage.

The pattern of development of inland navigation in this region was dictated by two basic factors, the physical characteristics of the area, and the absence of any great industrial conurbations to stimulate internal trade in heavy goods, as did Birmingham, Liverpool, Manchester or Leeds. The whole area from the Thames to the Humber has for centuries been involved in an agriculturally orientated economy and the main motive for trade has been the need to export agricultural products in return for the essential needs of the population. The relatively sluggish flow of the rivers encouraged this type of trade, by providing a highway for goods in areas where the marshy and clayey ground made land transport virtually impossible. Thus the origins of transport on the great rivers of the region, the Lee, Ouse, Nene and Welland, go back deep into history. And with such natural facilities available it is little wonder that rivers were used and improved rather than that time and money should be spent on planning and digging new canals which would be unlikely to provide any great financial return.

The reliance on natural watercourses led to the development of a series of isolated navigations instead of an integrated canal system as is found in the Midlands and the North of England. As the only means of passing from one of the eastern navigations to another was in many cases the open sea, or at best the estuarine portions of the Humber and the Thames, the types of vessel which developed were of a kind which could navigate in tidal waters as well as on the inland waterways and so the keels, wherries, and barges of the east are distinct types with different and special characteristics from the barges and narrow boats found elsewhere in the country. It is not the purpose of this book to deal with the technical design of these vessels, but it must be borne in mind that the interaction between the vessels and the navigations played its part in the history of eastern waterways.

It is also fundamental to the study of the waterways, particularly of Cambridgeshire and Lincolnshire, to remember that many of them were never primarily navigations even though they might carry a considerable amount of traffic. Their prime function was, and is, drainage and while it is difficult to disentangle the drainage from the navigation interest, the dominating concern throughout the history of the fens has been drainage. The cleavage time and time again has been between those who wanted to drain the land to improve it and those who opposed drainage on the grounds that it would deprive them of their livelihood, or that it would not yield the advantages claimed for it. The advantages of navigation might be used as an argument in the debate, but the central theme was always drainage. This was especially so in the case of the lower Ouse, Nene, Welland, and the Ancholme, for these rivers, particularly the first two, drain vast tracts of England far remote from their main navigable portions. In fact, as Defoe comments, 'All the water or most part of the water of thirteen counties falls into them'. And it was drainage that dictated to a great extent the pattern of the waterways.

It was this same dual concern, with the emphasis also on drainage, which led the Romans to carry out their civil engineering works on the Fossdyke, between Torksey and Lincoln, and on the Car Dyke in its great sweep round Cambridgeshire and Lincolnshire, so that the waters from the upland areas would be carried away more effectively to the sea instead of feeding the low lying lands round the Wash. In these early constructional activities we have the first recorded efforts in this country to tame natural water resources and use them to economic advantage, the advantage here being the availability of the drainage channels for transport purposes. In the centuries which followed, the use of water transport fluctuated with the pressing needs of the time, as for conveying heavy goods such as stone for the building of abbeys and churches; a need which could be translated into action by the power of the monastic establishments. But there was little known effort consciously to effect any lasting improvement to the waterways themselves.

Occasionally charters were granted, or authorizations given for special improvements, or commissions appointed to deal with a particular local problem, but it was not until 1424 that the first act of parliament was passed dealing with an individual waterway. This concerned the river Lee and so created a precedent which could be followed as the need arose elsewhere in the country. However, like most precedents, it was not followed immediately by a spate of legislation but rather the number of acts passed increased slowly, and at first intermittently, reaching a maximum in the eastern counties during the eighteenth century. These eighteenth-century acts belong mainly to the period of river improvements which preceded the canal age proper, although the canal mania elsewhere had its local effects in the eastern counties. Interest in water transport diminished, though it did not disappear, during the nineteenth century and into the twentieth. In fact the latest new canal to be dug in the United Kingdom, albeit a very short one, was opened in 1968 and provided a link between the Limehouse Cut, itself part of the river Lee system, and the then Regent's Canal Dock, now Limehouse Basin. It is perhaps coincidental that the first act and the latest canal should both be associated with the same river, but the 500-year span of its development reinforces the theme of the continuing importance of water transport.

The decline of commercial traffic on the waterways of eastern England was brought about by the development of rail transport in the nineteenth century and has been hastened by road improvements and the growth of door-to-door transport by twentieth-century road vehicles, but it has not disappeared altogether. Laden lighters can still be seen being towed along the Lee; barges still navigate the Ancholme to Brigg; and seagoing vessels still make their way to Norwich, King's Lynn, Wisbech and other places; but on the majority of those waterways which are still navigable it is leisure cruising which holds sway. Holidaymakers in their turn have realised that the eastern rivers pass through delightfully scenic stretches of countryside, just as John Constable recognised the essential nature of England and perpetuated the beauty of the river Stour in his immortal landscapes of the Essex—Suffolk border.

Eastern England does not have the dramatic, mountainous topography of other parts of the country and therefore there are few outstanding engineering works, but the waterways have a character that one only appreciates when one gets to know them intimately. But once that character is known, it becomes part of one's life, impossible to lose, pleasantly haunting both waking and sleeping, a realization that here is the essential England that gives every hope for the future.

CHAPTER II

The Lee and Stort

++◆++++++++++++++++++++++++++++++++++++++

River Lee

'Let the bounds of our dominions stretch to the River Thames and from thence to the water of Lee even unto the head of the same water'
(Treaty of Wedmore between King Alfred and the Danes, AD 879)

THE River Lee rises in the high ground near Luton on the western boundary of Hertfordshire and then flows eastward through Hertford to Ware. There it suddenly turns south and forms the eastern boundary of Hertfordshire and the old county of Middlesex with Essex. After splitting into a number of different channels between Homerton and Stratford in east London it reunites and drains into the Thames through Bow Creek. The lower reaches, between Hertford and the Thames, constitute one of the oldest navigations in the country. The date when vessels first navigated the Lee is lost in the mists of antiquity, for there is evidence of a lake dwelling community of the middle to late Bronze Age with an associated dugout canoe in the marshes of Walthamstow. And in the same marshes there were also found the remains of a Saxon barge. These remains are clearly associated with social and commercial utilization of the river. The value of the Lee as a means of defining the boundary of the Danelaw in the Treaty of Wedmore and the record of King Alfred's stratagem involving the stranding of the Danish fleet in AD 896 as quoted in the *Anglo-Saxon Chronicle* illuminate the early importance of the river. It is evident from these gossamer threads that boats have been employed on the Lee for over 2,000 years. The spelling 'Lee' is the one adopted in legal documents and for the official title of the river. 'Lea 'is used in other connections—eg Lea Valley, Lea Bridge.

The first contemporary written record of commercial activity is to be found in a licence given on 9 September 1190, or less likely 1191. In translation it reads

W. [presumably William Longchamp] by the Grace of God, Bishop of Ely and Chancellor of the Lord King, to the Sheriff of Essex; Know that we have given permission to the Abbot of Waltham to turn aside the course of the water of the Lee in the Town of Waltham as he wishes without harming anyone and for the advantage of navigation and therefore we order you to allow him to do this without impediment.[1]

A few years later a water conduit was being laid from Wormley in Hertfordshire to Waltham Abbey and the account of its construction includes the following comment:

They reached the great river with the water pipe . . . In the morrow of the decollation of Saint John [30 August 1221] they dug a ditch in the bottom of the great river transversely to a depth of two feet more than in the neighbouring land and in this they placed a long and strong pipe stretching beyond the river . . . they strengthened it and made it safe lest the pipe should be harmed in any way by the oars or poles of the watermen passing.[2]

These quotations show interest in navigation on the Lee even at this early date; this interest was further emphasized two hundred years later when, in 1424, there was passed the first act in this country for improving the navigable state of any river.[3] In this and the subsequent Act of 1430 commissions composed of local landowners were appointed to arrange for the scouring and improvement of the river and authorized to levy tolls to raise the necessary finance.[4]

So began the legislative control over the Lee which, in one form or another, has continued to the present day. When the river deteriorated, protests and petitions prodded the courts and the legislature into re-examining existing conditions and authorizing new measures to ease the traffic

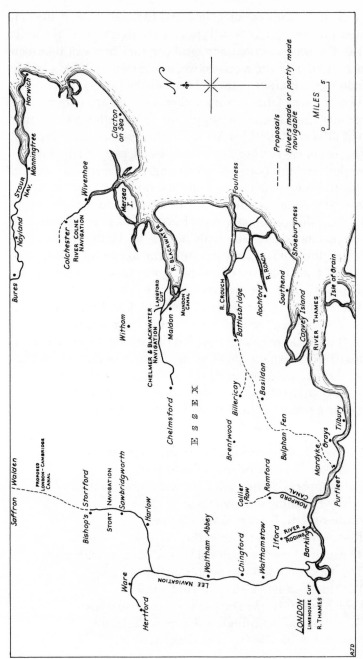

1. The Essex Navigations

flow. These inquiries, detached and judicial, related to such matters as the loads and types of goods carried, the tolls levied, the wages of boatmen, and disputes between boatmen and millers over their respective water rights. They provide valuable information about activities on the Lee.

The concern of the City of London to ensure an adequate and constant supply of grain to supply the metropolis led to another Act of 28 May 1571.[5] This Act also indicates that conveyance of both passengers and goods was then taking place on the Lee, for it empowered the Lord Mayor to improve the navigation and make additional cuts with walks on each side. No work was apparently done on a proposed cut from the river to the north side of London but shoals were cleared and a new cut with toll-free rights for barges was made nearer the Thames. It is probable that this cut was that section of the Lee between what are now Old Ford locks and Bow locks, also known as Bow river, which continues to retain its toll-free privileges.[6]

The conflicting demands of bargemen and millers over a limited water supply which was being extravagantly used to work flash-locks may well have led to the construction at Waltham Abbey of what is possibly the second pound-lock in England, the first on a river, and probably the first with mitre gates. The description of this lock is delightfully and graphically portrayed in a poem by Vallans, 'A Tale of Two Swannes', written in 1590.

Downe all along through Waltham street they passe
And wonder at the ruines of the Abbey
Late suppress'd, the walles, the walkes, the monuments,
And everie thing that there is to be seene.
Among them all a rare devise they see
But newly made, a waterworke, the locke
Through which the boates of Ware doe passe with malt.
This locke contains two double doores of wood
Within the same a cisterne all of Plancke
Which only fills when boates come there to passe
By opening of these mightie doores with sleight
And strange devise, but now decayed sore.

Apparently the construction was not particularly effective as the lock is described as both 'newly made' and 'decayed sore'. It was built in 1577 and was 70ft long × 24ft broad. Each side was composed of ten planks 70ft × 1ft × 3in and there were two gates at each end.

During the late sixteenth and seventeenth centuries there was a series of acrimonious, and at times violent, disputes between various parties. One was between the maltmen of Enfield, who claimed the right to carry malt to the London brewers by road, and the Lee bargemen, who claimed the right to carry it by water. In this case the bargemen appear to have come off best. Others were between the bargemen and the millers, and between the bargemen and the toll-owners. These disputes have left a legacy of documents which shed light on the day-to-day working of the navigation.

Despite their contentious ways the bargemen performed a very useful function and in 1665, the year of the great plague, they conveyed provisions to supply the citizens of London. In return for these services, often rendered at risk to themselves, they were granted special privileges, eg to navigate the Thames without the assistance of a Thames lighterman.[7]

Meanwhile a new threat to the navigation was just beginning. The growth of London's population in Elizabethan times posed the problem of an adequate water supply and in 1608 Hugh (later Sir Hugh) Myddleton, a City alderman, started to build at his own expense what was to be known as the New River to convey water from springs at Amwell and Chadwell, near Ware, through a contour channel to London. This great work, some 40 miles long because of its circuitous route, was completed in 1633. Very soon it was found that the flow from the springs was unable to keep pace with the growing demands of London and by the mid-seventeenth century it became necessary to abstract water from the Lee to maintain the service. This was bound to affect both millers and users of the navigation, and by the beginning of the eighteenth century it was clear that even a partial solution would require an act of parliament. It was this step that brought control of the river into its modern form.

Parliament was petitioned on 10 March 1736/7, based on an agreement worked out between the New River Company, Hertford Corporation, the inhabitants of Ware, maltsters, barge-owners, and farmers. It recognised the right of the New River Company to abstract water from the Lee, but laid down financial arrangements and stated the rights of the millers and the navigation. Between Hertford and Ware the Lee divided into two or three branches which reunited below Ware mill. The ancient channel was along what was known as the Manifold Ditch but the New River's staunch and feed had obstructed that route, so the navigation had been carried on for many years through the millstream to Ware mill and then through a lock. The New River Company agreed to purchase Ware mill and the lock and dedicate the millstream as a right of way. The route through the Manifold Ditch would then be abandoned. In parenthesis it might be mentioned that the lock at Ware is still owned by the Thames Water Authority, as successors to the Metropolitan Water Board, which absorbed the New River Company.

These arrangements were incorporated in the Act of 14 June 1739,[8] which also established a new pattern of control over the navigation. Instead of the old system of *ad hoc* commissions, which had not proved satisfactory where continuous and detailed oversight was necessary, a body of trustees was appointed to control the navigation through officers responsible to them.

The first general meeting of the new trust was held on 6 August 1739 at the Old Crown Inn at Ware and there the Act was formally read.[9] The first staff were also appointed. Bostock Toller of Hertford was to be clerk and would be paid £1 1s for attending each meeting and also reasonable charges and expenses. Thomas Martin was appointed receiver and treasurer. At their second meeting, this time at the Four Swans at Waltham Cross, the trustees decided to carry out a survey of the river between Hertford and Ware.

For this they called on William Whittenbury of Hertford, a carpenter, who had previously surveyed the river in 1733. Whittenbury later tendered for the erection of a flash-lock and his tender, which was accompanied by a model, was accepted. He must have created a good impression on the members of the trust, because by 4 August 1740 he was being referred to in the minutes as surveyor to the trust and not as carpenter. On the other hand there does not appear to have been any formal appointment of him as surveyor. He continued to serve until his death in 1757 when he was succeeded by John Clark.

A rather odd situation presented itself in 1741 when the trustees acting as commissioners received a complaint from one of the bargemen. They felt that the case was in such disorder that guidance ought to be given in the method of presentation but they were unsure how far they were legally able to assist. The question was referred to the Attorney General who expressed the opinion that the trustees could assist complainants by this form of legal aid to ensure that the matter was properly heard by themselves sitting as commissioners.

Another early problem which faced the trustees was the difficulty of navigation through Broxbourne Gull where barges frequently went aground. John ffrench, the occupier of Broxbourne mills, was averse to any alteration in the Gull but the trustees, after examining the site, decided that a flash-lock would not interfere with the mills and instructed their surveyor, Whittenbury, to draw up plans. These specified that the flash-lock should be 34ft wide with four gates. There would be one gate of 14ft for barges and three other gates of 6ft 8in each. The gates were to pen back 4ft 6in of water above the sill which in turn was to be 1ft 3in below the surface of the back water. The apron of the flash-lock was to be 24ft long, ie 12ft above the gates and 12ft below, framed out of single planks. There was to be a wheel and rolls to draw up the gates

> with friction wheels of iron in iron frames running on centres of tempered steel for the moving parts of the increased powers of the Great Wheel to move on and ease its motion.

The wheel was to be enclosed in a house to protect it from the weather and to prevent interference from passers-by. The flash-lock was completed and opened on 21 December 1741.

Slowly the navigation was improved, although there was still

the intractable dispute between millers and users of the navigation over their respective rights to the water. By the 1760s it became obvious that the trustees would have to acquire greater
powers if the navigation was to become reasonably efficient.
Therefore on 5 August 1765 John Smeaton was requested to
make a survey 'so as to settle the navigation on a new plan as
will be most conducive to the good of the public'. A second
request was made on 16 July 1766 and on this occasion Thomas
Yeoman was to assist. Yeoman, who had earlier been concerned with such navigations as the Nene, Stroudwater, Ivel
and Chelmer & Blackwater, was acting at this stage as a con-
sultant with Smeaton, and was later on 1 July 1767 appointed as
surveyor to the navigation.

Smeaton reported in September 1766. He summarized the
navigation's defects before proceeding to make recommendations for its improvement. He pointed out that as the
navigation was developed before the invention of locks or pen-
sluices with double pairs of gates it was not surprising that it was
defective. He recorded that there were flashes from eighteen
weirs and staunches, as well as a lock at Ware, and tide-gates
at Bromley (improperly called a lock) plus a cistern or lock
occasionally used at Hackney waterworks. He then recommended that a number of new cuts should be made, including
one from near Bromley lock to the Thames at Limehouse, and
cuts at Hackney, Edmonton and Waltham Abbey. With these
cuts and the replacement of the flash-locks with pound-locks
Smeaton estimated that a barge could travel from Bromley to
Hertford at an average speed of something over two miles per
hour.[10]

On the basis of this report the trustees petitioned Parliament
for an Act, but counter-petitions were entered by the trustees of
the Shoreditch to Enfield turnpike road, the proprietors of West
Ham waterworks, and the Waltons, the proprietors of the Waltham Abbey Gunpowder works, all on the grounds that the new
proposals would materially affect their rights. Royal assent was
given on 29 June 1767 and two days later on 1 July 1767 the new
trust held its first meeting at the Rose and Crown, Enfield.[11]
There new officers were elected, among whom was Thomas

Yeoman, surveyor and collector.

At this meeting, too, Yeoman was given his first instructions. He was to make a cut from Flanders weir, Chingford, to the tail of Walthamstow mill stream and so cut off some of the bends; to extend the navigation upstream from Folly bridge, Hertford, to the flood-gates of Hertford town mill; and to make preliminary investigations into the cutting of a new Limehouse section. The first of these projects was the start of what was later to become the Edmonton Cut. Within the next three months Yeoman was given many more tasks, including setting out the towing paths and giving directions for the construction of 35 towing bridges as well as reporting how best to make the cut from Bromley to Limehouse, the lock-gates and other works, and determining work priorities.

The construction of the Limehouse Cut was to claim a great deal of the trustees' time and concern during the next three years. On 14 September 1767 they agreed that Yeoman's proposed cut from Dingley's Wharf on the Thames at Limehouse to the Lee above Bromley lock would not only be useful but would also add to the safety of navigation by giving access to the Thames above the Isle of Dogs. Negotiations to buy the necessary land began almost immediately and the contract for cutting the channel was made with Charles Dingley, one of the trustees, at 10d per foot for the length between the Thames and Rose Lane and with Jeremiah Ilsley, a brickmaker from Hackney, for the remainder at 7d per foot. In order to get a costing for the lock into the Thames Mr Collard, another of the trustees, agreed to make a model and plan and on the basis of Collard's design the cost was estimated at £1,547 approx. After this had been agreed it was discovered that Collard had made his model and plan 16ft short, thus requiring a supplementary estimate of £149. By 1769 barges were being admitted to part of the cut and by May 1770 the work was so far advanced that the date of opening the complete canal was announced for 2 July 1770. There is no record in the minutes that the cut was opened on that date, for within a week there were still dams across the waterway because 60ft of brickwork had given way and fallen into the canal. This was quickly repaired and on 17 September

1770 the cut was opened throughout. Three weeks later the labourers who had worked on the cut were moved to begin work on the Edmonton Cut. But troubles on the Limehouse Cut were not over. On 22 December 1770 the bridge near the Windmill Field, Limehouse, collapsed into the cut and once more traffic was obstructed. Despite occurrences such as this traffic steadily increased so that in May 1772 a passing place was made. Even this was not sufficient, so in March 1773 it was decided to widen the Cut to allow two barges to pass each other anywhere. It was not, however, until June 1776 that the contract was let to Jeremiah Ilsley for £975, the work to be completed by 1 September 1777.

Meanwhile the trustees had decided to finance their improvements by raising a loan of £35,000. They advertised for subscribers in the *London Gazette* and other papers in September 1767, with the result that £161,500 was offered. Allocation was therefore by ballot. Most subscribers were from London and Hertfordshire and yet, while applications were received from places as far away as Chester, Whitby, and Cornwall, there were none from Essex.

The trustees, with extra capital available, were now able to arrange for work to start on the various cuts. Jeremiah Ilsley was awarded the contract for the Waltham Cut on 12 December 1767 and for the Hackney Cut on 18 January 1768, in both cases at 3d a yard. Since on 23 April 1768 he had also agreed to dig part of the Limehouse Cut at 7d per yard, Ilsley seems to be moving into the sphere of the public works contractor, for the time allowed for the Hackney Cut (four months) together with his other work must have necessitated a fairly substantial labour force.

Pressure was on other contractors too. Henry Holland, bricklayer, of Half Moon Street, Piccadilly, was given the contract to build the locks on the Waltham Cut on 26 December 1767 and on 23 April 1768 to build two locks on the Hackney Cut. Mr Cooper of Bromley, millwright, was instructed on 22 October 1768 to build Bromley lock and those between Newmans weir and Tottenham mills on the Edmonton Cut: Mr Scott of Cheshunt, carpenter, on the same date agreed to build

Broxbourne lock. All these contracts were to be completed by 1
March 1769. This suggests a tight schedule of work considering
that the construction was to be carried out by the last two contractors during the six winter months. The schedule, nevertheless, seems to have been well kept, for the cut from King's Weir
to Waltham Abbey was opened for barges passing up river on
Monday 20 March 1769 and in both directions on 3 June 1769;
and the Hackney Cut was opened for up and down traffic on 7
August 1769.

During this period the trustees realised that Yeoman was
being saddled with too much work for, on 25 February 1769,
Edward Rubie was appointed as his assistant at £80 pa plus £21
removal expenses from Portsmouth. As will be seen later,
Yeoman was also engineer to the Stort Navigation at this time
and as that navigation was opened on 24 October 1769 the Lee
works benefited it also. Yeoman continued as surveyor until
about the end of July 1771 when he apparently resigned, no
reason being given in the minutes.

This period of intensive activity following the 1767 Act resulted in the construction of about 11 miles of new cuts and at
least 12 new locks, some of which replaced existing flash-locks,
eg Stansted lock, while others were on the new cuts, eg Homerton and Picketts locks. The longest cut was the 5 miles of the
Edmonton Cut, followed by Limehouse Cut (1½ miles) and
Hackney Cut (2 miles) but perhaps the most interesting feature
was the construction of Aqueduct lock and the aqueduct over
the Cheshunt Mill stream on the three-mile-long cut between
King's Weir and Waltham Abbey.

For the next ten years maintenance and improvement of the
navigation continued without any major work being undertaken, but in 1779 the trustees' financial state gave rise to considerable concern. After thoroughly examining the accounts
they felt the practice of letting out by contract the care of the
navigation in different districts was undesirable.

The committee were concerned that the average outgoing for
7¾ years was £1,476 pa, yet 'notwithstanding these heavy
expenses the navigation is in such a state as to require a repair
of upwards of £2,600. It is therefore incumbent on the trustees

most seriously to think of putting their affairs on a much more economical footing. Whether this is done by the appointment of a standing committee of accompts this committee does not presume to determine.' One of the items criticized in the accounts was the large amount spent on liquor for the labourers and carpenters. Power to levy additional tolls and make other financial adjustments was included in another Act which received the Royal assent on 31 May 1779.[12]

One of the interesting outcomes of this self-examination was the preparation of a job specification for the surveyor:

1. To receive the Tolls from the collectors every week and pay the same to the Bankers every fortnight (except in such weeks in which the four Quarter Days may happen in which cases to receive and pay the Tolls up to such Quarter Days) or within three days afterwards, and to keep an Account of the Tolls received up to every Quarter Day; always examining the Collector's Book with the Bills of Lading and the Passage and Lading of Barges from one Collector's Book to another.

2. To report any irregularities and contraventions to the meeting.

3. To make a fortnightly survey and report on the navigation.

4. To make regular inspections and rectify minor defects up to a cost of £5 for any one instance.

5. Not to carry out new works or make alterations without sanction of the meeting.

6. Only to pay bills on the authority of the meeting.

7. Only to take orders for work at the meeting.

8. To ensure that the navigation is kept in repair and report any defects to the meeting.

9. To see that the mills, weirs, and tumbling bays, maintain their correct water levels.

10. To prevent as far as possible all stoppages on the navigation.

11. To supervise work carried out by others.

12. To attend the trustees meetings and receive such orders

are from time to time necessary.

Benjamin Lewis, who had succeeded Yeoman in 1771, was made the scapegoat for the unsatisfactory state of affairs and he was dismissed in December 1779, though he was retained temporarily to explain and show the navigation to his successor. He was also to prepare an inventory of the tools and materials belonging to the trust. His successor was John Glynn of Bishop's Stortford who was appointed at £120 pa, one of whose first tasks was to repair almost every lock. The navigation's ability to cope with a steady increase of traffic from this time suggests that the standard of maintenance improved.

Table showing annual toll receipts averaged over periods of five years

	£		£		£
1772–76	3,480	1797–1801	10,282	1817–21	12,920
1777–81	6,160	1802–06	11,079	1822–26	12.229
1782–86	8,297	1807–11	10,995	1827–31	10,350
1787–91	9,375	1812–16	11,185	1832–36	10,690
1792–96	10,382				

John Glynn died in August 1784 and was succeeded by his son, also John Glynn. By April 1791 James Griggs, ex-foreman, was acting surveyor because of Glynn's continued illness. By September 1791 Griggs was formally appointed surveyor and so began the reign of the Griggs, father and son, which was to last for sixty years until the death of the latter in 1852.

Meanwhile another scheme had been proposed for direct communication between Waltham Abbey and the north side of London without having to take boats onto the Thames. The advocate of this scheme was James Sharp, who commissioned Robert Whitworth to survey for a canal from Waltham Abbey running generally west of the present A10 to Stamford Hill, then through Clapton and Hackney and terminating in a basin at Moorfields. This basin, laid out as a pleasure garden, would have been for pleasure craft while goods would have been discharged at a larger basin at Holywell, about ½ mile before the end of the canal. The waterway, apart from a regulating lock at Waltham Abbey, was to be laid out on one level, but there would have been a short branch canal from Clapton to the Lee at Lea Bridge parallel with the present Lea Bridge Road. This branch would have required three locks to compensate for the difference in level between the new canal and the Lee. It was another of the might-have-beens.[13]

One of the cargoes regularly transported on the Lee was gunpowder. This was compounded at an extensive factory privately established at Waltham Abbey about 1650 and later taken over by the government. From the start water power was used for driving the various process mills and the availability of the leats for the millwheels suggested their further use for water transport purposes within the factory area. This ensured that the powder was not subjected to the jolting of land carriage with its attendant risks. Special boats, smaller than barges, 33ft × 8ft, with a semi-circular cover for most of the length, were developed for this purpose. In time an internal system of canals communicating with the Lee was created within the factory with two locks, one 90ft × 16ft and the other 50ft × 12ft, linking the two levels. The need for these two levels arose because of the head of water required for driving the wheels. The gunpowder was despatched from Waltham Abbey in barges down the Lee and after the takeover of the works by the government in 1787 specially designed Lee barges to minimize the possibility of an explosion were constructed in the nineteenth century. These were also used by the Royal Small Arms Factory at Enfield and there was close liaison between the two establishments to ensure that barges were available when required.

There is an interesting episode in the conveyance of gunpowder down the Lee much later in the century. On 14 September 1874 there was a fire at Bromley Flour Mills, and it was alleged that a gunpowder barge had been left moored unattended near the mills at the head of the Limehouse Cut so that there was a risk of falling embers igniting the cargo and so causing devastation in a built-up area. The Lee Conservancy wrote to the Gunpowder Works on 26 September and a reply was sent on 28 September saying that every precaution was being taken. On 2 October, less than a week later, the explosion occurred on the Regent's Canal and the next day George Corble, the Lee Conservancy clerk, wrote 'and need scarcely refer to the shocking explosion on the Regents Canal yesterday as a warning not to moor such craft in a thickly populated district'. Colonel Younghusband, the superintendent at the establishment, took immediate action to tighten the rules regarding the mooring of barges while they were waiting for the tide at Bow Creek. He also went further. Some of the gunpowder was being sent to the depot at Weedon via the Grand Junction Canal and this traffic was not in government barges. He felt that it would be preferable if he could be sure that full precautions were being observed throughout the journey. He therefore sent one of his bargemasters to walk to Weedon along the line of the canal to note whether there would be any impediments in the use of government barges for the whole journey. The bargemaster took five days over the trip and decided that the idea was impracticable.[14]

The defence departments became interested in the Lee much earlier in the century from another aspect. Following Napoleon's successes on the Continent there was a real fear that he would invade England and this led among other things to the building of the Royal Military Canal in Kent and Sussex. However it was also thought that he might invade through Essex and one possible line of defence for London would be the Lee valley. John Rennie was asked to survey the Lee to see whether it could be flooded in an emergency to form a barrier, pending a build-up of troops. His report was not encouraging. He pointed out that the fall in the Lee valley was not great and therefore there would have to be a large number of dams with a corresponding number of soldiers to defend them. He also pointed out that to get two feet of water in the shallowest places would take three months in ordinary times, rather less in times of flood, but that if the enemy cut the banks the whole would be drained in a short time. What he did not say was that if the valley were flooded the gunpowder works would be lost as well. He concluded 'If therefore I may take the liberty to give an opinion I have my doubts whether it would be worth the attention of the Government to expend so large a sum of money as this will cost without any certain benefits to be derived from it towards the defence of the Metropolis'. Despite his advice it was decided to go ahead with the plan, and work was still proceeding in 1807 when Major-General Sir Robert Brownrigg, Quartermaster-General, authorized payment on account of works so far completed. The work was never finished and in 1814 the Lee trustees were asking that the unfinished works should be removed as they were an impediment to navigation. No remains can be seen today.[15]

Meanwhile Rennie had also been retained by the trustees to make a survey of the whole line of the navigation primarily to consider what improvements could make the navigation and the mills less dependent on each other. On 15 September 1804 he made his report in which he recommended making two new cuts, 'the first to avoid Enfield, Tottenham, & Lee Bridge mills and mill streams, and the second to avoid that part of the navigation from Old Ford through Bow Bridge'. No action, however, followed. The following year an Act was passed regulating the depth of water for the mills and similar matters. It also specified a maximum loading of barges which in future must not exceed 40 tons.

An odd little sidelight on the trustees' care for their employees appeared in the minutes on 25 May 1809 when the payment of £3 7s 6d was authorized 'to Mr James, surgeon, of Hoddesdon for amputating two fingers of a labourer who met with an accident while working for the trust'. Another sign of the times was the decision in January 1812 for 'each collector to be provided with a pair of pistols and hanger for their protection and defence'. This concern was again shown in 1820 when a committee was appointed to 'consider the expediency of creating a superannuation fund' and as a result three of the trustees were appointed as trustees for the Fund for the Relief of Invalided Servants of the River Lee Trust.

During the 1820s certain trustees started taking a much closer look at the efficiency and integrity of their officers; as a result their clerk and solicitor were dismissed, their treasurer came in for a great deal of criticism, and their surveyor was considered to have been too prodigal with the repairs and alterations to the navigation—but he died before he could be disciplined.

By 1832 a substantial tonnage was being carried on the navigation, amounting in that year to 214,542 tons, of which over one-third was coal, and a quarter was malt, indicating a considerable freight in both directions. Other substantial cargoes were wheat and flour. The trustees were continually making improvements as the following items indicate. In 1833 it was decided to improve Carthagena lock and remove King's Weir lock. Various minor alterations were also effected. By 1838 the amount of traffic was increasing so much that they decided to appoint sub-collectors at the toll points to cope with the night traffic. In 1841 it was the turn of Ware to undergo improvements; Hadsley lock was removed and also it was decided to remove Ware half-lock, although this last was not done for some years. In order to deal with the increased traffic to Waltham Abbey a new dock was built—which still exists—in 1843 beside

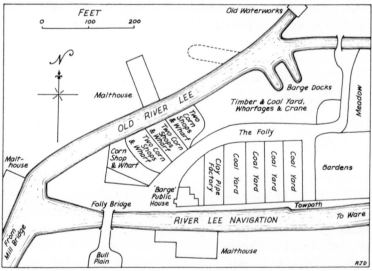

2. The Lee at Hertford, mid-nineteenth century

Waltham Town lock. Then in 1845 a decision was taken which illustrates the forward looking attitude of the trustees. This was to reconstruct Tottenham lock on a new site and to increase its capacity to take 100-ton barges. It must be remembered that at this time the requirements of the 1805 Act were in force limiting the maximum size of barge to 40-ton capacity.

In 1844 another survey had been carried out by Francis Giles, assisted by Griggs, the Lee surveyor. In it Giles recommended that the present number of locks, 25 principal and 3 half locks, should be reduced to 17 principal locks; this was a reduction to below the 18 inefficient flash-locks which Smeaton had referred to in his report as existing on the old unimproved river. Giles also recommended that the navigation should be 7ft deep throughout; and that the line be straightened to pass 100-ton barges. It was this last recommendation which had stimulated the trustees into rebuilding Tottenham lock to its new size. Other visiting craft were described as 'Coasting vessels of 100 tons burthen known as Billy Boys'.[16]

The timing of this survey and the recognition of the need for improvements had undoubtedly been influenced by the opening of a railway along the western bank of the river to Broxbourne as early as September 1840 and its extension to Hertford on 31 October 1843. The effect on the tolls was apparent in 1842 when the other section of the railway had been opened to Bishop's Stortford. The tolls for this period are as follows:

	£		£		£
1840	14,426	1844	10,545	1848	8,349
1841	15,306	1845	10,763	1849	8,512
1842	11,096	1846	8,249	1850	7,845
1843	10,096	1847	8,456	1851	5,799

As the rates of toll were continually being adjusted on the Lee the tolls above cannot be strictly compared with those at the beginning of the century nor can they be used as an accurate index of the tonnage carried. In fact the tonnage carried in 1848, 287,166 tons at a revenue of £8,349, exceeded that carried in 1838, 240,833 tons but with the higher revenue of £12,856.

On the basis of Giles' survey, which included various other recommendations, one of which is discussed in the next paragraph, the trustees went to Parliament and obtained a new Act on 14 August 1850.[17]

One of the recommendations was to build a proper poundlock at Bow tidal-gates, and it was immediately recognized that this could be an issue affecting the toll-free lengths of the navigation. The 1767 Act had authorized tolls on traffic passing specified points on the river but there was no mention of tolls on the Bow river, that is, that part of the navigation between Bow tidal-gates and what is now Old Ford lock; or on Bow Creek which is the present tidal portion of the Lee below the tidal-gates. Nor was there any mention of Bow Back Rivers which will be mentioned later. Up to 1850 therefore, traffic had passed, in the absence of a lock, from Bow Creek to Bow river through the tidal gates when the river and tide water were level. In 1850, in order to enable barges to pass at all states of the tide, it was proposed to build a lock. There was opposition to this on the part of the barge-owners as they were afraid that they would have to pay toll on the hitherto toll-free part of the navigation. In order to safeguard their interests—and to stifle their opposition—it was written into the Act that the section should remain toll-free.

However, when the lock was built, the trustees levied a toll for passing the lock. This, not surprisingly, led to disputes, although the barges could still pass through the tidal-gates without paying toll and, in fact, many of them did and still do. When their next Bill was before Parliament in 1868 the trustees sought to confirm their right to levy a lock toll. Parliament deleted the clause. Nevertheless agreement was reached between the trustees and the traders that a lock charge could be made, but access through the tidal-gates would remain free. Though the matter has been discussed several times subsequently with a view to obtaining authority to levy tolls on the Bow river, the position remains at the time of writing as it was in 1850.

With the passing of the 1850 Act the way was clear for the major improvements envisaged in Giles' report[18] and a subsequent report by M. Rendel,[19] but before they had really started Griggs died and was succeeded by Nicholas Beardmore. Beardmore had been appointed engineer on 7 September 1850 and was promoted to surveyor on 18 March 1851, Griggs remaining nominally in charge until his death in December 1852. It was at this time that a link between the Limehouse Cut and Regent's Canal dock was made. This necessitated the construction of a new lock on Limehouse Cut, primarily as a stop-lock, and this was built at Britannia bridge which carries Commercial Road over the Cut. The work also involved the reconstruction of the bridge itself. Limehouse lock was then recorded as being in a derelict condition. The construction of Bow tidal-lock was taking place at the same time.

These major engineering works, coinciding with the reduced income arising from tolls lowered to meet railway competition, placed the trustees in a difficult financial situation. This became so serious that in 1855 a Bill was proposed to transfer the whole undertaking to the New River Company.[20] This crisis was averted by economies and Beardmore was able to continue with the necessary works. These included the improved line between Waltham Abbey and Enfield involving the construction of Rammey Marsh lock, opened 10 September 1864.[21] Lea Bridge lock was also removed at this time and Old Ford lock constructed. By 1866 all locks between the Thames and Tottenham had been rebuilt to 100-ton standard.

During this period there were gradual changes taking place in the nature of the traffic being carried. Up to this time the cargoes had been mainly malt, wheat, flour and coal, but with the growth of trade in the London docks and the industrial development taking place in the Lea valley in the West Ham, Homerton, Leyton and Tottenham areas, there was a growing demand for the carriage of industrial goods. Though this was small to start with, by the 1880s, ie in thirty years, the toll receipts had risen from £5,799 to £15,468 pa. One rather unusual form of this traffic was by a man named Craven who had an engineering works, as well as coke ovens, at Clapton. He brought boilers from a works at Bow, where they were made, to Clapton by floating them behind barges along the navigation. At Clapton they were hoisted out of the water by a crane, put on to boiler trucks and drawn into the works by as many as twenty horses.[22] There was a brickworks here as well as one at Cheshunt but the one which appears to have generated most traffic was one at Ware, with its private branch canal running off at right angles to the main navigation.[23] In 1880, the Ware brickfields were despatching two or three barges loaded with bricks a day for East London.[24]

Plates 1 & 2 Lee Navigation: *(above)* the type of barge used to carry gunpowder from Waltham Abbey to the Thames; *(below)* the Conservators make their annual survey, 1890. Steam barge *Salisbury*

Plates 3 & 4 (above) a barge at Ware wharf on the Lee; (below) barges near Ilford bridge on the Roding Navigation, about 1900

To go back a little, in 1868, the Lee Conservancy Act of 31 July 1868 replaced the trustees by a board of 13 conservators each elected for four years.[25] Of these conservators, 5 represented landowners, 1 each barge-owners and local authorities, two each the New River Company and the East London Waterworks Company, and one each the Corporation of London and the Metropolitan Board of Works. The Act gave the conservators much wider powers, including control over sewage pollution, and it also empowered them to purchase the Stort Navigation.

Despite these powers, the Conservators were unable to prevent pollution of the Lee becoming a national disgrace, so that on 6 May 1867 a Select Committee on River Pollution (River Lee) was appointed. While much of the pollution came from the communities on the banks the evidence showed that a certain amount derived from the carriage of manure in leaky boats and it was also noted that when the manure was tipped on the banks as a fertiliser the rain water washed it back into the river. Following recommendations made by the committee the situation improved and the Lee was no longer an open sewer.[26]

As tonnages carried give a clearer indication of the steady increase of traffic than do toll receipts, the following figures show the growth over the 100 years from the 1850s to the 1950s:

	Tons		Tons		Tons
1851	212,633	1885	476,063	1915	617,890
1861	300,900	Av 1902–11	598,280	1949	1,814,000
1871	471,918	1912	621,764	1951	2,117,552
1881	532,651	1913	573,591	1953	2,047,614

A section of the Lee which has not yet been described is that group of waterways south of Hackney collectively known as the Bow or Stratford Back Rivers. These are a series of roughly parallel channels, most of which at one time or another have been used to drive watermills. Their origin is unknown, although a popular story associates them with the stranding of the Danish fleet in the River Lee by King Alfred. Over the years they have been used commercially in connection with the cornmills but as they were never part of the Lee Navigation *per se* they were toll-free and there was little incentive to the Lee trustees or the conservators to carry out the bare maintenance required. Each channel has a separate name and forms a section of the old channel of the River Lee; they are Pudding Mill river, City Mills river, Bow Back river, Waterworks river, Three Mills Wall river, Prescott Channel and Channelsea river. By the beginning of the century most of them were falling into decay and becoming a problem for the locality. They could not be closed because they are part of the flood relief system for the whole of the Lee catchment area but as they were getting choked they were putting a considerable area at risk from flooding. Prior to the twentieth century each one of them was used for commercial traffic but by the 1960s only the Channelsea river, the City Mills river, and the Bow Back river were carrying any traffic and today that, too, has almost ceased.

By the end of the 1920s the state of the Back Rivers had become desperate and with the high rate of unemployment in the West Ham area, West Ham Corporation jointly with the Lee Conservancy Board obtained money from the government under the unemployment relief scheme to carry out major improvements in the area. These involved the construction of a new lock at Bow, the reconstruction of Smeaton's Marshgate lock near the junction of the City Mills river with the Bow Back river, and the construction of a new lock at Carpenters Road near the junction of the City Mills river and the old channel of the Lee, together with a massive rehabilitation of the channels themselves. The work was carried out under the River Lee (Flood Relief) Act 1930[27] and started in 1931, being completed in 1935. While Marshgate lock was provided with normal mitre gates, Carpenters lock was provided with radial gates which work on the up-and-over principle by means of winches. Conditions have once again deteriorated and both locks are now virtually derelict. The old tidal doors are still in position at the Old Ford end of the old channel of the Lee but they, too, are in a derelict condition. There has been one further alteration, in that part of the Channelsea river was culverted in 1957–8 between High Street and Lett Road.

Although the Lee trustees were authorized in the 1868 Act to

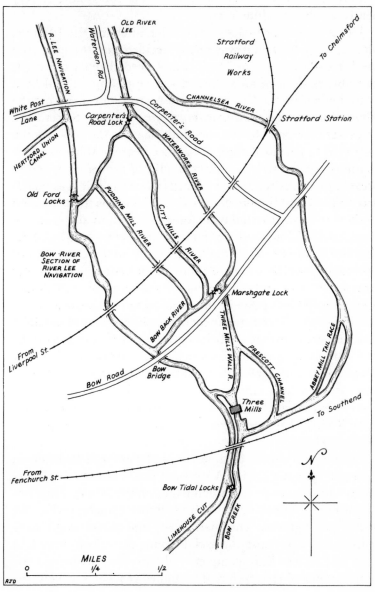

3. The Bow Back Rivers

purchase the Stort Navigation they showed no eagerness to acquire it until they were almost forced into taking it very nearly as a gift on 1 June 1911.

The other recent major construction affecting the Lee took place in 1967–8 when it was finally decided that the lock from the Limehouse Cut into the Thames needed replacement. It had always been in an awkward situation, approached by a sharp bend from the Cut and with a narrow entrance from the Thames under the road bridge carrying Narrow Street. The gates were operated by winches and chains as the area was too restricted to permit the use of balance beams. Above the lock chamber were a series of heavy baulks of timber designed to prevent the walls collapsing inwards when the tide was out. It was realised that the site of the existing lock was too congested to allow the construction of a larger lock and, in any case, the closure of the Limehouse Cut for the time necessary to build the new lock would be disastrous for the trade on the Cut. The answer to the problem was to reinstate the link constructed in 1852 between the Cut and the Regent's Canal dock but which had been removed and filled in 1864. Owing to the construction of new buildings the reinstatement of the old link was impossible. So a new length of canal, albeit only about 200ft, was dug for the first time for 84 years in the south of England and was formally opened on 1 April 1968 with the passage of the canal tug *Miriam* and a string of four lighters.[28] Limehouse lock was then filled in and one of the winches now finds a resting place beside Hampstead Road lock on the Regent's Canal as an industrial archaeological exhibit.

The Lee still carries commercial traffic as far as Brimsdown where, in 1969, the British Waterways Board opened a new terminal with 27,000sqft of warehouse accommodation. This traffic consists of imported goods and timber transhipped at the docks into lighters. The malt, coal, and flour trades have ceased. The modernisation and doubling of the locks from Old Ford to Ponders End, completed about 1960, has helped the continuation of this traffic. The upper reaches are now the haunt of pleasure craft and fishermen. No longer is it the noisome polluted river of the 1880s. It is instead the spine of the Lee

Valley Regional Park Authority which plans to make the whole valley into a linear park with facilities for a wide range of outdoor activities. The Lee is possibly the oldest navigation in the Eastern Counties but it still has a great future before it.

Stort Navigation

The Stort valley runs in a roughly southerly direction through Bishop's Stortford to Pishiobury Park just south of Sawbridgeworth. Here it turns abruptly west-south-west until it joins the Lee valley between Hoddesdon and Roydon. The streams which feed the Stort rise in the north-west uplands of Essex, which in turn form the watershed between the waters draining south to the Thames and those north to the Wash. This factor was of importance in proposals made at the end of the eighteenth century for linking the Thames and the Wash, which are dealt with later in this chapter.

The Stort itself was a sluggish stream following winding channels through an area which as far back as Domesday Book was described as 'inter pratum et marese', half meadow, half marsh. The ancient trackways avoided it, but early settlers dammed the streams and created channels to provide power for mills, some of the sites of which have continued in use to the present day.

During the early eighteenth century the malt trade in Bishop's Stortford increased and the townspeople and traders began to look for better transport facilities. With the example of the benefits derived by the maltmen of Ware following the 1739 Act for the Lee,[29] it was only to be expected that the practicability of using the Stort would be explored. A meeting to consider an application to Parliament for an Act was called for 11 December 1758 to be held at the Crown Inn, Hockerill, the proprietor of which, Thomas Adderley, seems to have been the prime mover in the scheme.[30] His memorial tablet in Bishop's Stortford church, which records his death on 1 April 1774 aged 67, carries the following eulogy:

He was equally zealous to serve his friends and Promote the

Publick Utility; Upon that Principle he first suggested the Idea in making the River Stort navigable up to this town, in which He had resided more than 45 years; and was Principally concerned in obtaining the Laws necessary for that purpose. He lived to see the good effect of those services, with respect to the Publick, and the Proprietors of the Navigation were so sensible of the benefit of his Advice throughout the course of the Arduous Undertaking that they were never wanting, as well before as since the completion of it, to pay him the respect due to his Zeal and to express their thankfull Acknowledgements.

The Act was obtained in March 1759 for making the Stort navigable from Bishop's Stortford to the Lee and commissioners were appointed who, *inter alia*, were to raise the necessary capital.[31] They held several meetings but, even though the benefits were obvious, they were unable to obtain the required money. Because nothing had been done and the powers had lapsed a further Bill was promoted in 1766 to enable the necessary works to be completed. This followed proposals made to the commissioners by Charles Dingley of Hampstead (himself a Lee trustee), George Jackson, and William Masterman that these three would provide the capital to develop the navigation within five years on condition that they could have the tolls. The Bill was passed on 30 April 1766 and the 1759 Act was thereby repealed.[32]

The new commissioners were to meet for the first time on 27 May 1766, again at the Crown Inn, Hockerill, but no record of this meeting has apparently survived. However, with capital now available, work started on 24 September 1766 and by the autumn of 1769 the navigation, including the construction of fifteen locks, was completed, well within the stipulated time. The engineer to the undertaking was Thomas Yeoman which reveals the fairly close relationship with the Lee Navigation, for Yeoman was at the same time the surveyor to that body.

The official opening took place on 24 October 1769 and George Jackson left a spirited account of the preparations and junketings of the day in his diary.[33] During the celebrations

Thomas Yeoman proudly announced 'Now the town of Stortford is open to all the ports of the world'.

George Jackson was also secretary to the Admiralty and
later MP for Weymouth. He was a friend and patron of Captain Cook who named Port Jackson in Australia and Point
Jackson in New Zealand after him. Later he changed his
name to his wife's maiden name, Duckett, in order to claim
an inheritance. He died in 1822 at the age of 97 and was succeeded in the baronetcy, which he had been awarded, by his
son, also Sir George Duckett. It was the second Sir George
who was responsible for the construction of the Hertford
Union Canal linking the river Lee and the Regent's Canal.[34]

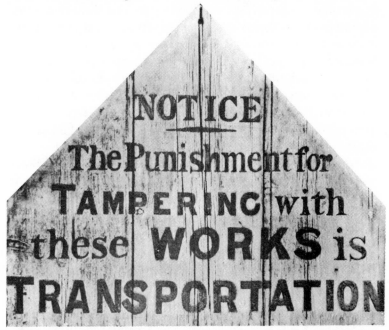

4. A notice from South Mill lock on the Stort. Deliberate damage done to navigation works was considered a serious crime against a community dependent
upon them for many necessities

The cost of construction is not known as it was financed
privately by the three undertakers, but Sir George Duckett
speaking in 1812 said that for the first twenty years it had not
been an advantageous concern. Nevertheless it fulfilled a need,

for a writer in the *Public Ledger* on 30 August 1770 remarked on the improvements made to Bishop's Stortford by a navigation opened into the River Thames for barges of 40-tons burthen. He went on to say that the direct communication with the metropolis had already drawn to it a considerable trade. That the Lee Navigation was not unaware of nor unresponsive to the improvements on the Stort is shown by the decision on 16 February 1774 to pay to the proprietors of the Stort £105 for improvements done at the mouth of their river.[35]

By the end of the eighteenth century trade was increasing, influenced by the effect of the French wars. In 1791 between 18,000 and 19,000 tons were carried, including 19,500 sacks of flour and 97,000 quarters of malt sent to London. By 1811 these quantities had increased to 40,000 tons, including more than 50,000 sacks of flour and more than 203,000 quarters of malt. An interesting feature of the times was the roundabout way some goods were carried to take advantage of water transport. In the winter of 1811–12, 20,000 quarters of barley were purchased at Norwich, sent round by sea to the Thames and then up the rivers Lee and Stort to Bishop's Stortford to be made into malt for the London trade.[36]

Against the background of the growth of trade on the Stort and contemporary realization of its further growth potential, it is necessary to look at what proved in the end to be an abortive concept, unfortunate both for the general development of commercial water transport as well as for the late-twentieth-century popularity of pleasure boating. This was the proposal to link the Stort at Bishop's Stortford to the Cam at Cambridge and thus establish a direct waterway system between London and the Wash.

Preliminary thought as to the possibility of the link must have started within a few years of the completion of the Stort navigation, for a sufficiently strong pattern of ideas had formed by 1779 for the City of London itself to take a practical interest in its feasibility. Who had been instrumental in stimulating the City's interest is not known, but George Jackson with his parliamentary connections was probably a powerful influence. At its meeting on 4 November 1779, the City's Thames and Canal

Committee empowered its surveyor 'to prepare a plan of a navigable canal from Bishop's Stortford to Cambridge together
with a section and profile and to report his opinion of the probable expenses of carrying the same into execution and that Mr.
Whitworth may be directed to report his opinion whether any
more desirable line can be found for a new communication from
Cambridge to any other part of the river Lee and that the
expence therefore do not exceed £250'.

Robert Whitworth received his instructions on 16 November
1779 but his report was not produced until 6 December 1780.[37]
He took the most favourable route along the valley of the Stort
to near Elsenham and then across the watershed into the valley
of the Granta and so to Cambridge. Unfortunately this route
passed across the grounds and in front of the house of Audley
End, then the home of the most powerful landowner in north-
west Essex, Lord Howard de Walden. The proposal immediately attracted violent opposition from Lord Howard and his
neighbours. A meeting was held at Great Chesterford on the
border of Essex and Cambridgeshire on 22 November 1781. The
Thames and Canal Committee considered that one of its members should have attended, but there was apparently no authority for this to be done. In any case there was dispute at the
meeting as to why it had been called and who had called it, so
for the time being the project was dropped.

In 1785 John Phillips published a new proposal for opening
up the counties of Essex, Suffolk, and Norfolk by linking
London with Lynn via Ongar, Chelmsford, Braintree, Lavenham, Eye, and Diss and then across southern and western Norfolk to Lynn using the beds of natural rivers where possible; and
also by a branch from Great Ellingham in central Norfolk easterly to Norwich. He further proposed a line from Bishop's
Stortford to Cambridge passing the estates of Shotgrove and
Audley End on the west and thereby negating the objections of
the owners of those estates to the earlier proposal which would
have affected them. He supported his proposals with a fervent
advocacy for the benefits of canals in general and his scheme in
particular. His costings and anticipated revenue both appear
wildly optimistic. The estimated cost for a 36ft wide canal was

£212,800 and the revenue £32,800 pa. In addition he suggested a number of branch canals including one to the River Colne at Chappel and then to the sea via Colchester. Even with his special pleadings the ideas were still-born.[38]

George Jackson had not lost interest, and on 1 May 1788 he suggested to the Thames and Canal Committee that it would be possible to carry the canal behind Lord Howard's estate to Saffron Walden, 'where it would be of essential service as great quantities of corn and other grain are sent from thence'. Jackson also suggested that Samuel Weston (who had worked on the Oxford and Chester Canals) should be invited to act for Whitworth as the latter was engaged in canal works in Scotland, and make the necessary survey of the line via Saffron Walden. Following this survey a meeting was held at the Crown at Great Chesterford under the chairmanship of Alderman Richard Clark of the City of London. It was estimated that about 500 were present, including Lord Howard de Walden who maintained his opposition to the scheme by saying that he had laid out nearly £100,000 upon improvements at Audley End that would be destroyed.[39] Opposition, too, came from the corporation of the Bedford Level.

A year later, however, in 1789, a further meeting at the Crown authorized an application for an Act to make a canal from Bishop's Stortford via Saffron Walden to the Brandon (Little Ouse) river by Wilton Ferry, with branches to Cambridge and Burwell Lode. This was the line proposed by John Rennie who, in submitting his suggestions, opened by these remarks: 'In the course of my report I shall deliver my ideas with all the perspicuity I am Master of and to make myself better understood shall in the first place give a separate description of the different lines I have surveyed and afterwards make my comparisons'. However in conclusion he suggested a further survey 'from the single circumstance of the Ground having been covered with snow to a considerable depth it is possible some things may have escaped my notice such as I should wish to correct and this I guess cannot require much time'.[40] His estimate to Brandon, including the reservoirs at Elsenham, Henham, and Newport, was £168,257.[41] The amended plan was supported by the City of

London but the opposition grew in strength. At a meeting on Saturday, 2 January 1790, a fund was opened to fight the Bill and support was promised from landowners including Lords Howard, Bristol, and Egremont, Cambridge University, the town of Cambridge, the conservators of the Cam, the corporation of Bedford Level, and millowners. The University, in presenting its case, pointed out that the price of wheat between January 1789 and January 1790 had been higher in Newmarket than in London, and the price of barley the same, 'which proves that the canal cannot be of any utility in opening communication with the Metropolis for grain, which is the principal thing on which they found their expectation of tonnage'.[42] In the end the opposition was sufficiently strong to secure the Bill's rejection. It was at one time proposed to raise the money necessary for carrying out the works by a tontine, but the committee finally decided that fund-raising should be by normal subscription list.

There was an even longer interval before the next attempt was made. This time Sir George Jackson, or Duckett, as he had now become, had found a powerful supporter in the Earl of Hardwicke, and at a meeting on 11 January 1811, presided over by the Earl, it was decided that steps should be taken to make the canal. The new proposal was based on a re-survey carried out by Netlam and Francis Giles under John Rennie's direction, and included a branch canal to Shefford on the river Ivel.[43] A Bill was introduced in 1811 and received a second reading before being thrown out in committee. The promoters, on this occasion, did not waste much time in returning to the attack, for leave to bring in another Bill was given on 29 January 1812, though the branch to the Ivel was shortened to Whaddon adjacent to the Earl of Hardwicke's estate at Wimpole. This reduced the lockage required.

Meanwhile the Earl of Hardwicke had been gathering additional information. He asked Rennie about the suitability and practicability of barges navigating through from London to Lynn. Rennie replied:

The Lee and Stort barges are very long, flat and of great capacity for stowage and draw from 2 feet to $2\frac{1}{2}$ feet of water. These barges are too slender a make to bear the swells of water which frequently take place at Lynn or to lie aground on the uneven bottom of the channel there. Consequently such barges are not suited to a through navigation between London and Lynn; they would navigate with perfect safety from London to Denver Sluice or even to St Germains. But although the river Lee barges cannot navigate to Lynn except in fine weather when the water is smooth, yet those from Lynn to Cambridge could with safety go from Lynn to London.[44]

Once again there was considerable opposition to the Bill and the second reading went to a division, the voting being 84 for and 30 against. Some of the opposition was mollified by the insertion of special clauses, such as the one to protect Hobson's Conduit at Cambridge, or the ones to protect the tolls and rights of the Cam conservators and the estates of landowners. Nevertheless there was an attempt on 22 May 1812 to defer the Bill for six months, but this was defeated by 93 votes to 28. It received the royal assent on 9 June 1812, nearly 35 years after the idea was first seriously mooted.[45]

Work was not to begin until £425,250 had been raised, the total capital authorized being £870,000. There were to be three tunnels, one nearly $1\frac{1}{4}$ miles long, 52 locks on the main line and 13 on the branch to Whaddon. The required amount to commence work was not forthcoming, and a further Act was obtained in 1814 to permit the construction of the length between the Cam and Saffron Walden and also the Whaddon branch, which had been authorized under the 1812 Act, using the money—£121,300—which had been subscribed.[46] But it was not to be; no work was carried out and the scheme was dropped. Sir George Duckett the second still clung to the hope that a canal would be built and on 3 February 1824 he wrote to the Earl of Hardwicke

My Lord,

Your Lordship is so thoroughly aware that the present is or ought to be the best period for promoting the Cambridge

Canal that I have endeavoured to excite the attention of the town of Bishop's Stortford to the subject trusting that by temperance and judgments all parties may finally be circulated. I cannot however boast of much success. In the meantime, my Lord, I have given notice of an intention to apply to Parliament for powers to make at my own expense a cut between the Regents Canal and the Lee Navigation and I do myself the Honour of sending you a sketch.

It is my hope that the benefit to the Regents Canal will induce that company to look to Cambridgeshire as an essential source of profit and improvement.

For this purpose no better present method perhaps exists than the improvements which are now either in execution or agitation at the two ends of the great line, Lynn and London.[47]

So ended the hope of a link between the Cam and the Stort. Its potentialities were present when it was first mooted and today it would have been of inestimable value for pleasure traffic. It must go down in history as one of the great might-have-beens.

The Stort continued to carry a considerable amount of traffic during the saga of the London & Cambridge Junction Canal but its association with the Duckett family ceased after 1832 following the failure of Duckett, Morland & Company, bankers, and the bankruptcy of Sir George Duckett. It was estimated that, considering that the navigation was free of all taxes and all conveyances were free of stamp duty, the navigation, warehouses, wharfs, land, etc bringing in an annual revenue of £5,000 would be worth £150,000. It ultimately came into the hands of a firm, Birbecks, who had granted a mortgage on the concern for £40,000 and then foreclosed the mortgage,[48] from whom it passed to the bankers, Gurney & Co of Norwich.

With the opening of the Northern & Eastern Railway to Bishop's Stortford on 16 May 1842 with its track parallel to the river for most of the way and several of the stations literally on its banks, there was a sudden decline in the amount of waterborne traffic, from £5,477 in 1838 to £2,593 in 1848. Thereafter for the next 20 years the revenue remained fairly constant. It was only to be expected that the Lee Navigation would be interested in acquiring the Stort and so purchase powers were included in the Lee Acts of 1868 and 1874. However, although surveys and valuations had been made on three separate occasions, the conservators considered that because of the bad condition of the locks and works, the amount of dredging required, and the falling off of trade, only a nominal offer should be made and this was rejected. In 1886 they considered that it would be better to lose the tolls the Stort brought to the Lee than to take over the concern and be compelled to keep it in an efficient condition.[49]

In 1873 the undertaking was sold by Gurney & Co to Truman, Hanbury & Co, brewers of Spitalfields, who clearly must have thought it of value for the transport of their malt requirements.[50] It later passed into the hands of Sir Walter Gilbey who, in 1905, formed the Stort Navigation Company Ltd, his own family being a majority of the directors.[51] The company's fortunes declining, he resumed negotiations with the Lee. In January 1909 Bishop's Stortford Urban District Council, who still hoped that the navigation could be improved, offered £170 towards the purchase price provided other local authorities would also make contributions. Before discussions could be completed an incident occurred which changed the situation. At 11pm on 20 April 1909 one side of Brick lock, Roydon, collapsed; as this was the last but one lock before the Stort joined the Lee it virtually blocked the navigation.[52] As a result Sir Walter decided to cut his losses and offered the navigation to the Lee Navigation free of charge provided he could have the local authority contributions. A fortnight later the Lee board noted that all the Stort barges except one were trapped above Brick lock and at the rate of progress by the six men employed by the Stort on reconstructing Brick lock it would be many months before the navigation reopened to traffic.[53] They therefore offered the services of some of their men to speed up work. In fact the lock was reopened on 4 October 1909.

Meanwhile the Lee board had again been looking at the cost of taking over the Stort. They considered that capital expenditure of £10,800 would be required to bring it up to a standard suitable for 60–65 ton barges. They also noted that the tolls received had steadily fallen from £927 in 1901 to £615 in 1904 and £319 in 1907. Against this background the negotiations dragged on until finally in 1911 Sir Walter sold out to the Lee for five shillings (25p) and the Stort became the property of the Lee Conservancy Board on 1 June 1911.

Before the transfer the Lee board had decided to apply to the development commissioners under the Development and Road Improvement Funds Act 1909 for a loan to cover the cost of repairs.[53] A loan of £12,500 payable in annual instalments of £2,500 over a period of five years was granted, this being interest-free and non-refundable whilst the works were in progress. If no profit occurred then the loan would be continued on the same terms. When a net profit was made then interest and repayments would commence. The work started in 1913 with the most urgent tasks—mainly the reconstruction of the locks—but then the Great War intervened and put a stop to all but the most urgent work. The tolls for the year ending 31 March 1913 had fallen to less than £72 which did not augur well for the future, and they were to fall still further the next year.[54]

Eventually repairs were completed and there was a grand reopening on 4 July 1924 officially performed by the Minister of Transport, the Rt Hon Harry Gosling, MP.[55] Commercial traffic recovered to a degree, mainly in timber, grain and malt, but after the Second World War it gradually died away and the last commercial boat, at the time of writing, to penetrate the Stort was in the autumn of 1972 when a load of stone was brought from Atherstone for repairs to Little Hallingbury mill.[56]

The decline of commercial traffic has not meant the decay of the navigation, for the Stort is now a well used cruising river with a marina at Little Hallingbury mill and developments taking place elsewhere along the waterway.

There used to be an inscription on Latton lockhouse, originally the residence of the clerk of the Navigation: 'Man may come and man may go, but the river goes on for ever'. Regrettably the house was destroyed by fire in the 1950s but the sentiment expressed in that inscription is still appropriate for rivers in general and the Stort in particular.

CHAPTER III

The Essex Navigations

THE county of Essex, bounded on the west by the ancient navigable Lee and on the south and east by the irregular and, in places, deeply indented coastline of the Thames estuary and the North Sea, has always been favourably placed with regard to navigable water. The improvement of the Stour on the northern boundary at the beginning of the eighteenth century served many of those parts which were remote from water transport, so that by 1710 only the very rural area in north-west Essex was dependent on the packhorse for journeys of more than fifteen miles. Furthermore, there were no mineral resources to demand sophisticated transport arrangements to carry bulk supplies to their consumers. The old cutlery industry of Thaxted had long since disappeared. The old woollen industry in the east and north east was decaying for reasons other than the absence of transport facilities and the factory system which transformed the Stroud valley and the West Riding had no counterpart in Essex.

Because of this background, as with the rest of the eastern counties, the pattern of development was the improvement of the short and slow-running rivers, each an individual effort, linked only by the tidal waters of the Thames or the North Sea. The real industrial development of Essex is a product of the later age of the railway and the motor vehicle.

Roding Navigation

With the exception of the Lee, the Roding (or Rodon as it was known in the early eighteenth century) is the most westerly of the Essex rivers entering the Thames and, like so many Essex creeks, navigation of the tidal portion as far as Barking had a long history. The town quay at the head of the creek lies close to the remains of Barking Abbey and was under its control until the sixteenth century. A document of 1601 records that it had been much used by boats carrying provisions to the Abbey and corn and meal to the watermills.[1] The river trade also included shipment of provisions to Greenwich and London.

Barking was still the head of the navigation at the beginning of the eighteenth century but Ilford, higher up the river on the Great Essex Road was developing. So in 1736 Joseph Goodman, of 'the Precinct of St Catherine's near the Tower', convinced the local landowners that it would be an advantage to all concerned to extend the navigation upstream from Barking mill to Ilford bridge. He formalized the arrangement with an indenture dated 22 May 1736 by which the landowners gave permission for Goodman to 'come upon their lands for the cleaning the river in order to make it navigable and for removing any impediments therein'. The agreement also provided for the river to be widened to 30ft. It was only when work was under way that Goodman realized that he would have to get legal sanction for the improvements because some of the lands were held by 'infants or feme-coverts or under some intail or settlement' and these persons could clearly not be bound by the indenture.[2] Accordingly on 9 March 1736/7 he petitioned Parliament for an Act to make the Roding navigable to Ilford bridge, which was passed on 21 June 1737.[3] An interesting amendment had been made to one of the clauses of the draft Bill during its passage through Parliament. It had originally been proposed that 'if any boatman obstructed the waterway with boats then on proof of the matter is hereby authorised and required to order such person and persons *to be put in the common stocks within the same Parish where the same matter or offence shall be committed by the space of Two Hours*'. The words in italics were deleted and the penalty substituted was 'a fine of five pounds payable to Joseph Goodman and if that were not paid in ten days then the boatman or boatmen were to be sent to the House of Correction without Bail or Mainprize for the space of One

Month as a Punishment for such his and their Obstinacy and Perverseness'.

The Act authorized Goodman and his assigns to make the river navigable from Barking to Ilford. Goodman also obtained land to make a wharf at Ilford beside the bridge on a lease of 81 years. Following the Act, work was resumed but although some progress was made on this very short navigation of 1¾ miles Goodman died before completion. The navigation and wharf were acquired by John Webb, who was a Quaker and apparently rather impetuously agreed to purchase the navigation before a survey had been carried out, for he wrote on 26 July 1757 from the Stockyard, London, to John Campion at Harwich

Friend John Campion,

Very lately a Friend of mine was at Illford (and Survey'd the River) who advised me well to consider, whether the expence of making it Navigable, Building a Wharfe and Wharehouses would answer my intention of Purchasing such a hazardous adventure. Also if it would be completed according to my desire, whether the coal merchants at Barking (who have Colliers come up to the Town) would not under sell me in the Price of Coals?—and as there is no land belonging to it. What value will the River be if there is not water enough for the Navigation.

These considerations has had some weight with me, and altho I have still some Inclination to try the Experiment, therefore will not go back from my word provided there is no other Incumbrences Intail'd to it besides the repairs of Cowbridge.

The Inclosed letter I have lately received from our Friend William Goodman but it will not suit me to stay until he comes to Town for several reasons: and being willing to act consistent with justice and Honour (Supposing that I have been the cause of they signing that agreement about the repairs of Cowbridge) therefore take this opportunity to acquaint thee that if thou thinks well of accepting those terms which I have proposed I am ready to fulfill my word and I desire thou wilt please to send me answer in writing by the bearer.

Which will much oblige

Thy Real Friend

John Webb.[4]

Negotiations were protracted, but the navigation was conveyed to Webb on 30 October 1764 and he was then able to complete the works. He is recorded as having been the first person to have coals on the wharf at Ilford bridge. After Webb died his widow, in partnership with a Mr Chalk, carried on the business and subsequently the rights were sold to one Carrington who later disposed of them to Rose, Pratt and Daldry.

In an action at the Essex Lent assizes at Chelmsford on 14 March 1822 between Sir Charles Hulse, Lord of the Manor and Messrs Rose, Pratt and Daldry (there described as coal merchants occupying a wharf and land used for their business at Ilford), whereby Sir Charles Hulse sought to recover the land, evidence of the construction of the navigation was given by aged witnesses;[5] one was 82-year-old Sarah Ross.

Q. Do you remember the wharf?

A. Very well sir and I have been playing on it many times when I was a little girl.

Q. Do you remember Mrs Webb using that piece of ground where the cage used to stand?

A. Very well for I used to be a washerwoman to Mrs Webb. . . .

Q. Who had the wharf after Mr Webb?

A. Mrs Webb and Mr Chalk were in partnership and then after Mr Carrington.

Q. Do you remember Mr Goodman?

A. Yes very well and Mrs Goodman and her three sons.

Another witness, Thomas Miller, stated that he was 78 and remembered driving a coal wagon on to the wharf over 50 years earlier.

Sir Charles Hulse won his case for the wharf and later on 25 February 1835 he purchased the navigation rights from the then partners for £3,780.[6] About the time of the case vessels were regularly trading between St Katherine dock, London and Ilford and between 1826 and 1833 the tolls averaged £387 12s pa. By the end of the century receipts were steadily increasing.

	1897	£560
	1898	£742
	1899	£940
January–May	1900	£1,151

The navigation today is still in use under the control of the Barking & Ilford Navigation Co (1961) Ltd which acquired the river charter and freehold land for £5,764 in 1961 but there is now little traffic on it. It is still entered through a single pair of gates out of Barking Creek when the tide is at a level with the river and for this reason there is no limit to the length of vessels using it, but the width is restricted to 17ft and the depth to 7ft 6in. The navigation company, which is jointly owned by Thames Plywood Manufacturers Ltd and Younghusband Stephens & Co Ltd, describes its principal activity as the collection of river dues and operating the lock-gates.[7]

Romford Canal

Before the eastern urban and industrial sprawl of London had engulfed the countryside lying in the valleys of the Lee, Roding and Beam (or Rom), western Essex was an important centre for the supply of potatoes and other vegetables for the London market. This agricultural produce was normally transported by waggon along the feeder roads to the Great Essex Road (which linked London with Harwich and the Continent) and thence by Ilford and Stratford to London. According to a broadsheet issued in 1825 little use had, even then, been made of the available means of water transport from Rainham on the Thames, or from Ilford or Barking on the Roding to carry agricultural produce to London because, it was suggested, 'of the greater liability to damage and of Thames dues payable in the port of London'.[8]

Nevertheless a proposal was made on 28 September 1809 in the form of a map signed by Ralph Walker, entitled *Plan for Proposed Canal from Romford to the River Thames*.[9] This was the forerunner of several schemes mooted during the next sixteen years which emphasized the advantages of water carriage for agricultural products. The 1809 scheme, as well as the subsequent 1812 proposal, suggested a canal from Rainham Creek with an entrance lock from the Thames and a basin followed by a cut leading to the River Beam. The canal would then have turned in a more northerly direction along the river valley to a terminal basin adjacent to the Great Essex Road approximately where Ind Coope's brewery now stands in Romford.

Owing to other commitments Walker was unable to produce a further map until September 1812.[10] This showed a canal $4\frac{3}{4}$ miles long from Rainham Creek to Romford with six locks having a total rise of 34ft. A petition was presented to Parliament on 18 December 1812, but the scheme was then apparently dropped.

Interest in a canal revived in 1818 when a new proposal was put forward by the engineer Robert Vazie and a promoter from Hornchurch named E. Y. Hancock, who at a meeting on 23 September 1818 stated that the scheme had originated with himself.[11] Hancock was obviously a go-getter and not only did he try to whip up enthusiasm for the project among the local landowners and farmers but he approached the commissioners for the Crown Estates who were responsible for the administration of Hainault Forest close to the upper end of the proposed canal. He suggested that 'the canal, will materially increase the value of the Crown Lands and will open a ready communication for the conveyance of timber from Hainault Forest to H. M. Dockyards'. In this he hoped to get financial assistance from the government. His letter was referred by the commissioners to a firm of surveyors, A. & C. Driver, for comment and they were anything but impressed by the scheme. They replied that they did 'not anticipate that it would be a lucrative or even profitable concern' though they felt that there might be some advantage to the Crown in the removal of their timber but they could not 'see any advantage is likely to be derived by their contributing their support in a pecuniary way'. They concluded by saying that they were 'very doubtful whether the projectors will be able to accomplish their object'. How right they were![12]

Nor did the scheme meet with the approval of many of the local landowners for, on 31 October 1818, following a meeting on 16 October at Romford Town Hall, a printed circular *Observations on the Romford Canal* was issued giving reasons for their opposition to the project.[13] In the prospectus the estimated cost of construction was £46,053, but by 16 February 1819 this had been revised to £80,000, an increase which justified the opposition's scepticism.

The plan envisaged a canal 36ft wide and 5ft deep capable of taking barges of 40 to 60 tons. On an assumed daily traffic of five barges and tolls at 1s 4d per ton the annual income was estimated at £4,000, which would be sufficient to pay off the capital and provide a dividend.[14] The route would have been from Dagenham on the Thames to a basin near what is now the White Hart, Collier Row, in the valley of the Bourne Brook. Ten locks and a river lock would have been required for the rise of 60ft. However, because of local opposition and lack of subscriptions this scheme, too, was dropped.

The canal project that was revived in 1820 took into account fears of possible inundations arising from breaching the Thames embankment to form a lock. It was proposed that there should be a double inclined plane whereby barges would be hauled out of the river, over the embankment, and then lowered into the canal on the other side. Boats leaving the canal would follow the reverse procedure. The new plan also eliminated locks on the remainder of the canal in favour of five inclined planes. The proposed method of operation of these planes is unknown but the *Chelmsford Chronicle* stated that the 'barges shall be drawn over the said embankments by similar means to those which have been successfully applied for many years on the Coal Brook Dale Canal in Shropshire . . . and by a like application to pass the barges from the different levels of the canal'.[15] This scheme foundered largely on the depressed state of agriculture at the time.

Yet another plan was issued in 1824 after trade had improved. Locks were now proposed, and it was noted by the opposition that 'the hazardous experiment of cutting the embankment and admitting a free ingress of the tide' had been revived. In announcing the new plan Robert Vazie estimated the cost as under £60,000 ie £20,000 less than the revised estimate of 1819, which was to be raised in shares of £50. Vazie suggested that the locks should be made to admit the largest lighters constructed to navigate the Thames, Lee, and Regent's Canal.[16] This time the opposition used a fresh argument, that of potential competition from the new railways, in addition to that of the risk of flooding, to counter the proposals and again the opposition was successful for the plan was withdrawn and the concept of a canal lay dormant for nearly fifty years.

In 1874, interest was revived by the publication of a notice of intention to apply for an Act incorporating a company to construct a canal from Romford to the Thames at a point about 220ft south-westward from Havering Great Sluice through which the river Beam enters the Thames. Surprisingly there was apparently no opposition to the proposal and the Act was passed on 19 July 1875.[17] This empowered the company to raise £80,000 in £10 shares and a further £19,000 by borrowing. The directors were not local men and the engineers were Russ and Minns of Victoria Chambers, London. This absence of local interest suggests that the proposal was a purely speculative venture.

The rather fulsome prospectus issued after the Act was passed, apart from indicating the need for improved transport facilities, also suggested that as the Nuisance Act, ie the Public Health Act, had come into operation varnish manufacturers and others would have to move from London and would want sites on the canal banks. It was hoped that the canal would be open for traffic in twelve months although the permitted time for completion was five years.[18] The estimated profit was very optimistically assessed at 15 per cent pa.

The maximum tolls laid down in the schedule of the Act included 'for each and every bull, bullock, cow, heifer, horse, and mule the sum of two shillings: Provided that if any number less than five be conveyed in any boat, tolls as for five may be taken'. The mind boggles at the thought of five bulls in a boat on the canal.

Six locks, including the tidal-lock into the Thames, rising to Romford were to be built on the $4\frac{1}{2}$ mile canal and construction commenced soon after the passing of the Act. Part of the cut was built, together with one lock, apparently in mass concrete, 135ft × 16ft 6in, just to the north of the present A13. A tunnel under the Barking to Upminster section of the London, Tilbury & Southend Railway was made but when the line was widened to accommodate the District Line extension to Upminster the new embankment was made solid over the line of the canal. This tunnel half-way under the present embankment together with traces of the lock are two of the few remaining pieces of evidence that the canal was ever started.

The company obtained a second Act on 24 July 1876 empowering it to raise a further £16,000[19], although the final call on the original issue of shares was not made until 1 May 1877[20] on the grounds that the company had already constructed a great part of the works but required further money for completion. Work apparently ceased in about 1877 and although a third Act was obtained in 1880[21] to extend the time for completion until 1883, no further work appears to have been carried out. In 1910 the company was officially liquidated and in 1912 the lands acquired by the company were auctioned by order of the trustees.

So ended a canal which, even in its early days, could not have been a particularly viable undertaking and certainly when construction started in the hey-day of railways, seemed doomed to failure.

Mardyke Canal

Another local Essex scheme which attracted attention spasmodically over a very long period was the possibility of canalising the Mardyke. This stream—it can hardly be designated a river—rises in Bulphan Fen to the north of Grays and drains that marshy area. It flows generally westward and discharges into the Thames at Purfleet, through the area of what was then the government powder magazine. Following the establishment of the magazine about 1760, the lower part of the Mardyke to its junction with the Thames was used for the unloading of barges from gunpowder works at Waltham Abbey and elsewhere and for the shipment of gunpowder to the services.

The first proposal for establishing a navigation beyond the magazine came in July 1776 when John Swinden, a surveyor, submitted an estimate for making the Mardyke navigable at a cost of £15,746 'from Poorfleet Sluice to beyond Bulphan Fen to a bridge near Childerditch Church'.[22] This is not far from Thorndon Hall, then the seat of Lord Petre, one of the most important landowners in Essex and a supporter of the Chelmer & Blackwater Navigation. The total length of the canal was to be $9\frac{1}{2}$ miles with a fall of some 50ft. Swinden proposed five locks, including that from the Thames into the Mardyke. The pound from this Thames lock to the second lock was five miles and the second to fifth locks were to be constructed in the next $4\frac{1}{4}$ miles. There was to be a basin at the Childerditch end.

The scheme did not attract sufficient support and so the idea was dropped for over half a century. Then on 17 October 1833 a meeting of landowners and tenants of property near the Mardyke was held at the White Hart Inn, Brentwood, to consider a Parliamentary application for power to construct a canal on the line of the Mardyke, from Purfleet to Puddle Dock bridge in Great Warley. A list to defray expenses was opened, which was headed by Lord Petre with a subscription of £10. The meeting felt that there was a favourable prospect for the scheme and they agreed to appoint Edward Lapidge, who had already made a partial survey, as engineer to make a complete survey of the line and submit an estimate. The proposal received the blessing of the local press who trusted 'that no opposition will be offered to the carrying into effect a design so evidently fraught with utility, possessing such natural means of facility for carrying it into execution'. Lapidge produced his scheme on 19 November 1833.[23]

But it was not to be. On 19 August 1834 Lapidge wrote to C.

Comyns Parker, a land agent and one of the supporters of the scheme:

> Sir,
>
> As you mentioned at the last meeting at Brentwood that it was your intention to speak to some of the owners of the land on the banks of the Mardyke Drain, on being furnished with a list of them; it now appearing that the project of making the drain into a canal has been abandoned by the parties who originated it, I beg to acquaint you of that circumstance that you may not attend to no purpose on Thursday next, the day that was appointed for the next meeting.
>
> I am, Sir
E. Lapidge.[24]

So once more the scheme died, only to be revived again seventy years later as a suggestion in two letters in the *Grays and Tilbury Gazette* in January 1905 claiming that a navigation would benefit farmers in transporting their produce and that the establishment of factories along the Mardyke would be encouraged. The day of local canals had long since passed and this was the last stirring of an idea which was first mooted 130 years before.

Nevertheless, despite the failure to obtain statutory powers for making the Mardyke navigable, in about the 1870s barges used to ply between Purfleet and the farms in Orsett Fen. The craft, known as 'dumpy' barges, were operated by a Mr Bannister and used to collect manure from London stables and streets at a transhipment point at Rainham.[25] This was then taken along the Mardyke to the various farms in the fen for spreading on the land. The return cargo was corn and fodder for London horses. Access to the individual farms was by wide shallow ditches fanning off from the Mardyke along which the barges were poled, in some cases nearly a mile from the main stream. Today these ditches are no more than deep cut drains and it seems incredible that they were ever large enough to carry traffic.[26]

Billericay Canal Project

In 1825 a scheme complementary to the Mardyke proposals was prepared by Alexander Clark, engineer, and J. & H. Clayton, surveyors, and the statutory documents were forwarded to the county on 30 November 1825. This was 'An intended canal from the River Crouch near Battlesbridge to Purfleet and also of an intended branch canal from the said canal to Billericay'.[27] The branch canal was to rise 181ft in 7¼ miles. It was proposed to enter the canal at sea level by an entrance lock and then to rise through 5 locks almost immediately. There would then follow 7 intermediate locks and the final rise of 100ft in 1¼ miles would require 16 locks before the terminal basin was reached. Billericay's trade could never have justified the expense involved in constructing such a series of locks and nothing more was heard of the scheme.

Mundon or White House Farm Canal

About two miles south-east of Maldon there is a short canal approximately 1¼ miles long running from Southey Creek on the river Blackwater in a southerly direction to White House Farm, Mundon. This canal, which is now at the upper end little more than a rush-filled cut with a few inches of water in the bottom, was built as a private venture without Parliamentary sanction by the owner of the land, James Marriage. It was dug in the autumn of 1832 and is described in a property survey made 5 January 1833 as follows:

> A canal has lately been dug from the River Wall to the Homestead with the intention of forming a wharf for coals, chalk, and other Manure, also Materials for the repair of the roads. This when finished will add to the value of the property.[28]

A basin was constructed near the house at the upper end of the canal and it seems that a lock and lockhouse were built at the entrance of the canal from the creek. The remains of the lock chamber and gates were removed in 1974 when the Essex River

Authority converted the lower part of the canal into a drainage channel. The lock floor and walls were said to be of red brick and timber and the cill was an 8in-square pine baulk. Unfortunately no photographic or other record was made at the time of clearance.

Goods were carried on the canal in a 15-ton lighter and navigation continued for about fifty years, but in the 1880s it ceased to be a navigable waterway.

There is no evidence from the parish records that it was ever used for the conveyance of road materials and its sole traffic was probably agricultural goods to Maldon and other coastwise places and manure from London.

Chelmer & Blackwater Navigation

The River Chelmer is not one of the great rivers of England. It flows gently through the Essex countryside with no dramatic overtones, but its fall has been sufficient to provide the necessary power for the waterwheels of the many mills established over the centuries on its course. It has its source in the north of the county and flows in a generally southerly direction to Chelmsford, where it is joined by the Can and the Wid, then turns to the east to meet the Blackwater near Beeleigh Abbey and finally enters the broadening tidal section of the Blackwater at Maldon.

Despite the obvious advantages which would accrue from making a navigation along the fourteen miles of the River Chelmer it was 120 years from the first proposal until the vested interests which opposed it were overcome and the navigation completed. The main opposition throughout this time came from the port of Maldon which feared the loss of revenue if traffic were permitted to travel direct to Chelmsford. The opposition also found active support among the owners and tenants of the watermills who were dependent on the flow of the Chelmer for their power supply.

The first concept of a navigation between the two towns came from that prolific innovator Andrew Yarranton who, in 1677 in his work *England's Improvement by Sea and Land*, recorded the results of a survey he had made. He estimated that the cost of making the river navigable, including damages to land-owners, would be £8,000. A plan based on his proposals includ-ing the brief of a Bill was prepared, but because of Maldon's opposition nothing more was heard of the scheme.

Nearly half a century later, on 13 and 14 July 1733, John Hore surveyed for a navigation. This John Hore (or Hoar) was also concerned with the Kennet, Stroudwater and Avon (Bristol) Navigations.[29] He propounded two schemes, the first to make the river navigable for £9,355, and the second to cut a canal on a new line for £12,870.[30] Despite the considerable difference in cost between the two schemes, Hore advocated the latter as in the interest of the landowners and millers. Hore justified his ap-proach by an analysis of the probable returns, which showed a profit of £382 pa; while those opposing the scheme with equal positiveness and equally unproven figures showed a loss of £430 10s to the proprietors. Maldon also objected to the scheme on the ground that the canal would reduce materially the income Maldon derived from tolls, duties and wharfage. The objec-tions proving more powerful than the proposals, the scheme was abandoned.

In 1762 the idea of a navigation was again revived and surveys were carried out by both John Smeaton and Thomas Yeoman. Smeaton's estimate was £16,697 and Yeoman's was close to this figure. The proposals were supported by Chelmsford and again opposed by Maldon. The latter had as its spokesman John Strutt, who later became MP for Maldon.[31] In 1765 Yeoman produced yet another plan and this was the basis of the appli-cation to Parliament for a Bill.[32] He recommended widening the river at the surface to 30ft and at the bottom to 20ft with a constant depth of 4ft, locks to be 70ft × 14ft 1in. His estimate was £13,000. The opposition were under no illusions regarding Yeoman's position in the civil engineering field and they there-fore sought someone equally illustrious to prepare a scheme to counter Yeoman's proposals. They made approaches to Smea-ton, Brindley, Grundy, Langley Edwards, and Nickalls but all refused on the grounds that they were too busy. Eventually they secured the services of two brothers, Ferdinando Stratford and

William Stratford. Ferdinando Stratford was at this time also working on the proposed Chippenham extension of the Avon Navigation from Bristol.[33] The lot of engineers was no easy one for both the Stratford brothers contracted ague and fever on the Chelmer survey—Ferdinando died as a result on 28 April 1766 and William was ill for twelve months before recovering. Meanwhile Yeoman had his problems too, as the following extract from a letter of 19 June 1764 to John Smeaton demonstrates:

> . . . Now Suppose I should tell you that I am not paid for what I have done will you believe me and if I should add that the under Sheriff took it in his head two Days to attend the Survey with Company and order'd provision & to the Water Sides, lay all night at Danbury at my Inn, and left me to pay every thing even so much as his and his friends Corn and Hay for their Horses, will you give credence to it? but so it is my Friend and so it must be, until they take it in their Heads to pay; Should not I charge two Years Interest in September next? . . .
>
>   I beg that my best wishes be acceptable to Mrs Smeaton, Children and Self and am with sincerity
>   Dear Sir
>   Your most obedient and obliged humble Servt
>   Thos Yeoman.[34]

Stratford, too, had been carrying out his investigations to build up a case for the opposition. He wrote to Strutt advising him to stipulate that the locks should be built with stone walls and not constructed with timber and planked. He pointed out that the material was not durable enough and at Weybridge in Surrey 'which has been one of the worst navigations in that respect the proprietors are rebuilding of them [the locks] with stone'. He continued 'that when Yeoman undertook the Northampton Navigation he promised security, but in the end eight subscribers were obliged to be the security for £4,000. Probably the same game may be played again for Mr Yeoman had some hand in that affair.'[35]

On the basis of Yeoman's 1765 plan an Act was passed on 6 June 1766 'for making the River Chelmer navigable from the

Port of Maldon, to the Town of Chelmsford'. The term during which the improvements might be effected was limited to twelve years, but no work was to be done until 25 per cent of the cost had been advanced. Despite efforts made at several meetings it was found impossible to raise the £13,000 required.

On 2 October 1772 Peter Muilman of Stapleford Tawney, a man of Dutch origin, invited the minister, churchwardens, and principal inhabitants to a meeting at the Chelmsford Coffee House, and proposed to revive the idea of making the Chelmer navigable. However, at a later meeting on 17 October 1772 it was decided not to follow that proposal but instead to make a new cut from Maldon to Chelmsford. Muilman rather naively announced that

> by this plan we shall at once remove every complaint and save a considerable expense; as, by proceeding on this plan, we shall want few or may be no locks at all. This being resolved on, the next step is to take Counsel of the ingenious in this kind of navigation.[36]

Unfortunately he does not disclose how he intended to cope with the fall from Chelmsford to Maldon without locks. He proposed to ask Whitworth to make a survey at his expense and then he would undertake the navigation himself. After this the scheme again went into limbo and in parenthesis it might be mentioned that Muilman committed suicide in 1790.

The success of inland navigation in other parts of the country and the increasing economic expansion towards the close of the eighteenth century caused the inhabitants of Chelmsford to feel that they were becoming unnecessarily isolated. So, in 1792, interest again began to be taken in the possibility of water communication between the county town and the coast. The continued opposition of Maldon had now over-reached itself for the new proposal envisaged the navigation terminating not at Maldon, but a little to the north between Heybridge and Goldhanger at the place now known as Heybridge Basin on a stretch of the Blackwater called Colliers' Reach. This new line was surveyed by Charles Wedge under the direction of John Rennie;[37] and a further survey was carried out, again under Rennie's direction, in 1793 by Matthew Hall.[38] These surveys showed that by by-passing Maldon the length of the navigation would be increased by two miles to 13¾ miles.

The submission of a Parliamentary petition for a Bill led to the publication of a pamphlet expressing Maldon's ire and indignation. *Observations on the Chelmer Navigation Bill now pending in Parliament* criticized in round terms what was termed the 'Manifest Impropriety of passing any Bill under these Circumstances in the present Sessions'.[39] The pamphlet alleged that the proposals were unsupported by evidence of public utility or expediency, but the issue which seems to have goaded the writers of the pamphlet more than anything else was the apparent failure on the part of the promoters of the Bill to have any kind of consultation with the Maldon people. Despite this opposition the Bill received the Royal assent on 17 June 1793.[40]

The Act established 'The Company of the Proprietors of the Chelmer and Blackwater Navigation', listing 147 names as proprietors, and empowered the making of a navigation between Chelmsford and Colliers' Reach; but it did not refer in its title to Maldon. The proprietors were authorized to raise among themselves £40,000 in £100 shares and a further £20,000 could be raised either by the issue of new shares or by borrowing money on the tolls.

The tolls were laid down on a mileage basis (milestones were to be erected by the side of the navigation) and they ranged from ¼d per mile per quarter for oats, malt and other grain not otherwise specified to 2d per mile per chaldron for coal and 2½d per mile per ton for all other goods. Stone etc for roadmaking, other than for turnpikes, was to be carried free. Landowners' pleasure boats were to be toll-free on condition they did not pass through any lock. The Act was to come into effect on 15 July 1793 and work began soon afterwards on improving the existing river in the reaches near Chelmsford. Construction was nominally under the direction of John Rennie, but was actually controlled by his assistant, Richard Coates, who had also assisted on the works on the Ipswich & Stowmarket Navigation.

Plates 5 & 6 Chelmer & Blackwater Navigation: *(above)* a funeral party on its way to the canal-served cemetery at Heybridge, c. 1905-10; *(below)* a barge near Little Baddow

Plates 7 & 8 On the Stour near Wormingford before World War I: *(above)* horse towing; *(below)* a steam tug and lighter

Apart from the long cut of 2½ miles between Beeleigh and
Heybridge basin, and the shorter cut from the river to the
terminal basin at Chelmsford, a distance of about half a mile,
a number of short cuts accommodated the locks provided to
compensate for the mill falls. Altogether 13 locks were constructed, including the sea-lock at Heybridge Basin. They are,
from the Chelmsford basin, Springfield, Barnes Mill, Sandford,
Cuton, Stonehouse, Little Baddow, Paper Mill, Rushes or
Weir, Hoe Mill, Ricketts, two at Beeleigh, and the sea-lock.
The two at Beeleigh were required because the navigation
diverges from the course of the Chelmer through a short cut to
join the Blackwater along which the line of the canal continues
before entering another cut to Heybridge Basin and Colliers'
Reach. Following the construction of the navigation the water
of the Blackwater was diverted into the Chelmer at Beeleigh

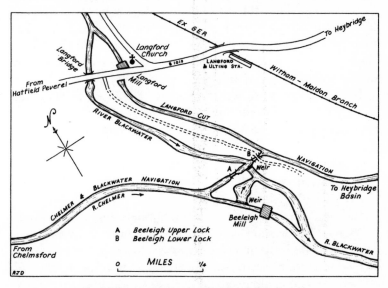

5. Beeleigh crossing on the Chelmer & Blackwater

Falls. The two locks at Beeleigh are therefore sited one on each
side of the present course of the Blackwater so that the navigation is protected to a great degree in both flood and drought
conditions. The total fall from Chelmsford to Heybridge is approximately 75ft.

Meanwhile, as the early stages of construction began, Maldon re-examined its position. It had failed to prevent the passing of the Act and it now sought to retrieve something from the loss. Benjamin Henry Latrobe, who had studied engineering under Smeaton and had worked on the Basingstoke Canal, was called in to advise. Latrobe was later to gain eminence as an architect in the United States, designing Baltimore cathedral, and beginning the Capitol at Washington. Latrobe submitted two reports.[41] The first in 1793 recommended the deepening of the Blackwater and straightening its course as far as Fullbridge where the road linking Maldon to Heybridge crosses the river. His second report in 1794 improved on his earlier proposals and this, together with a suggested improvement of the Blackwater upstream to its junction with the Chelmer, was incorporated in a Parliamentary petition presented on 3 March 1794.[42] The proprietors of the navigation at once realized that if this proposal were accomplished it would mean that their expensive cut from Beeleigh to Heybridge, and Heybridge Basin itself, would be valueless. It was therefore rigorously opposed and in the end dropped.

By April 1796 work was sufficiently advanced to allow the lower part of the navigation to be used for traffic. The *Chelmsford Chronicle* reported that on Saturday 23 April 1796 there

arrived in the grand bason at the entrance to the Chelmer Navigation near Collier's Reach the good brig '*Fortunes Increase*', Robert Parker, master, laden with 150 chaldrons of the best Burnmore coals from Sunderland, consigned to Messrs. Bryde and Coates, the first adventurers in that navigation. This is the first shipload of coals which the navigation has received. It may be worthy of remark that the '*Fortunes Increase*' is a good old brig and during her journeys on the seas about 40 years has never experienced any misfortune. Yesterday three wagons loaded with coals from a coal yard at Boreham, stocked by the Chelmer Navigation arrived here [Chelmsford] with their horses decorated with coloured ribbons as being the first carted coals from that navigation. On Tuesday last, [26 April 1796] a barge was loaded with near

150 sacks of flour at Hoe Mill from whence it proceeded by the new navigation to Collier's Reach for the London Market. This appears to be the first barge load of flour conveyed upon that navigation.

By 3 June 1796 advertisements had started appearing in the local press offering coals for sale at Baddow Mill coal wharf. Three weeks later it was announced that as the coal merchants had reduced their prices by 2s per chaldron, there would also be a reduction at Baddow Wharf. Price cutting had begun.

The final stretch of the navigation to be completed was the cut from the river to the terminal basin at Chelmsford and this took almost another year. On 5 and 6 September 1796 two barges of foreign wheat were brought up to Mr Marriage's mill about $\frac{3}{4}$ mile from Chelmsford and it was hoped soon to see that 'beneficial undertaking completed'. But it was not until 2 June 1797 that an anticipatory news item appeared in the *Chelmsford Chronicle*.

The navigation from Collier's Reach near Maldon to this town being completed all the barges now ready with coals etc. will on Saturday morning 3 June 1797 arrive at the last lock in Springfield Mead and at one o'clock proceed in grand procession with colours flying etc. into the bason near Springfield Bridge, the ground around, which is now divided and let to different persons for wharfs, will in a few days after opening be plentifully stored with coals, lime, chalk, cinders, etc.

By the time the navigation was complete the cost had risen to approximately £50,000, a far cry from Yarranton's £8,000 even allowing for changing values.

Troubles were not long in coming. In December 1797 heavy rainfall caused serious flooding and shoals were formed to such an extent that barges were impeded and coal stocks were depleted in Chelmsford.[43] This problem increased with every flood until on 20 March 1799 at a meeting of the navigation committee the following resolution was passed:

Whereas the Chelmer and Blackwater Navigation appears to be in many parts very defective particularly at and near

Paper Mill, Richards [sic] Lock and Hoe Mill insomuch that from the gathering of shoals after every flood the Navigation nearly becomes impassable and has not of late been navigable for vessels carrying more than 10 tons, and whereas it appears to the Committee that these impediments have arisen from a defect in the original survey by not foreseeing the inconveniences and bad consequences of passing so near the mills; Resolved that Lord Petre be requested to see Mr Rennie and state to him the said defects of the navigation together with the opinion of the Committee that they think they have a claim upon Mr Rennie to take a survey of the line of the navigation and point out a remedy for the defects without any further expense to the Company.

Rennie accepted these strictures and carried out a survey on 25 May 1799. In his report of 5 June 1799 he made the comment:

I lament that it was not in my power to plan and lay out this navigation in the first instance. Had it been so I trust the alteration now proposed would not have been wanted, but as the matter now stands I am ready and willing to contribute my time to the rectification of the defects discovered and I trust when rectified the trade which will be caused on this navigation will reward the proprietors for the great expenditure.[44]

In 1805 further problems arose when the millers at each of the six mills on the navigation, Moulsham, Barnes, Sandford, Little Baddow, Paper and Hoe, complained of the loss of water used by barges in passing the locks near each mill, and the leakage and bad condition of the locks, and requested damages. Rennie was again engaged and, following a survey on 25 November 1805, he recommended improvements costing £4,918 for settling the differences with the millers. In spite of these efforts the millers were still trying to get satisfaction in 1807.

Traffic started to increase right from the opening of the navigation. The early months of 1799 brought severe weather and by 8 February the navigation was completely frozen over and it was reported that because of this coals were very dear in

Chelmsford, a remark which would hardly have been made unless the price had already been lowered because of the navigation.[45] It was not until 1 March that the waterway was open again. The facility of cheap transport of coals also led to the establishment of a gasworks in Chelmsford in 1819—this was the second constructed in Essex and the first one at an inland situation. The Chelmsford Gas Light Co purchased 'a convenient spot beside the Chelmer Navigation for the receipt of coals' and today the Eastern Gas Board still occupy the site by the canal.

Examples of dividends paid are as follows:

	per cent		per cent
1811	2½	1848	3
1818	5	1858	3
1828	5	1868	3¼
1838	4	1920	1½

In 1846 £100 shares were selling for £66 but by 1918 they had fallen to £17 10s. The fall after 1838 was undoubtedly due to the opening of the Eastern Counties Railway through Chelmsford in March 1843, but the navigation benefited from the fact that there was never a direct line between Maldon and Chelmsford; the only route, a roundabout one through Witham, was opened for traffic on 15 August 1848.

Goods carried included not only coal but timber, bricks, stone, and general cargo inwards and grain and flour outwards. To help in the distribution there were local wharves near the villages of Little Baddow, Boreham, Ulting, and Heybridge, as well as the terminal ones at Chelmsford and Heybridge Basin. The barges used, of 25 tons capacity, were a special type being flat-bottomed with a very shallow draught. The navigation had the distinction of being the shallowest of any in the country on which commercial traffic was regularly carried. The barges were 60ft × 16ft, with a draught of 2ft, the maximum size which could pass through the locks. The barges, which are all day boats with no cabin accommodation, were horse drawn until the 1960s but later diesel-powered with an outboard motor.

The sea-lock is of much greater capacity. It was constructed to take vessels 107ft × 26ft, giving access for vessels drawing 8ft at neap tides and 12ft at springs. The lock has been lengthened since the World War II in order to accommodate coasters bringing in timber from the Continent.

There was one short branch canal originally called Mr Westcomb's Navigation because it ran across his land and consequently did not require Parliamentary sanction for its construction. The branch leaves the main line just below the lower of the two Beeleigh locks and runs for about half a mile in a north-westerly direction to the Heybridge—Hatfield Peverel road near Langford church. It served Langford mill and therefore later became known as Langford Cut. It was opened at the same time as the main navigation and carried a substantial traffic during the first half of the nineteenth century and as late as the 1870s. As far as can be ascertained the last barge to traverse it carried 100 quarters of wheat to the mill on 9 August 1881.

There is no doubt that the canalization of the river has justified the foresight of the original promoters by helping Chelmsford to grow from a small market town to the stage where it was able to take advantage of the railway and become the important centre that it is today. It was the availability of land beside the Chelmer & Blackwater Navigation, with transport facilities for the import of raw materials and the export of finished goods, that led William Bentall to establish in 1804 his works at Heybridge which became, during the nineteenth century, one of the most important agricultural engineering firms in Essex.

The navigation was in use commercially until 1972 although, latterly, the only traffic was the carriage of timber from the wharf where the coasters discharged at Heybridge Basin to the sawmills and timber yard of Brown and Son Ltd at the Chelmsford basin, and the barges made the return journey empty. The section between Heybridge and the sea has been used for some time for the mooring of pleasure craft, but until the cessation of commercial traffic pleasure craft were not allowed to pass through the locks. Now a limited number may do so. The proprietors are also aware of the leisure potential of this attractive waterway and have themselves started operating a trip boat during the summer months. The navigation was not nationalized, and remains an independent body owned by the Company of the Proprietors of the Chelmer and Blackwater

Navigation Ltd. This company still maintains the old tradition of a formal inspection of the navigation by the proprietors and their friends.

Colne Navigation

Colchester, the oldest recorded town in Britain, lies on the river Colne and its importance in Roman times was probably due to its position at the head of the navigable tidal section of that river. Though the corporation created by a charter of Richard I, had jurisdiction over the river as far as St Osyth, some eleven miles downstream, it was concerned primarily with landing fees etc, and restrictions over landing places, rather than with the maintenance of a navigation.

This legal defect was first rectified by an Act of 1623, but later in the century it was clear that more improvements were necessary. A further Act to cleanse and make navigable the channel from the Hythe at Colchester to Wivenhoe, a distance of about four miles, received the royal assent on 16 May 1698.[46] This authorized the levy of tolls and the borrowing of money for the maintenance of the navigation and as it was soon found that the tolls were inadequate for the purpose, large sums were borrowed. Commissioners were appointed to oversee the work and to negotiate between the corporation and the landowners.

The provisions were to remain in force for 21 years and when they expired in 1719 Colchester obtained a renewal for a further 21 years.[47] This renewal, while it authorized the raising of additional funds and the construction of towpaths on both sides of the river, also extended the representation on the governing body to include individuals other than members of the corporation. As events turned out this was a vitally important and far-sighted provision which proved invaluable in 1750. Soon after 1719 a lock was constructed about half-a-mile south of Hythe bridge which created a non-tidal basin at the Hythe. A further renewal of the Act was obtained in 1740 which made the powers of the previous Acts, together with additional powers, perpetual.[48] This continued concern for the navigation seemed to augur well for its future but, as has been pointed out, 'the slump of the early decades shattered not only the cloth trade but the town's confidence in itself and its future'. This slump resulted in the collapse of the power and authority of the mayor and commonalty and the consequent failure of control over the navigation had by 1749 led to its decay and the collapse of the lock.[49] In the absence of the borough court there was no sanction to compel the payment of river dues, and money which ought to have been spent on repairs remained in the hands of the late receiver-general and was not available.

Fortunately the 1719 Act had authorized the appointment of non-corporation representatives in the commission and they in 1750 were able to obtain a further Act which vested the powers of the commission in the justices of the East Division of Essex for thirty years.[50] This Act also levied an additional 3d a chaldron on coals for thirty years to help to pay for repairs and maintenance. The Act was extended again in 1781 for another 40 years when members of the corporation were permitted to act as commissioners though the corporation itself was precluded from acting in a corporate capacity.[51] Yet a further Act repealed the foregoing in 1811 but by this time the navigation was on a much sounder financial basis.[52]

Throughout this period there had apparently been no thought of radically improving or extending the navigation beyond maintaining the lock which served the dual purpose of providing safe berthing facilities at the Hythe and acting as a dam and sluice to ensure a head of water for scouring the tidal part of the channel to the sea. In 1842 Peter Bruff, the engineer, deposited a plan for a ship canal running parallel to and on the east side of the river from Wivenhoe to the Hythe where it would terminate in a dock. Entry to the canal was to be by a sea-lock at Wivenhoe and the canal would thus have bypassed the existing lock below the Hythe.[53] Bruff also proposed a barge canal from the Hythe along the Colne valley to land owned by the Eastern Counties Railway at Lexden, north of the present A12 Colchester bypass. On this $2\frac{1}{4}$ mile canal there were to be locks at East and Middle Mills and also one between the barge canal and the proposed ship canal dock. It was apparently intended that the Eastern Counties Railway should build a short branch from their main line to the terminal basin.[54]

On 9 May 1846 a report drew attention to the derelict state of the navigation and the encroachment of wharves and warehouses into the channel. The concern aroused by this report led to a public inquiry by Ellis and Brooks, two surveying officers appointed by the Admiralty, into the question of the improvement of the navigation.[55] At this inquiry plans submitted by three engineers were considered but there was no further mention of the barge canal. Each plan included the construction of a new lock and a non-tidal dock, though varying in details.

In the end none of these schemes came to fruition for on 31 March 1847 the Colchester, Stour Valley, Sudbury & Halstead Railway opened the 1¾-mile Hythe branch linking the E.C.R. east of Colchester station with the Hythe. Instead the river was widened and deepened and the old lock removed. In 1892 after a lapse of over 100 years the navigation reverted to Colchester corporation. Today Colchester is a busy port handling a regular traffic in small motor coastal vessels, but the river remains tidal and strictly it can no longer be regarded as an inland waterway.

CHAPTER IV

The Stour and Suffolk Navigations

◆◆◆◆◆◆◆◆◆◆◆◆◆◆◆◆◆◆◆◆◆◆◆◆◆◆◆◆◆◆◆◆◆◆◆◆◆ ◆ ◆◆◆◆◆◆◆◆◆◆◆◆◆◆◆◆◆◆◆◆◆◆◆◆◆◆◆◆◆◆◆◆◆◆◆◆◆

Stour Navigation

THE Stour rises at Wratting Common in Cambridgeshire, and, flowing in a generally easterly direction, forms for many miles in its lower reaches the boundary between Essex and Suffolk. It broadens out into a long estuary which unites with another long estuary, that of the Orwell, just before the joint waters reach the open sea between Landguard Point and Harwich. In its passage between Essex and Suffolk it winds through a wide valley set in an unspoilt and particularly attractive countryside and its beauty was the inspiration for many of John Constable's paintings which are not only superb works of art but also an accurate pictorial record of many aspects of this navigable waterway.

As with other rivers in the eastern counties it may well have carried in earlier times a certain amount of local traffic without there being any formal or legal arrangements but in the absence of known records it is impossible to determine its extent. In the early seventeenth century the practicalities of a proper navigation were being canvassed, for in 1634 the mayor of Sudbury, Daniel Biatt, spent 2s 'at the Chequer in wyne with Mr. Doctor Warren and Mr. Spenser when did wee meete about making the river navigable'.[1] Mr Spenser was Arnold Spencer who was also interested in improving the river Ouse. Following the meeting with the mayor of Sudbury he obtained Letters Patent on 11 December 1638 for making the Stour navigable from Sudbury to Manningtree at the head of the estuary.

Possibly because of the troubled times prior to the outbreak of the Civil War combined with Spencer's concern with the

Ouse improvements, together with his financial difficulties of 1644, no action appears to have been taken on improving the Stour at this stage. A further proposal in 1658, about the time that Spencer died, by a Mr Maynard to open up the river from Sudbury to Manningtree towards which the Corporation of Sudbury offered £5 also failed to generate any activity. Before the end of the century the Letters Patent had been assigned to John Little and Benjamin Dodd who later stated that they had spent great sums on completing the navigation.

The results of their efforts could not have been particularly effective for in 1703 the mayor and corporation of Sudbury were themselves promoting a Bill for making the Stour navigable to Sudbury. Little and Dodd petitioned Parliament against the Bill on 10 January 1704 on the grounds that their rights under the Letters Patent might be prejudiced and they requested that there should be some provision in the Bill to safeguard them.[2] The petition was rejected, which suggests that their rights were minimal.

The Bill had an uneventful passage and was passed on 16 February 1705.[3] It nominated the mayor and aldermen of Sudbury together with ten named gentlemen to be the undertakers. Arbitration of differences was placed in the hands of the usual lengthy list of commissioners. The necessary works for making the river navigable were to be started before 24 June 1708 and completed before 24 June 1713. The commissioners had the right to appoint other undertakers if the work were not completed in time. Millers between Manningtree and Sudbury had the right of toll-free carriage of millstones and building materials to their mills. This was clearly a concession designed to limit the amount of opposition from the millowners. While a good deal of the traffic was expected to be under sail the Act stated that 'it will be necessary in some places, to hale or tow up barges . . . by the strength of men, horses, engines or other means'. To provide for this it seems that towpaths were laid down in a rather ad hoc fashion depending on the willingness of landowners to allow the passage of men and horses along the edges of their fields, and this discontinuous nature of the paths led to problems in later years.

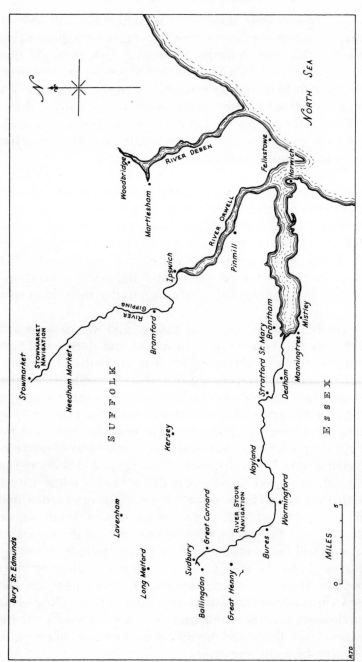

6. The Stour and Ipswich & Stowmarket Navigations

Authority was also given for the 'setting up and use of winches and other engines in convenient places for towing or haling the vessels and men to go on the banks to operate these winches'. These winches were provided to haul the barges through the flash-locks or staunches of which there were thirteen. They were constructed as follows:

Two substantial posts with a bottom cross cill were fixed at a given distance apart sufficient to permit a boat to pass easily between them. Upon one of these posts was a beam turning on its centre and long enough to span the opening. When the staunch was used the boatmen turned the beam across the opening and placed vertically in the stream a number of narrow planks resting against the bottom cill and the swinging beam thus forming a weir which raised the water in the stream about 5 feet high; the boards were then withdrawn, the swinging beam turned back, and all the boats which had been collected above were carried by the flash over the shallow below. By repeating this operation at given intervals the boats were able to proceed a distance of 23 miles in two or three days.[4]

In addition to the staunches thirteen pound-locks were constructed and these, too, were of a distinctive type. The gates were pintle hung, ie like field gates, instead of having the more usual heel post. This method of hanging throws a strain on the land posts making them liable to collapse inwards. To prevent this on the Stour the land posts were carried well above ground level and a lintel fitted between their upper ends across the entrance to the lock. The sides of the locks were originally earth but later they were constructed in timber. In the nineteenth century the staunches were eliminated and the locks reconstructed so that ultimately there were 15 locks between Sudbury and the sea.

Nothing was said in the Act about financial arrangements. In fact the capital was created by the issue of 48 shares of £100 each, half of which was acquired by one London merchant, Cornelius Denn, while the other half was divided between another London merchant, Dean Cock, and several Sudbury clothiers. The two London merchants were authorized by the undertakers in 1706 to execute the necessary works. The capital raised proved inadequate and further calls were made on the shareholders which raised the final amount to £9,000. This included £800 for 16 barges as well as £6,500 for the actual navigation works. The remaining £1,700 was for warehouses etc. Despite the additional cost, the works could not have been very extensive, which suggests that some of the work may have been rehabilitation rather than new construction.

The date of opening to Sudbury is not known but in May 1709 2,211 tons of north-east coast coals were carried up river from Manningtree to Sudbury. In 1710 an agreement was made between Cornelius Denn and a boatman, John Ricklingham, of Whitby, master and mate of 'ye good ship called ye Ryall of Whitby of ye burthen 150 toynes'. Ricklingham agreed to carry coal from Sunderland to Manningtree at 24 shillings per chaldron. At Manningtree the coal was transferred to barges and sent up river.[5]

The early promise of a successful navigation was not fulfilled and further calls had to be made on the proprietors to provide additional capital. When Daniel Defoe visited the eastern counties in 1722 he wrote that 'the navigation does not answer the charge, at least not to advantage'. By 1734 the lack of capital had so restricted their activities that the proprietors were unable to maintain a transport service on the navigation. They therefore arranged with one George Elliott that he would bring a 1,000 tons of coal up the navigation while the company would allow the use of their barges and distribute and sell the coal in Sudbury and Ballingdon, in return for which Elliott would pay the company 6s a ton. This arrangement lasted only two years and then the company decided that anyone could use the river upon payment of the appropriate tolls.

Some idea of the toll receipts and expenditure is given in the table opposite for years for which figures have survived.

Although the 1705 Act had empowered the commissioners to elect others when vacancies occurred, this power had not been properly used, so that by the end of the 1770s only two were left. As the 1705 Act required a quorum of fifteen to elect new commissioners a new Act had to be obtained nominating new commissioners. This was done in 1781[6] and among the appointments were Golding Constable, miller of Dedham, father of the painter, John Constable, and Samuel and John Gainsborough, brothers of Thomas Gainsborough, the other great Stour valley painter. The opportunity was also taken of including in the new Act powers to enable the commissioners to prescribe towing paths and to make the proprietors responsible for upkeep of bridges, gates, stiles, etc.

Year	Tolls	Expenditure
	£	£
1736–7	399	428
1743–4	329	360
1744–5	299	317
1750–1	395	297
1752–4 (two years)	697	858
1754–5	540	540
1755–6	630	607

The first meeting of the commissioners under the new Act was held at the Queens Head, Nayland, on 24 September 1781 and after a discussion on the desirability of making a complete survey of the river it was arranged that Golding Constable and William Strutt should carry out this task.[7] They reported back on 30 September 1782 on the need for extensive dredging. This was the start of a much more positive attitude towards maintaining the efficiency of the navigation and consequently the use of the river increased. Trade on the Stour between 1782 and 1817 doubled, rising from £700 in 1782 to £1,400 in 1817 with a peak in 1812 of £1,600. In order to keep pace with this increase warehouses were constructed in Sudbury in 1791 and 1806. The demand for coal grew during this period and the proprietors attributed this to 'the deficiency in wood and the general mode of living requiring a greater use of coal'.[8] Coal was indeed one of the important commodities carried on the Stour, the others being grain, flour, malt, and later bricks. The coal trade was a vital factor in the revenue of the Sudbury trade, for while 50–65 per cent of the weight carried on the Stour went to Sudbury, the toll structure was such that that weight provided no less than 85 per cent of the total revenue derived from the carriage of coal. It was therefore in the proprietors' best interests to develop the Sudbury coal trade.[9]

It was also during this period, when the promotion of canals was taking place elsewhere, that proposals were made to provide navigable links between the Stour and Hadleigh to the south and Boxford to the north. Neither proposal came to fruition, nor did a similar one in 1833 for linking Lavenham and the Stour.[10] A very short branch, constructed at this period, was later known as the Ballingdon Cut. This served some brickworks and limekilns on the south side of the river opposite Sudbury. It was this cut that was used over a century later to sink a fleet of barges, one of which has recently been recovered and is being restored by the River Stour Trust.

Trade continued to improve and by 1817 the dividend paid was 11 per cent, but as early as 1836 the coming shadows of the railway system were causing concern to the proprietors and they sought the advice of William Cubitt. His reply makes interesting reading. 'The bill on the projected Eastern Counties Railway will not pass the Commons and Lords as the scheme is too ruinous for even the gullibility of Englishmen.' He also averred that 'he can prove that heavy goods can be taken as cheap or cheaper from the various ports on the coast; that iron is risen in price 25 per cent; and that he has lately been examining the Liverpool and Manchester Railway and finds that it is in a very unsound condition, and in consequence no heavy goods are now carried as they find they do not pay for the wear and tear; the Bridgwater Canal which runs in the same direction as the railway now does more business than before'.[11] Cubitt's view at that time was that rail carriage could never compete with water carriage. Nevertheless the Stour proprietors' surveyor considered that the navigation should be made as competitive as possible. He suggested modernization of the locks and a cut at Wormingford to eliminate a considerable loop in the river. Traces of that cut and the two locks constructed on it still remain. He also recommended that the proprietors should acquire haling rights wherever possible so that adequate and continuous towing paths could be provided. The modernization programme cost some £12,000 but it placed the navigation once more on an efficient working basis. It was now possible for barges to navigate the 22 miles to Mistley in 12 hours and return in 14.

Reform of the toll structure took place at this time, and making the navigation competitive as well as efficient enabled it to remain in a very flourishing condition with the share value of £100 shares running at £800 in the years around 1840. A serious proposal was also made in 1842 to extend the navigation 8 miles further upstream to Clare but as this would have required 10 locks and cost £30,000 the scheme was dropped.

A year later the Eastern Counties Railway from London to Colchester was completed leaving Sudbury some 11 miles to the north—and a suitable prize for another railway promoter. Before long the Colchester, Stour Valley, Sudbury & Halstead Railway was projected and the promoters, seeing the successful Stour Navigation as a rival, sought to buy the shares. The asking price of £1,000 per £100 share was considered excessive, however, and the deal was rejected. While the railway was being built the navigation continued to thrive and in fact reached a peak in 1848, when the toll receipts amounted to £3,400, the year before the railway opened from Marks Tey to Sudbury. After that the tolls slumped to £1,400 in 1852.

Another matter, peculiar to the Stour, came to the fore at this period. From the early days of the navigation horse towage had been impeded by the discontinuous nature of the towpath; discontinuous partly because it changed banks frequently with no adequate crossing places such as turnover bridges as are found on other canals, and partly because the towpath itself was crossed by the boundary fences of each piece of land. These fences were ungated on the towpath and the situation is well illustrated in Constable's painting 'The Leaping Horse' which shows a barge horse jumping one of them. The problem from the landowner's point of view was referred to much earlier on 24 September 1810 when complaints were received by the commissioners that the jumps, as they were so called, were too low to keep out cattle etc. An order was made that the jumps were to be 3ft high, though this was modified on 10 May 1811 to 2ft 10in.

If there could have been a Grand National for barge horses, those which worked the Stour Navigation would have been prime contenders. Constable is recorded as saying that the horses were in finer condition than the wretched animals that towed the barges near London. Nevertheless, in a survey made on 31 July and 1 August 1850 it was found that there were no less than 123 jumps between Sudbury and Manningtree and in addition 20 boating places. These were places where the horse had to be ferried across the river because the towpath changed sides. The barge would be steered close to the bank and at the critical moment the horse would leap onto the barge while the latter was still under way. Then the steersman would immediately swing the barge over to the other bank where the horse would leap ashore and continue towing the barge from the other bank. That the jumps were not all easy ones may be seen from the surveyor's comments: 'Jump no. 46 in Wiston Head where there is a tree standing in an inconvenient place and should come down to give room for the barge horses. . . . Jumps no. 112–120, these eight jumps are much too high and cannot be used without great danger to the barge horses. The same should be reduced to a reasonable height or gates substituted.' A particularly intriguing comment refers to jump no. 102: 'At Mr. Hardy's meadow where the horse was compelled to swim across the river.'[12]

Despite the tradition of the past and the reluctance of the riparian owners to institute change the surveyors, who included Abraham Constable, made the following recommendations: 'We deprecate the use of jumps in all cases except where absolutely necessary and strongly recommend the adoption of gates in lieu of jumps in all places where the banks are of sufficient height. We make the recommendations with a view to the protection of the land from depredation and trespasses of stock, the preservation of the barge horses from accidents and other injuries and the saving of labour to the animal. Also for facilitating the transit of merchandize and at the same time promoting the interest of the proprietors.' On the question of boatings they had this to say: 'Just below Bures bridge there are three boatings. This repetition of boatings within so short a distance ought to be avoided by removing the haling path to the opposite side of the river. There have been in the course of a few years several horses lost at this place.' The horses may have been good jumpers but like Grand National favourites they sometimes failed. Gradually over the years the jumps and the boatings were replaced by a more humane way of treating the horses.

Ten years later ways were still being sought to improve the facilities and to this end two of the proprietors made a tour of several canals where steam barges were being used and were impressed by their advantages. The question was further discussed in 1862 but the first price quoted (£600 plus extras) rather frightened them and the matter was shelved. However later in the year on 27 August they 'Resolved that Mr. Jeffries C. E. having produced models of an iron barge fitted with machinery for steam apparatus be engaged under a proper agreement to make one barge with steam engine and apparatus and attach the same to the proprietors wooden barge to be completed on or before 25 December 1862 for £400'.[13] The steam barge was not delivered to time and when it did arrive in 1863 it was found to be most unsatisfactory. Continued attempts were made to bring it into a serviceable condition and eventually in April 1864 a Mr Salter was called in to advise. He made experiments with the screw but finally concluded that paddles would be more efficient on the Stour.[14] The proprietors asked him to look further into the possibility of converting the barge into a paddle boat but after checking paddle boats elsewhere he realised that there was insufficient headroom under the Stour bridges.[15] As a last resort an additional screw was added and the shape of the boat altered at a cost of an extra £250. This seemed to do the trick and by December the barge was in working order. It had a short life as even after modification it was not a success and in December 1867 it was offered for sale at £750.[16] Its reputation must have been widely known for there were no offers then or for some time subsequently. Eventually it was sold in 1873 for £150.[17]

Although in the early 1860s traffic was being maintained, as in the year ending April 1864 when 17,591 tons of coal, 32,786 quarters of wheat, 42,899 sacks of flour, 5,080 quarters of malt, 2,007 quarters of barley and oats, and nearly $3\frac{1}{2}$ million bricks were carried, after that period there was a steady fall and in 1868 only flour and bricks had not been affected by the 50 per cent drop in cargoes. Dividends, too, had dropped from 10 per cent in the early 1860s to 2 per cent in 1873.[18] As was also to be expected in a declining situation the standard of maintenance on the navigation was falling. An attempt to arrest this was made in 1879 when a self-acting dredging crane was purchased from Priestman Brothers of Hull.[19] This proved quite an asset. On one occasion it was reported that had the work it had performed been done by hand, the navigation would have had to be dried for three months.[20]

In 1882 an analysis of the traffic was made and this showed that it could be divided into three parts: (1) the trade between Sudbury and Mistley taking bricks and malt downstream and returning with coal and maize. The coal part of this trade was depressed because current Sudbury demand was for low-priced rail-borne coal from the Midland counties. (2) the trade from Nayland and Wiston to Mistley, consisting of flour for London and returning with coal and foreign wheat; and (3) the trade from Stratford and Dedham to Mistley again with flour for London and with similar return cargoes to (2).[21]

The brick trade in particular had been a very important one. For years the bricks, many of which had been produced in the brickfields adjacent to the Ballingdon Cut, had been sent to Mistley where they were transhipped for onward transit to Angerstein's wharf in Deptford, South London. From there they were distributed as required by rail or local transport. A considerable part of the nineteenth-century building boom in South London depended on these bricks and examples are also to be found in the Albert Hall and Liverpool Street station. In 1859 Allens, who owned the brickworks, were operating a fleet of 22 barges. Because of their dominant position in the Stour trade the Allens exercised a considerable influence over the navigation and by the end of the nineteenth century were virtually in control. But the sheer economic advantages of rail transport of this time began to curtail the brick traffic and with the decline of that the whole viability of the navigation began to be questioned. In 1892 the proprietors applied to the Board of Trade for a warrant of abandonment under the 1888 Railway & Canal Traffic Act, but this was refused on the grounds that the navigation had not been disused for at least three years.[22]

As an abandonment order could not be obtained the proprietors decided to form themselves into a limited company under the title of the River Stour Navigation Company Ltd and the company was formally incorporated on 31 December 1892, the nominal capital being 60 shares of £100. Trade continued to decline until by 1906 the annual expenditure involved in essential repairs, eg to locks, had begun to exceed the toll revenue. Eventually on 8 October 1914 the Company went into voluntary liquidation with assets of £46 and unsecured creditors of £65.

With the Great War still in its early days there was a proposal that the navigation should be taken over by the Government and improved so as to take 100-ton barges but the idea was dropped. Nevertheless a stay of execution was secured to prevent the formal winding up of the company and the shareholders became a trust, a small amount of traffic continuing to use the lower reaches of the navigation. It was the presence of this traffic which was responsible for the reconstruction of the locks at Brantham, Flatford, Stratford, and Dedham in 1928 by the South Essex Waterworks Company at a cost of £5,000 each though the subsequent usage did not justify the cost. The last barge went through to Sudbury in the early years of the Great War, probably about 1916, but Clovers, the millers at Dedham continued to use the river until 1930. In 1935 the Registrar of Joint Stock Companies was notified the 'the company is not now carrying on business or in operation . . . . . . River Stour has long since ceased to be used for navigation . . . . . . desired you will put into operation the provisions of Section 295 of the Companies Act 1929 by taking the name of the company off your Register'. The final statement came in 1937: 'The River Stour Navigation (Trust) Co. Ltd. was dissolved by notice in the London Gazette dated 19 March 1937'.

That was still not the end. In September 1968 a new company

was formed, The River Stour Trust Ltd, a company limited by guarantee and with no share capital, having for its objects 'the preservation, maintenance etc. of rivers and inland waterways for the use of the public . . .'. This Trust is now doing a very useful work in restoring, rehabilitating, and publicizing what is perhaps the most attractive river in the Eastern Counties, both in its associations and in its natural beauty, and ensuring that its history and traditions are not forgotten.

Legislative control is never static and in 1976 the Anglian Water Authority was empowered to become the navigation authority for the Stour. Time will show how this will affect the use of this lovely waterway.

Ipswich and Stowmarket Navigation

The north-westerly arm of the two creeks which join and enter the North Sea between Harwich to the south and Felixstowe to the north is the river Orwell. At the head of this tidal river lies Ipswich and it is here that the river Gipping, which has flowed from the higher ground to the south-west of Mendlesham in East Suffolk, changes its name from Gipping to Orwell.

The Gipping passes through only one town of any size, Stowmarket, and it was the stretch between Stowmarket and Ipswich which was to become canalized in the late eighteenth century. Occasional earlier use had, however, been made of the river, as when flat-bottomed boats were used to convey stone to Rattlesden in the thirteenth century for Bury St Edmunds abbey, or when the bells of Stowmarket church were taken downstream in the seventeenth century to be recast.[23]

Tentative proposals for making the river navigable about 1719 were dropped because of the objections of Ipswich Corporation who were afraid that their trade might be prejudiced. Towards the end of the century, however, the need for improved communication was becoming paramount and so in 1789 William Jessop was commissioned by several local landowners to survey the Gipping valley with a view to making the river navigable. The survey was made by Lenny and on the basis of his report, endorsed by Jessop, Parliament was petitioned on 17 February 1790 for leave to bring in a Bill to make a navigation from Stowupland bridge at Stowmarket to Hanford bridge in Ipswich and so by a navigable cut into the Orwell. Power was also sought to cleanse, scour and improve the navigation of the Orwell from the cut to Stoke bridge. Additionally, authority was requested to extend the navigation by $\frac{3}{4}$ mile from Stowupland bridge to the turnpike to Bury St Edmunds should this later become necessary—an extension that was never made. Jessop gave evidence at committee stage, and the Bill passed uneventfully on 1 April 1790.[24]

The Act named six trustees, all local gentry, who were empowered to borrow £14,300 on the credit of the undertaking and raise another £6,000 by mortgage or otherwise if required. The waterway including the towpath was to be limited to 18yd in width except where the banks were more than three feet above the water or where places were made for boats to turn or pass, in which case the limit was raised to 20yd. An unusual clause laid a penalty of £5 on a vessel carrying fishing tackle. The first meeting of the new company was to be held at the King's Head inn, Stowmarket, on the third Monday after the passing of the Act.

This took place on 19 April 1790 and it was arranged that Jessop would prepare detailed drawings and specifications which would be the basis for the submission of tenders. It was also agreed to advertise for a surveyor and at the following meeting on 7 June James Smith of Reading was appointed at a salary of £300 for the period from 21 July 1790 to 1 October 1791, by which time it was hoped that the navigation would be complete. At this meeting also Messrs Dyson and Pinkerton were awarded the contract for the construction and Mr Baynes of Stowmarket was authorized to 'conduct the law business'.

In the matter of appointments the trustees got off to a bad start. Within a month, on 5 July, they felt it necessary to rescind Baynes' appointment as they were dissatisfied with 'his unaccommodating and improper behaviour'. Unfortunately there is no elaboration of the reason for this decision. Then on 6 November they wrote to Dyson and Pinkerton forbidding them to enter any lands to carry out any work on the navigation, apparently because they had been trespassing on lands over which the trustees had no control. This ban on the contractors, who had started work at the Ipswich end of the navigation, led to legal action which effectively delayed work on the river for some time and also involved the trustees in considerable unforeseen expenditure.[25]

Work did not entirely cease during the period of the lawsuit, for on 15 January 1791 Smith was ordered to set up a brickworks at Hanford bridge and on 9 June 1791 an agreement was made with Samuel Wright of Ipswich for the building of six locks. However the delayed completion at the Ipswich end and the consequent loss of the possibility of water transport upstream led to heavy materials being transported overland to the Stowmarket end.

The lawsuit was settled on 14 November 1791, though it is not clear how the verdict went. As a result of these difficulties together with those arising in the normal course of the work the trustees consulted John Rennie, asking him to make a survey of the works. This he did, jointly with the trustees, on 13–15 December 1791 and reported back to them a week later. He found that the upper section from Stowmarket to Needham Market was nearly finished but noted that alterations would be required including raising the level of the towpath to allow for floodwater coming down the Gipping. He also recommended that swing bridges should be provided for small roads, fixed timber bridges for large roads, and brick ones for public roads.

He then went on to give some sage advice to the trustees:

In every work it is a wise maxim to lay down a proper plan on the first outset and to pursue the same with diligence afterwards. In this case the general outlines previous to obtaining the Act of Parliament seem to have been well pointed out by Mr Jessop but the proper steps to be pursued afterwards have been neglected. A regular survey of the river should have been taken and the works to be executed properly laid down. The original survey is very incorrect. I am surprised that Mr Lenny should have paid so little attention to accuracy—this renders it necessary to set about a new survey soon and to lay down the true form of the river with the different works to be proposed.

He then advised that though the three completed timber locks should stand the remaining locks should be in brick owing to the decay of timber in such damp conditions.[26] Rennie again reported to the trustees on 23 April 1792 and estimated that it would cost £12,762 to complete the navigation, including £6,600 for 12 locks at £550 each.[27]

On 4 May 1792 he was again in touch with the trustees having examined the lower end of the navigation. He considered, after looking at various sites, that the best junction with the Orwell was the one Jessop had proposed. He again expressed his concern about the timber locks but in the end recommended reconstruction 'when the navigation begins to pay'. He also advised that application should be made for power to raise more money.[28]

The trustees took this advice and applied to parliament for a second Bill on 28 December 1792 to raise a further £15,000. On this occasion John Rennie gave evidence before the committee. Despite some delay on procedure, the Bill passed on 28 March 1793.[29]

Completion of the works followed without further delay, the money having been raised from the original trustees and shareholders, and they were opened throughout on 14 September 1793. The navigation was slightly less than 17 miles long and had a fall from Stowmarket of just under 90ft. There were 15 locks designed to take barges of 52ft 6in × 13ft 6in with a maximum draught of 3ft 4½in.[30]

At first only two to four barges were employed and between the date of opening and July 1794 the tolls amounted to £460. The number of barges increased to ten during the next year but the navigation suffered severe damage in the early months of 1795 from frost and floods which cost some £1,000 to repair and caused a serious diminution from an expected £400 to £103 in the amount of tolls received in that period. Despite this setback the total received for the year July 1794–5 was £937.

A period of consolidation and regular trading now followed, with local agricultural produce moving downstream and coal and heavy goods in the opposite direction. Unfortunately the trustees did not record their toll receipts in the minutes so that there is no financial yardstick to measure progress. Nevertheless by the early 1800s the number of barge trips had increased to over 30 per week, the average journey time being about seven hours in each direction. The even progress was briefly disturbed in 1805 when James Austin, the surveyor appointed on 10 October 1804, another of the trustees' mistaken character assessments, absconded and the trustees advertised in the Cambridge papers offering a ten guinea reward for his apprehension and safe lodgement in jail.

Another indication of the continuing success of the navigation was found in a meeting held in January 1819 at Eye. At this meeting, chaired by Marquis Cornwallis, two reports were considered for making a canal from Ipswich to Eye. In the first William Cubitt proposed a line that involved a tunnel through the hills at Mendlesham, the cost being estimated at over £100,000. The second plan was to carry the navigation over instead of through the hills, but the estimate for this was nearly £80,000. Both proposals were rejected on the grounds of expense. The meeting, however, accepted an alternative suggestion, that the new navigation would branch off the Stowmarket Navigation at a point just above the paper mill at Needham Market and proceed along the valley through the Creetings to Stonham. A terminal basin was proposed there adjoining the turnpike road. Waggons from the Eye area would then be able to do the round trip to Stonham in one day instead of taking two days to Ipswich as was the regular practice. The cost of this proposal was £12,000, but although shares were offered and taken at this meeting the scheme did not come to fruition.[31]

The navigation continued to thrive but in 1844 the trustees learned of the proposal of the Eastern Union Extension Railway to build a line up the Gipping valley from Ipswich to Stowmarket. Ignoring or forgetting the prohibition in their Act of 1790 forbidding them to lease the navigation, the trustees started tentative negotiations with the railway promoters for this very purpose. They wisely stipulated that the waterway should be maintained by the lessees. They felt that the letting of the navigation would be beneficial to both the shareholders and the public and there is little doubt that they regarded the negotiations as of value to the railway board in stifling opposition to the latter's proposals from an influential quarter. So on 8 February 1845 they wrote to the railway board offering a basis for negotiation. This was immediately accepted by the board, subject to agreement on details, on 12 February and ten days later the navigation bondholders had also given their consent. It was only then that the trustees realized the legal hurdle, for on 1 March their parliamentary agent pointed out the limitations under the 1790 Act on leasing the navigation. It also appeared unexpectedly that the railway company was placing a lower valuation on the navigation than the trustees themselves.

Negotiations proceeded throughout the summer of 1845 and eventually on 27 September agreement was reached whereby each company would seek parliamentary powers oversetting the 1790 Act. The terms agreed were as follows:

> The rent of the navigation for the first 21 years would be £1,070 per annum. For the next 21 years it would be £850 per annum, being 4% interest for the shareholders plus £15 for the trustees annual expenses. The term to commence on 1 January 1846 to allow the trustees to make up their accounts to that time, the Company being allowed the profits arising from carrying any materials &c on the navigation for the railway works in the meantime.[32]

This left the question of new legislation to be resolved. Accordingly the trustees on 5 February 1846 petitioned parliament for a new Bill. In the draft it was stipulated that the lease should contain a covenant by the lessees to maintain the navigation. This did not satisfy the House of Lords, for after 'maintain the said Navigation' they added the words 'in as good a State and Condition as the same shall be at the Time of Passing of this Act'. This later proved to be a most valuable addition to the Act. It received the royal assent on 26 June 1846.[33] Although the railway company initially included a similar clause in their draft Bill the clause was dropped during its passage through Parliament. The Railway Commissioners were very critical of the way the railway company had obtained powers over a navigation without having included any part of the arrangements in their own Act. In the Commissioners' 1847 Report to Parliament they said that they 'feel it to be their duty to call attention to the circumstances under which this interferance has taken place with the tolls of a Navigation Company by a Railway Company'.[34]

There the interest of Parliament and the Commissioners rested and for the next 42 years the trustees settled down to a period of regular dividends, though they did not altogether relax their concern for the wellbeing of the navigation. In 1869, at their annual survey, they noted the lack of maintenance and prodded the Great Eastern Railway, as the Eastern Union had become, into restoring the defective sections.

Towards the end of the period of the lease they wrote to the G.E.R. on 11 March 1887 enquiring about the latter's intentions regarding renewal. This brought a swift response from the G.E.R. directors on 17 March saying that they 'have no intention of renewing the lease because in these days when so much is being said about railway companies being owners of canals they do not think it likely that Parliament would sanction such renewal'. The real reason was no doubt that they realized that they were paying out regular dividends against which they were deriving a very limited income, and that by now any competition or opposition from the canal company would be negligible.[35]

The matter remained in abeyance until later in the year when at a meeting between the two parties held on 22 November the directors firmly declined to renew the lease. There remained, however, the fulfilment of the amended clause in the 1846 Act relating to reinstatement. The navigation was evidently in a run-down condition and there seems to have been very little traffic, a factor recognized by both sides, for on 3 January 1888 the railway directors offered £2,000 in full settlement of any claims for repairs; and two days later the trustees accepted the offer, the cheque being paid over on 23 March.

With the navigation back in their own hands the trustees tried to keep the undertaking viable but by the end of the century the trade to Stowmarket was limited to an occasional cargo of manure to Prentice's, returning with guncotton from the explosives works. There was, however, rather more traffic between Ipswich and Bramford to Fison's and Packard's. Had it not been for these two companies the navigation would have been abandoned earlier than it was, for they helped to maintain the lock-gates and clear the weeds in the lower section for which they received abatement of the dues. The barges used were 30-ton capacity and a steam barge was used to tow two other barges on regular trips between Ipswich and Bramford. This practice created difficulties in working the three barges through the four locks in this stretch of the navigation. Mr Walter Packard, late vice-chairman of Fison's, recalls that the barges often worked through during the dark as they could only pass from Ipswich docks to the navigation at high water.

Traffic continued to decline until in 1917 the trustees critically examined the financial position. They found that the current account balance had dropped to just over £25 and the only other funds were £54 in a deposit account, £76 in a dilapidation account, and £642 in India $3\frac{1}{2}$ per cent stock. Their current rate of expenditure was £480 pa whilst the total income was approximately £220 pa. Stringent measures were taken; the labour employed on the navigation was reduced to a minimum, the payment of towpath rents was suspended, the dilapidation account was closed, and the engineer was asked to accept half salary. Even these measures were not sufficient to halt the decline, for in December 1921 the current account was overdrawn and the only funds left were £60 on deposit.

At the trustees' meeting on 16 May 1922 the deficiency had increased to £47 and it was resolved that 'in view of the financial position of the navigation the same be closed down from 3 June 1922 but without prejudice to the rights of the trustees to dues and the employees being given notice accordingly. The barges and other property of the trustees to be locked up and made as secure as possible.'[36]

There was no further meeting until 25 November 1930 and by

9 August 1932 it was resolved that 'no objection be taken to the proposed draft order for the revocation of the powers etc of the trustees'. The closing order was made under section 41 of the Land Drainage Act 1930 on 29 August 1932 and confirmed by the Minister of Agriculture & Fisheries, after consultation with the Minister of Transport, on 5 October 1932.

The end came on 16 March 1934 when, at a meeting held at Lloyds Bank, Cornhill, Ipswich, it was decided 'that the funds after payment of debts should be divided equally between the Catchment Board and the East Suffolk County Council and all books and papers relating to the navigation should be handed over to the Clerk of the Catchment Board'. The final minute was a pleasant farewell gesture: 'A vote of thanks was passed to the clerk for the attention he has always given to the business of the navigation.'[37]

River Blyth or Halesworth Navigation

On the Suffolk coast some 35 miles north of Ipswich lies Southwold at the seaward end of a 5-mile-long tidal creek bridged at its western or inland end at Blythburgh. This creek forms the mouth of the short and slow-running river Blyth. The only town of local importance on the river is the old market town of Halesworth, 9 miles upstream from Blythburgh bridge. At one time, unlike today, the creek broadened out between Southwold and Blythburgh forming a large area of saltings which were covered every tide, and it was the tidal scour from this large area of water that was the vital factor in enabling Southwold to develop over the years as a minor though important port on this part of the Suffolk coast. It was the later ill-conceived reclamation of the saltings in the nineteenth century and the consequential diminution of the scour which led to the formation of a bar at the harbour mouth and then ultimately to the decay of the harbour and the failure of the Halesworth navigation which had been constructed in the eighteenth century to link Halesworth and Southwold.

The possibility of making the Blyth navigable from Halesworth to Blythburgh had been mooted in the 1740s, the prime

mover in the scheme being Thomas Knights, a brewer in Halesworth. It was clear that before there could be any success to the
navigation the harbour and harbour entrance at Southwold
would have to be improved and this was done. That the harbour improvements had a beneficent effect is shown by the increase in the harbour dues from £110 in 1747–8 following the
passing of the first harbour Act[38] to £284 in 1753–4 when
Knights was once again canvassing the need for the navigation.

The first proper plan for river improvement was prepared by
Benjamin Reeve in 1753 and this included a branch to Ubbes-
ton to the south-west of Halesworth in addition to the main
line.[39] No further consideration was given to this proposed
branch. An estimate by John Reynolds for making the river
navigable of £4,614 11s was submitted on 4 May 1753. This included the provision of three locks at £517 each.[40]

No immediate action was taken and Knights was reminded
of the urgency of proceeding with the preliminaries on 25
October 1753 when another of the supporters, Robert Buxton of
Darsham, pointed out the expediency of getting the Bill
through the current session of Parliament. However, the Bill
was not proceeded with until 1757 when R. Yeates, one of the
Clerks of the House of Commons, wrote on 23 December 1756
asking whether Knights was going to draft the Bill himself or
whether he would like Yeates to draft it on the lines of the Brandon and Waveney Act. As Yeates was subsequently paid £186
'for soliciting the bill and all other fees and charges for the
Act . . .' it seems that he prepared it for presentation.[41]

Parliament was petitioned on 1 February 1757 by the inhabitants of Halesworth and also the trustees of Southwold Harbour
who had found that their Act of 1746 had not been broad
enough to cover the intended purposes and so wished to increase their powers. Subsequently Knights himself and
Thomas Manning, engineer, gave evidence that the river could
easily be made navigable. There was no opposition and the
royal assent was given on 1 April 1757.[42]

At the first statutory meeting on 8 June 1757 held at the
Angel, Halesworth, the commissioners decided that whoever
was appointed to make a survey preparatory to starting the

work should also be required to undertake the work according to his estimate. At this meeting, too, they considered a letter tendering for the work which in its way is a masterpiece of pious hope and is here quoted in full:

Gentlemen,

Meeting with an Advertisement from your Honners Relating to makeing the River Blyth Navigable from Halesworth Bridge into the Haven of Southwould in Suffolk onley on this Day and fiending your Apoyented time for puting it oute to be on Wednesday next ye 8th instant fiend the time toow short for me to make a survey of it to give in an Estimate of the Charge. this to Ackquaint you if plese to take in evereys ones Estimates that offers and I will Undertake aneything of that or aneything of that kinde at one forth part less than the Lowest Estemate given in. if your Honners think proper to Poestpone Actualley Contracting with aney till you can Sig-- nify your Plesure to me and I will God willing come and Undertake it by an Estimate that I shall make or as above proposed by a Machine of my owne Invention for witch I have a Patent under Solisetation for it Cost me upwards of twentey years Study and have been at a Considerable Expence your Honers—Signifying to me your Pleasure on this Affaire will lay me under an Obligatiori to waite on you should it fit and ame your Honners Humble Obedient Servant though Unknown

Wm. Cawdren.

P.S. plese to dyrect for me at the Register Office on the Terris in Snt James's Markit London.

June ye 4th 1757.[43]

Not surprisingly no action was taken on this letter but later one of the commissioners applied to Langley Edwards to make a survey and this was done. On 10 August at the next meeting Edwards regretted—the first of many regrets that he had not had 'the time to reduce the same to writing'—but he thought the cost would be about £3,000. He later produced his report, the estimated cost being exactly £3,000. This estimate was based on improving the river,

Plates 9 & 10   (above)
Wormingford, showing the
construction of a Stour lock;
(below) the steam tug *Trent
River* and a barge at
Bramford lock on the
Ipswich & Stowmarket
Navigation in the 1920s

Plates 11 & 12 Broadland about 1890: *(above)* wherries at a maltings, probably Ranworth; *(below)* the wharves at Acle bridge

building bridges, and constructing locks capable of passing boats 50ft long × 12ft beam. Also included in the estimate was the purchase of Wenhaston watermill for £150.[44]

A subscription list was opened and slowly money was offered until by 1759 £3,600 had been received from 38 people—most came from the immediate locality, demonstrating that it was very much a local venture. At the annual meeting on 6 June 1759 the commissioners considered a second opinion desirable and sought the advice of John Grundy. He replied on 18 June setting out his terms but adding that 'he was not at that time available because he had engagements in West Cheshire and Yorkshire'. The commissioners were rather shaken by his charges and decided that the 'terms were too expensive and it would not be proper to employ him'. After this abortive attempt to obtain further advice the commissioners asked Edwards to make a resurvey and he again quoted £3,000.

Edwards was requested to attend meetings with the commissioners when certain matters were under discussion but on 30 October 1759 he sent his regrets from Biggleswade, 'an unforeseen event has prevented my being with the commissioners at their meeting'. In his absence the commissioners agreed with Andrew Chandler that he would build a lock of brick and timber for £450 and also certain bridges. Two tenders were received for the earthworks but they felt that both were extravagant and refused to accept either; though at a subsequent meeting on 3 November at which Edwards was present they agreed to accept one of them on condition the contractor started work by 19 November and agreed to employ not less than 40 men.

Having got the organization of the work under way the commissioners decided to meet monthly as from 5 December so that they could keep the progress of the works under review. It was as well they did for on 30 July 1760 it was noted that there were defects in the newly constructed bridges and Chandler, the contractor, suggested that this was due to miscalculations in the design. The commissioners immediately sought an explanation from Edwards but Samuel Jones, Edwards' assistant, said he did not know where he was. The commissioners were rightly perturbed that Edwards did not 'attend more closely to the works'. His whereabouts having been discovered he was ordered to attend a meeting on 9 August 1760, but on 5 August he wrote from Bardney, near Lincoln, that 'he was surprised at the account of the brickwork as I have had many built of the same dimensions of wall and have never yet had one failed. As to my being at Halesworth on the 9 August it is impossible as I am on business which will detain me here until that time.' He promised to be with them by the end of the following week.

The commissioners called another meeting on 20 August but Edwards once again failed to appear. The meeting was adjourned until 3 September and although he had written from Boston on 23 August saying he was sorry he had not attended the last meeting he still did not appear on 3 September. This time the commissioners decided to send their clerk, John Woods, to find Edwards and bring him back. If he then did not come he was to be told that they, the commissioners, would have nothing more to do with him. On 10 September Edwards at last appeared. He apologized by saying that he had arrived at Halesworth the day after the last meeting and this was due to his having been taken ill on the road and he had had other jobs to complete. His excuse for not attending the next meeting was that he had fallen from his horse and had hurt himself and the next time was because his horse had been taken lame on the road.

By 13 May 1761 the commissioners were thoroughly dissatisfied with Edwards' failures to attend and decided that on this occasion they would publicly advertise in the papers to ensure his attendance. However before the end of the meeting Edwards arrived and again apologized. The navigation was now nearing completion but cash was running short and to overcome this they agreed that there should be a second subscription for another 10 per cent on the original subscription.

The opening took place on 23 July 1761:

This day we had the pleasure of receiving into our bason a keel from Southwold laden with coals and drawing upwards of 3 feet of water. We can assure the publick that the works for facilitating the navigation of our river are constructed and finished with the greatest art, and as they afford the most pleasing probability of a particular benefit to this town, so do they no less promise to the country round a more extensive influence.

The barge was attended from the Town lock up to the great bason by a numerous concourse of people, assembled not more to satisfy their curiosity at the novelty of the sight than to join in the general joy and triumph on the occasion.[45]

The major works on the navigation were four locks of galley-beam type as on the Stour, and a tidal staunch above Blyth-burgh bridge. Another lock was later built at Halesworth to take the navigation out of the cut and back into the stream to give access to a maltings. The only bridge of importance was one at Blythburgh carrying the main road from Ipswich to Lowestoft, the cost of which was partially borne by the county justices. The final cost of the navigation was £3,822, which was roughly half way between Edwards' estimate of £3,000 and Reynolds's of £4,614.

With the completion of the works the commissioners turned to the day-to-day management of the undertaking. Their first action was to appoint Samuel Jones, who had been Edwards's assistant and who undoubtedly had been responsible for over-seeing the construction, as toll-collector, surveyor of works, lockkeeper and warehouse-keeper for three years at a salary of £45 pa. At the end of this term when his contract was renewed for another year his salary was reduced to £42 per annum. At the end of the next year the commissioners were prepared to extend the contract but at a still further reduced salary. As Jones was not willing to accept less than £40 per annum his ser-vices were terminated. Jones' assistant William Bickers, a labourer from Wenhaston, was prepared to undertake the work for £21 per annum and he was duly appointed, being well re-commended 'on the grounds of honesty and sobriety'. His main recommendation, however, seems to be his willingness to accept a low salary!

Trade steadily increased and during the eighteenth century the navigation justified itself as a communication between

Halesworth and Southwold. The tolls averaged £134 pa between 1765 and 1798 with a minimum in 1782 of £81 and a maximum in 1793 of £280. In the majority of years the figure was between £120 and £150. The return journey between Halesworth and Southwold generally took two days and the vessels used at first were keels but their place was gradually taken by wherries. It was at the time of this change that the one and only wherry built at Halesworth was launched in 1772. This was named the *Halesworth* in honour of its construction.[46]

In the early years of the nineteenth century growing concern was felt about the deterioration of Southwold harbour and the increasing difficulties wherries were finding in crossing its bar. This was having a consequential effect on the working of the navigation. Accordingly advice was sought from John Rennie who presented a very lengthy and technical report dated 6 January 1820 and in it he pinpointed the embanking of the saltings as the cause of the deterioration, but as the destruction of the embankments was out of the question, he could give no useful advice.

Despite the silting up of the harbour trade continued to flourish during the next 15 years with the tolls averaging £405 per annum between 1823 and 1833.[47] There were quays at Roydon, 1½ miles from Southwold, and at Blackshore, ½ mile upstream from the bar, and this was the transhipment point between the sea-going wherries and those vessels which could reach Halesworth. The main cargoes carried were coal, averaging at this period 4,311 chaldrons pa, and corn, averaging 9,536 quarters. Other cargoes were chalk and shop goods. There was even a proposal in 1837 that the navigation should be extended from the basin at Halesworth up to the town bridge, but the hey-day of the navigation was nearly over. In 1839 the harbour was completely blocked for some time and the wherries inside could not get out, and those outside could not get in. One of the latter was lost while waiting for the harbour to be opened.

Because of the concern about the condition of the harbour and its serious effect on the trade of the port, a further survey was carried out by John R. Wright, under the direction of James Walker, in 1840. It was calculated that 1,504 acres of land had been reclaimed from the marshes and this had led to the exclusion of no less than 148,296,490 cu ft of tidal water at each tide. It is therefore not surprising that the scouring effect of the tide had been manifestly diminished.[48]

From 1850 to 1883 there was a steady decline in trade and on 9 September 1884 a notice was inserted in the papers: 'Notice is hereby given that this river having ceased to be used as a navigable river pursuant to the Act etc. the Commissioners have ceased to derive any income from the tolls or duties which have been accustomed to be received for the carriage of goods and merchandise and have no means of keeping the bridges and the banks and sides of the river in repair and henceforth decline all responsibility in respect of such repairs.'

Ten years later on 18 September 1894 it was proposed that a memorial be presented to the Board of Trade for their warrant authorizing the abandonment of the river Blyth as a canal on the grounds that it is no longer necessary for the purposes of public navigation. Although this was passed by the commissioners unanimously it was still not the end, for in the early years of this century a Halesworth man, Fred G. Lambert, bought the wherry, the *Star*, from Oulton Broad and traded on the Blyth carrying coal from the occasional vessels which managed to put into Southwold harbour. Lambert estimated that £1,000 would have put the whole navigation into working order but he could not raise the money. He continued working until 1911 and then finally he left the *Star* on the hard at Walberswick to be broken up.[49]

The formal end of the navigation came with an order of abandonment dated 19 February 1934 made under the Land Drainage Act 1930 s41.

Today the Blyth still flows through Halesworth and there are still a few remains as evidence that there used to be a navigation up to this town but it is hard to believe that the little water that flows once carried trading wherries.

CHAPTER V

Broadland and the East Norfolk Navigations

✦✦✦✦✦✦✦✦✦✦✦✦✦✦✦✦✦✦✦✦✦✦✦✦✦✦✦✦✦✦✦✦✦✦✦✦✦◆✦✦✦✦✦✦✦✦✦✦✦✦✦✦✦✦✦✦✦✦✦✦✦✦✦✦✦✦✦✦✦

The Broads are probably the best known inland waterway area in the whole country. As seen by the casual visitor they seem so much part of the typical Norfolk landscape that it is hard to realize that they are a product of human activity of centuries ago. When the land was higher than it is today the local inhabitants dug out large quantities of peat over a period of several centuries, but after the fourteenth century when the land started subsiding the peat holes became waterlogged and ultimately flooded. Over the last hundred years there has been a natural tendency for silting to take place, but recently there has been a recovery operation by the Bure & Waveney Commissioners and places like Sutton Broad, Ranworth Broad, and Dilham Dike have been rehabilitated. Although given over today to leisure activities, these artificial lakes and their associated natural rivers carried a considerable amount of commercial traffic for several hundred years.

This system of Broads and natural rivers had, and still has, three main arteries; the Bure and Ant draining north-east Norfolk; the Yare or Wensum linking Norwich and Yarmouth; and the Waveney flowing along the Suffolk—Norfolk boundary until it turns north to Yarmouth. Each of these arteries had its series of associated veins of smaller waterways so that the whole flow of traffic connected to the heart at Yarmouth. Pursuing the metaphor, the aorta was Breydon Water to which each of the arteries was joined. This created a water-based transport economy for the whole of east Norfolk with virtually every village, hamlet, and farm having its staithe—often a parish staithe (ie one for the common use of the parish)—on either Broad or river. In many cases it was impossible to reach the destination by any other means than water transport, eg the Berney Arms on the Yare, and the system provided almost door-to-door transport between any two points in the area. That this system has a long history is shown by the case of Norwich suing Yarmouth in 1249 for not permitting their ships to come laden with their goods to the city as they always did in time past;[1] and by the placing of an order by Edward III in 1372 for a balinger to be built in Norwich.

The peculiarities of the waterways, arising partly from their variable depth and partly from the fact that at one stage in a journey a boat would be traversing a fairly narrow, and possibly winding, channel whereas at another it would be crossing an open sheet of water which could be treacherous in a high wind, led to the development of special types of trading vessel. For a long time this was the keel, though different from the Humber keel, with its mast stepped amidships and carrying a square sail, but gradually, and particularly after the late eighteenth century, the keel was superseded by the wherry with its mast stepped for'ard and a black or dark brown gaff sail. It is the wherry which is popularly associated with the trade on the Broads. The wherries varied in size from the small 14 tonners which worked on the narrower rivers to the 40 tonners and larger which were to be found on the Yare and the Waveney.

Though the trading wherries serving this large complex of waterways from Bungay in the south to Antingham in the north carried every conceivable kind of cargo—even including bodies for burial—certain freights constituted the regular traffic. Large quantities of coal were imported through Yarmouth, over 10,000 tons pa of which had its origin in collieries served by the Aire & Calder Navigation in the early 1850s. A common feature on the staithes on both the Broads and the rivers was the coal bin for supplying the local customers. In the reverse direction grain (over 15,000 qrs pa in the 1850s[2]) was collected from the various staithes and despatched via Yarmouth to cornmills served by the Aire & Calder. Two of the more unusual cargoes were reeds and ice. The former were gathered from the edges of the smaller Broads and rivers in reed lighters and transferred to

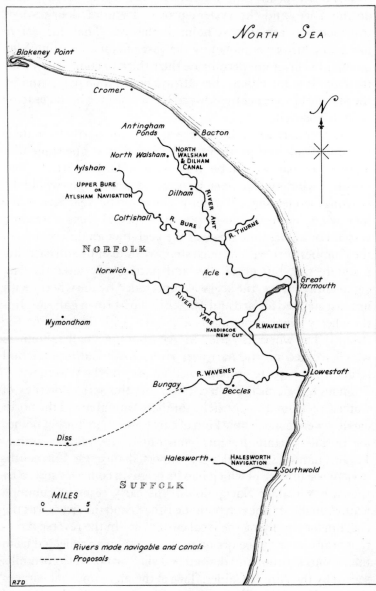

7. The Broadland Navigations

the wherries to sail to various parts of the navigation system for roof thatching. The latter was dug out of the frozen waterways in times of severe frost and taken in the holds of the wherries to Yarmouth for the preservation of fish before the days of refrigeration.

With such an integrated natural waterway system it is not surprising that attempts were made to extend it from the earlier days of river improvement proposals. So apart from the general oversight of the Yarmouth Haven & Pier Commissioners there were extensions involving the construction of locks on the Waveney to Bungay; on the Bure to Aylsham; and on the Ant to North Walsham and Antingham. In addition there was a battle by Norwich to secure an outlet to the sea via Lowestoft to overcome the Yarmouth monopoly. This led to the construction of Haddiscoe New Cut and the provision of through navigation via Oulton Broad, Lake Lothing, and the sea at Lowestoft. Each of these improvements is dealt with separately.

Rivers Waveney and Yare

The earliest Act giving authority to improve one of the Norfolk rivers was passed on 17 March 1670 only a fortnight after the first reading, empowering Thomas Walcott, William Barker, Robert London, John Gouche, and John Girling of Bungay and John Saverie of Downham Market to improve the navigation of the Waveney.[3] This Act also provided for the improvement of the river Brandon, or Little Ouse, which flows westward from the same watershed and falls into the Ouse south of Denver Sluice (see the next chapter). Duties were laid on commissioners appointed under the Act which included the power to ascertain the amount of damage done to the banks of the river by the bank-haling of vessels. The point was also made that at one time 'lighters and keeles and other boats of considerable burden' could navigate to Bungay, a populous place, but for the 'want of navigation whereof hath reduced the inhabitants to great poverty', whereas now the vessels 'because of clogging and landing up' can only get to Beccles. Three locks were built on this short stretch of the Waveney between Bungay and Beccles on what was a private navigation separate from the control of the Yarmouth Commissioners. These were at Wainford, Ellingham, and Geldeston or Shipmeadow.

This section at the end of the eighteenth and the beginning of the nineteenth century was in the hands of Matthias Kerrison, a wealthy Bungay merchant. On his death it was bought by William Butcher, an auctioneer, who gave evidence at an enquiry into the reconstruction of St Olave's bridge in 1847, saying that though he owned the navigation he did not know much about it as he had let it and the dues were settled by the judges at Bury Assizes.[4] The following year Butcher promoted the Bungay Navigation Tontine Co with a proposed capital of £21,000 divided into 210 shares of £100 for the purchase by means of a tontine of the right of levying tolls, and of the premises and trade to and from Beccles and Bungay.[5] The company did not become viable. Later in 1889 the navigation passed into the hands of W. D. Walker of Messrs W. D. and A. E. Walker, maltsters and merchants of Bungay.[6] This firm were the original owners of the *Albion*, the wherry now owned by the Norfolk Wherry Trust. In 1919 control passed to Watney, Combe, Reid & Co who retained it until the navigation closed in 1934.

While the rest of the Waveney remained relatively free from trouble, silting was creating problems further north in relation to the Yare and Yarmouth Haven and in order to ease the difficulty another Act was passed in 1698 with power to levy duties on coal to pay for improvements to both the river and the harbour.[7] This led to harbour improvements but the Yare continued to be neglected and further Acts in 1722[8], 1747[9], and 1749[10] failed to alleviate the difficulties. It was perhaps natural that the Commissioners in Yarmouth should consider their harbour the first priority. Yet another Act in 1772 tackled the problem in a different way.[11] This time it was clearly laid down how the toll receipts were to be distributed. Norwich was to receive 3/20ths for improving the Yare between Norwich and Hardly Cross; Norfolk magistrates had 2/20th for improvements to the rivers Bure, Ant, and Thurne; Suffolk magistrates 1/20th for improvement of the Waveney; Yarmouth 1/20th for repairing the bridge and the public quays; Yarmouth again

5/20ths for the improvement of the Yare from Yarmouth to Hardly Cross; and the remaining 8/20ths were for the improvement of Yarmouth Harbour. This Act helped the situation temporarily but a permanent solution was still some time in the future.

Despite the fact that virtually every place on the Yare and the Waveney had its staithe where goods could be loaded and unloaded—and there were many staithes remote from any village—thus providing a comprehensive system for local trade, the gnawing canker at the hearts of the Norwich merchants, and to a lesser degree the Beccles merchants, was their dependance on Yarmouth as their outlet to the sea. The shallow stretch of Breydon Water made it essential that all goods brought from beyond the immediate area of the Yare and Waveney had to be transhipped at Yarmouth. As trading vessels became larger so did the problem increase until in 1814 Alderman Crisp Brown and the Norwich merchants decided to take action. They asked William Cubitt to advise, and he suggested that the cheapest and easiest way of improving conditions would be to dredge a channel to the south side of Breydon Water and generally improve the Yare at a cost of £35,000. Once the plan had been published in 1818 Yarmouth raised immediate objection and John Rennie was called in by the Corporation. His view was that this would reduce the scour from Breydon Water and lead to the silting up of Yarmouth Harbour, a condition which the Yarmouth people had tried for years to prevent.[12] Cubitt then carried out another survey to determine the feasibility of providing an alternative exit to the sea at Lowestoft. This proposal was estimated to cost more than double the original plan but owing to the intransigence of Yarmouth over both plans it was decided to go ahead with the latter. Both Telford and James Walker expressed their views that improving the navigational facilities to Norwich would not harm Yarmouth but to no avail.

Application was made to Parliament in 1826 for an Act to permit the Norwich & Lowestoft Navigation Company to carry out the following works: deepen the Yare between Norwich and Reedham; build a canal 2½ miles long from Reedham

to Haddiscoe on the Waveney; and enlarge Oulton Dyke and
create a link between Oulton Broad and Lake Lothing, thus
gaining an exit to the North Sea at Lowestoft. A formal enquiry
into the Bill was held between 10 April and 1 May 1826 at which
six eminent civil engineers of the period gave evidence, William
Cubitt, Alexander Nimmo, William Chapman, Thomas Telford, James Walker, and Benjamin Bevan. William Cubitt out-
lined the scheme, mentioning his proposal for a double lock at
Mutford bridge with gates pointing both ways, and proposing
to use a steam tug on the navigation as steam boats were
already being used between Yarmouth and Norwich. During
the course of the cross-examination there was an interesting
exchange which throws some light on the surveying methods of
the time.

Q. By whom were they (the levels) taken?
A. In the first place those at Reedham were made by a
young man of the name of George Baynes; I can bring
better evidence of it than my own; the other young man
at the Haddiscoe end of the Cut was Elliott.
Q. Are those people in your own service?
A. No.
Q. Did you employ them?
A. I did.
Q. What are they, are they engineers or surveyors?
A. No. They are persons who can read and write and when
the scale was nailed up in the river they could write down
the height of the water at each hour.
Q. Did you know anything of them before?
A. No, but I found them competent to the business and in
their class of life respectable.
Q. They gave you the account?
A. We ruled a book and ruled the lines and wrote the hours
and they put in the figures; whenever I have been down
and measured the tides myself I have found them agree
with the numbers set down by those persons and have no
doubt they took them accurately.[13]

Evidence was given by a number of other people including the

masters of some Leith and Berwick smacks who thought that
the provision of a harbour at Lowestoft would be very valuable.
In support of the Yare traders Alderman Crisp Brown of Norwich gave details of the traffic, pointing out that he had been a
trader for 33 years. Despite the evidence, the opposition of Yarmouth and the timid owners of the marshlands, who had been
adequately schooled by the opposition into fearing an inundation if the Bill were successful, was sufficient to secure a rejection of the Bill by a slender majority of five.

A similar Bill was re-introduced next session and again
opposed by Yarmouth, who spent £8,000 in their attempt to secure its defeat. Evidence given in Committee sheds interesting
light on several aspects of the proposals. William Cubitt estimated the cost at £100,000 including the new cut from Reedham
to Haddiscoe, and he was asked 'Do you know any one place in
the whole kingdom of England so fit for canal navigation?' and
his succinct reply was 'I do not'.

Alexander Nimmo was examined, mainly on the currents etc
at the mouth at Lowestoft, and he made a very interesting ob-
servation on the subject of puddling:

> Query: Is it proposed to puddle the Reedham Cut?
> Answer: I believe there has been a good deal of discussion
> upon that. I think it is quite unnecessary to puddle it. I have
> my reasons for that not only from my own experience but the
> universal experience of Holland where there never was a
> bank puddled from the days of Caesar to the present hour. I
> know they know nothing about it. It is an English fashion en-
> tirely.

It was also argued in support of the Bill that pilferage would
be reduced when sea-going vessels could reach Norwich by the
new navigation. William Slack, a partner in a dyeing business
in Norwich, said that over the previous four years he had
imported 1,000 chaldrons of coal pa, which had to be transhipped at Yarmouth, so adding an additional freight charge of
2s 3d per chaldron on top of his annual Yarmouth dues of £120
per annum. In addition he also lost a considerable amount of
coal due to theft when the lighters or wherries were crossing the

marshes. John Althoe also stated that he had lost wine through the cargoes being broached during the passage between Yarmouth and Norwich. Alderman Crisp Brown, the leading protagonist for the navigation and himself a Norwich merchant and maltster, estimated that by avoiding Yarmouth he could save 5s per chaldron on coal and an equivalent amount on grain. This would be effected by bringing ships direct to Norwich and thus saving the expense of wherries and middlemen. He also recounted how he had been robbed, having been informed of the thefts by a series of anonymous letters in 1820 as a result of which a watch was set up by putting a man in a wicker basket so that he could see through the wickerwork. The man heard all the conversations and kept an account of all the goods which were taken away. No less than 18 men and the receiver were convicted. He further stated that the amount of coal being imported into Norwich was between 50 and 54,000 chaldrons (40,000 tons) pa. In cross-examination he admitted being the originator of the scheme, but he had sold his shares to prevent objections to his evidence. He also agreed that the scheme would not eliminate transhipment at Norwich as it would be impossible for sea-going vessels to negotiate the Norwich bridges. There would, indeed, be tug charges but the metage charges (ie charges for measuring the coal) at Yarmouth would be outflanked.[14]

Elsewhere it was reported that the traffic in the 1820s between Norwich and Yarmouth amounted to about 300,000 quarters of corn and 50,000 sacks of flour per annum downstream, and, in addition to the coal, about 40,000 tons of other goods upstream.[15] This time the Bill was passed on 28 May 1827.[16] The authorized capital was £100,000, with power to raise a further £50,000 from various sources including the Exchequer Bill Loan Commissioners. There were great celebrations in Norwich when the promoters returned from London bearing the news of their success over their Yarmouth rivals. The horses were detached and their coach was drawn by men in triumph into Norwich where there were bonfires and general junketings. The first sod was cut by Alderman Brown in the autumn of 1827, and by 1828 a ¼-mile channel had been cut between Lake

Lothing and the sea. During 1829 the lock and sluice between Oulton Broad and Lake Lothing at Mutford bridge were constructed, the lock being 150ft long × 50ft wide. The first vessel to enter the new harbour at Lowestoft was the yacht *Ruby* (50 tons) on 3 June 1831.

A demonstration was carried out the same evening to prove the effectiveness of the sluicing arrangements, using the water from Oulton Broad to clear the channel through Lake Lothing to the sea:

> The culverts being opened the gates gradually moved back, a tremendous rush of the waters to the sea from the lake took place, the stream running at a velocity of eight to ten miles an hour, carrying stones, silth, and shingle with a bubbling roar of waters to the ocean, the impetus of which might be distinctly perceived at least half a mile from the shore, and the rattle of stones along the bottom of the cut, might be heard down to the mouth of the opening; the whole effect far exceeding the statements made before the House of Commons, as to this very point, of the power that could be obtained of clearing the opening by sluicing from the lake. The effect of the first sluicing was such as to sweep out with one rush of the mighty torrent upwards of 3,000 tons of beach and shingle into the ocean. This, and four subsequent sluicings, it is estimated, have cleared out nearly 10,000 tons.[17]

Having completed the Lowestoft end of the navigation the engineer William Cubitt continued with the important task of finalizing the link to Norwich through the New Cut. The costs of the work were now running above money available, partly owing to the high parliamentary expenses, partly to the increased cost of the sea-lock, and partly to the failure of certain of the subscribers to pay their calls resulting in forfeiture of shares. Application was made to the Exchequer Bill Loan Commissioners for a loan to complete the work, and £50,000 was granted. With this help the New Cut was completed in 1832 and the whole 32 miles from Norwich to Lowestoft was ready for formal opening in the autumn of 1833. This was celebrated in great style, reminiscent of the gaiety of some of the eighteenth-century openings.

NORWICH A PORT.

LONDON
TRADERS.

REDUCED
FREIGHTS.

LONDON, LOWESTOFT, AND NORWICH
SHIPPING COMPANY.

A REGULAR LINE OF VESSELS IS NOW ESTABLISHED FROM
GRIFFIN'S WHARF, LONDON,
TO NORWICH DIRECT;
And, to prevent delay, a STEAM TUG of 27-Horse Power has been engaged.

VESSELS will load every WEDNESDAY, at GRIFFIN'S WHARF, and at R. and S. RUDRUM'S WHARF, every THURSDAY. The Committee of the above Company respectfully invite the Shippers of Norwich to support this undertaking, and they beg to announce that it is their intention to Start TWO Vessels from each end every Week.   (1517

For Freight apply to R. and S. RUDRUM, King Street, Norwich,
W. V. BARNARD, Lowestoft,
THOS. FARNCOMB, Griffin's Wharf, London,

Norwich, 1st October, 1833.   **AGENTS TO THE COMPANY.**

8. Norwich a Port: from the *Norwich Mercury* of Saturday 5 October 1833. The date at the foot is the day after the opening of the Haddiscoe New Cut which completed the Norwich & Lowestoft Navigation.

Monday last 30 September 1833 has been rendered ever memorable in our local history by its being the day on which Norwich really became a Port. And this too from circumstances rather unexpected for it was not until the preceding evening that intelligence was received .... that the *Squire*, London trader, had arrived on Saturday at Lowestoft and (with the *City of Norwich* trader lying there) would proceed (through the New Cut) to Norwich on the following day. .... The *Jarrow* (Capt. Wilkinson) of Newcastle lying at Yarmouth was to tow the two vessels to Norwich.

But here Norwich had not reckoned with the sense of injustice under which Yarmouth still suffered. It was Sunday and the *Jarrow* had to pass through Yarmouth bridge. In a spirit of non-cooperation Yarmouth refused to open the bridge. This caused delay but not complete obstruction, because eventually the captain cut down the funnel and was able to take the tug under the bridge. Unfortunately the *Jarrow* was further delayed because she had missed the tide and was held up by the shallowness of Breydon Water. Meanwhile another tug, the *Susanna*, had brought the two vessels as far as the New Cut but could not proceed further owing to lack of power occasioned partly by her inadequate engines and partly by shortage of coal on board. It was at the entrance to the New Cut that the *Jarrow* met the little fleet.

The VIPs at Norwich went downstream on Monday morning on the paddle-steamer *Tickler* to await the convoy from Lowestoft which approached 'with all their sails set and decorated with signal flags and streamers'. Unfortunately the rejoicing as the convoy met the reception party was marred by a fatal accident which stemmed from a fit of petulance on the part of the master of the *Susanna* who, when he learned that he was not to lead the convoy with the *Squire* into Norwich, cast off and refused to proceed. The son of the master of the *City of Norwich*, Robert Allerton, then attempted to take a tow rope to the *Squire* by using a small boat, but he overbalanced out of the boat and, striking his head on the side of the *Squire*, was stunned and drowned.

This accident did not affect the reception the convoy was given when it reached Norwich, for some 10,000 people were lining the river banks cheering them on. The final function of the day was a dinner for the directors, and in the words of the reporter 'it was a good one considering the short notice that had been given'.[18]

The high hopes entertained for the new navigation via the Haddiscoe New Cut were not sustained, although at first it seemed that the vessels of the Norwich, Lowestoft & London

Shipping Company, to which the *Squire* and the *City of Norwich* belonged, would be the start of a new era. But operating costs were in excess of the revenue and it was impossible to repay the Exchequer Bill Loan Commissioners. The coming of railways into the area also aggravated the situation. In 1842 the Commissioners took over the navigation from the company and ultimately decided to sell it. They found a purchaser in Sir Morton Peto, who wanted the navigation partly to eliminate competition with the railway he was planning and partly to provide the estate required to develop his industrial ideas in Lowestoft itself. Soon afterwards, in 1848, Norwich promoted a Bill to acquire the navigation, but though it had the support of the Admiralty opposition from Yarmouth and elsewhere caused it to be withdrawn.[19] By this time, too, the traders of Beccles were finding that their best transport route, despite the difficulties, was once again via Yarmouth. The main reason for this was that Lake Lothing had silted up. The long-term sluicing effect through Lowestoft harbour was not as adequate as the demonstration on 3 June 1831 had suggested.

Sir Morton Peto, who had acquired the Haddiscoe New Cut among the other properties from the Exchequer Bill Loan Commissioners, was also connected with the Lowestoft Railway & Harbour Company and these were the *de facto* owners of the New Cut. They in turn leased their company to the Norfolk Railway, which in turn became part of the Great Eastern Railway. Thus in due course the ownership of the New Cut came to the British Transport Commission. In 1954, following the 1953 floods, which caused considerable damage to the banks, the Commission sought powers to close the Cut, but this drew forth such protests from the yachting associations and others that the Cut has been saved.[20] In 1957 it was transferred to the East Suffolk and Norfolk River Board (now the Anglian Water Authority). It is little used for commercial traffic but forms a very useful link for pleasure craft between the Yare and the Waveney.

The concept of Norwich as a port still lived on after the decay of the Norwich & Lowestoft Navigation, for in 1908 a Mr Botterell gave a lecture at Norwich entitled 'The Coming of the Ship

Canal and the Premier Naval Dock'. He conceived a ship canal between Norwich and Yarmouth with an 8-acre commercial dock at Whitlingham. The scheme was also to include a naval base at Rockland Broad, some 11 miles by river east of Norwich, by expanding Rockland Broad from 60 to 400 acres and moving everything from Woolwich as part of the scheme. He took the view that it would be in the national interest to move naval installations away from London because of the gathering clouds in the pre-1914 period.[21]

Up to the 1960s coal was brought to Norwich in barges hauled by steam tugs but that traffic has now ceased; Norwich commercial traffic is today represented by small sea-going coasters which are important to the city's trade, but these now come via Yarmouth and not via Lowestoft and the Haddiscoe New Cut.

Although most of the branches now never see commercial vessels—for instance, the last trading wherry traversed the river Chet to Loddon about 1938—the majority of them are regularly used by pleasure craft and they are now probably busier than they have ever been.

It must not be forgotten, too, that there have been a number of schemes at various times to link the south Norfolk rivers with the navigations to the west. In 1773 there was a proposal to build a canal from King's Lynn to Norwich via Swaffham and East Dereham to facilitate the passage of long wool supplies (an important commodity in the Norwich trade) from the Midlands and the return traffic of manufactured goods for export via King's Lynn.[22] Another proposal suggested a link between Norwich and Downham Market and on to the Ouse to tap the corn and wool growing regions of Northampton, Huntingdon, and Cambridge, but owing to the opposition of established river and coastal interests it was abandoned.[23] A revival of the idea of a connection with East Dereham was made in 1819 but although a subscription list was opened nothing more was heard of the idea.[24] Finally there have been regular suggestions for a link between the Waveney at Bungay and the Little Ouse at Thetford which, if it could be achieved, would be an excellent route for pleasure craft passing between the Broads and the inland waterway system of the rest of the country.

Bure Navigation

The River Bure, the northernmost of the three main Broadland rivers, rises in the higher lands of northern Norfolk near Melton Constable and flows generally eastward via Aylsham and Coltishall to Wroxham where it enters the stretch of Broadland which includes among others Wroxham, Hoveton, and Ranworth Broads. It then accepts the rivers Ant and Thurne on its northern bank and traverses marshland for another 14¼ miles until it meets the Yare at Runham, Yarmouth, at the eastern end of Breydon Water. The lower section of 31¼ miles below Horstead mill was commercially navigable for many years, for it was recorded in 1685 that the river a mile from the manor house of Meyton was used for the carriage of coal, corn, timber etc and could be made navigable up to the house. As the river beyond that point was not navigable, goods for Aylsham had to be transferred from wherries to waggons at Coltishall or else taken by sea to Cromer and then by waggon.

It was not, however, until 1773, nearly a hundred years later, that positive steps were taken to extend the navigation beyond Horstead mill. On 27 January 1773 Parliament was petitioned for a Bill to permit the extension of the Bure navigation, otherwise known as the North river, to Aylsham. John Adey, later to become clerk to the commissioners at £25 pa, estimated the cost at £6,000 of which £1,300 had been received by voluntary gifts and £200 to £300 more was expected.[25] The remainder was to be raised by subscription. The Bill had a rapid passage through Parliament without opposition and was passed on 7 April 1773.[26]

Construction began on 29 June 1774 and a revealing sidelight on local interest occurred on 29 November when Mrs William Hardy of Coltishall recorded in her diary: 'Tuesday, Mr Mrs and Miss Smith went with us to the new river to see the lock; carried the men 2 bottles of gin. Mrs Ives gave the men a barell of beer at J Neaves and he forced them to drink it abroad.' Whether Neaves had had previous experience of the consequences of the navvies drinking habits or whether he was relying on their reputation and thus being ultra careful is not recorded. The lock visited by Mrs Hardy was on the short cut at Coltishall which by-passed Horstead Mill. On 16 March 1775 the first boat, Mr Ansell's *Crampus*, passed through the lock and three days later Mr Simon's keel of Yarmouth passed it with a cargo of bricks, pavements, coales, cinders and salt.[27]

Work proceeded slowly on the remaining locks at Buxton mill, Oxnead mill, Burgh-near-Aylsham mill and Aylsham. In October 1777 when the work was still a long way from completion John Smith the engineer reported that some £3,600 had been spent and another £2,951 was necessary to complete the navigation. Eighteen local landowners and traders rallied round with loans of £50 to £150 each and Smith agreed on 25 February 1778 to continue. In March 1779 when the work was nearing completion John Green of Wroxham became joint engineer. The navigation was finally opened throughout in October 1779. The commissioners then made a survey of the river on 9 November 1779 but found the working depth of 3ft had already decreased by the formation of shoals. Clearance of the river bed was a regular task if depth were to be maintained, as is shown by a commissioners' note of 7 May 1782:

> ordered that Thos Durrant Esq., Treasurer pay Joseph Bell and Rob. Rose seven pounds ten shillings being a quarter of a year's pay due to them the 2nd instant for didling the navigation[28]

To didle or dydle is to clean the bottom of a river with a scoop or dredge otherwise called a didle, possibly a corruption of dike-delve. The didle is a tool having a straight cutting edge about eighteen inches long behind which is a bag made of rope attached to a frame. The assembly is so arranged as to gather the cut material into the bag and thus facilitate its removal from the river bed. The didle has a long metal spike at right angles to the cutting edge and frame to take a long wooden handle and the person using it has the appearance of hoeing the bed of the river.[29]

The traffic was carried in 13-ton wherries with a draught of

2ft 4in to 2ft 6in, of which about 26 operated on the river, some being built at Aylsham and Coltishall. The main traffic was agricultural produce and flour together with coal and timber as well as bricks from a brickyard near Oxnead. There was also a special local cargo which had been shipped from Horstead on the lower section of the river long before the Aylsham navigation was built. This was marl obtained on the Horstead Hall estate from at least the sixteenth century and was to continue until about 1870. The pits from which the marl was dug were served by a navigable dike parallel with the river and linked to it by cross-dikes, some of them navigable.

A rather odd arrangement for toll collection was made in 1810 when notice was given

> that every person having charge of any vessel passing up the navigation from Great Yarmouth is to obtain at the house of Elizabeth Pratt, one of the Wharfingers of the navigation in Great Yarmouth, a ticket to be given to Elizabeth Gant, one of the collectors of the tolls in Coltishall, before passing through Horstead Lock. Those coming down to get their ticket at the Counting House of Parmeter and Dent in Aylsham. Those from between Burgh Bridge and Oxnead Bridge to get it from the Counting House of Thomas Boulter, Burgh-Mill, and below Oxnead Bridge to get it from the Counting House of William Palgrave of Buxton Mill. The tickets to be given to Elizabeth Gant.[30]

The original course of the river was generally followed except at the mills where short cuts were made to accommodate the locks and at Aylsham itself where a lateral canal was made for about a mile on the north side of the river. At the Aylsham end of this canal a bonemill was established and there was also a grouping of warehouses by the terminal basin. This basin was linked by a short cut to the pool at the tail of Aylsham mill so that wherries could deliver grain and receive flour at the mill itself.

Although the improvement in communications to Aylsham was generally acceptable there were some critics such as Dr

Gaye who said in 1788 that the navigation had been opened

> to the prejudice of the Trade of Horstead mill . . . and the
> Great Damage of T.J. Batchelor Esq.'s meadows and royalty
> from Coltishall to Meyton Bridge: the land being frequently
> flooded and the Fish and swans disturbed or stolen.[31]

The navigation continued to play a major role in the community during most of the nineteenth century until its near-
monopoly was hit by the opening in 1879 and 1880 by the East
Norfolk Railway, later part of the Great Eastern Railway, of
the line from Wroxham to Aylsham which roughly followed the
Bure valley. Further railway competition occurred in 1883 with
the opening on 5 April by the Eastern & Midlands Railway, the
successor of the Yarmouth & North Norfolk Railway, and later
to become part of the Midland & Great Northern Railway, of
the line from North Walsham to Melton Constable which had a
station at Aylsham near the terminal basin of the navigation.

Despite railway competition wherries continued to use the
navigation until its death blow fell in the great flood of 1912. The
locks were badly damaged and it was estimated that it would
cost over £4,000 to repair them. The commissioners with their
depleted funds were unable to find such a large amount and as
there was no available source of compensation the undertaking
was abandoned although formal abandonment did not take
place until 1928. Today Buxton lock has completely disappeared, having been filled in in 1933; its site is now a car park.
The gates at the other locks have been replaced by sluices but
some of the old warehouse buildings at Aylsham still stand.

One other memory of this navigation will remain in the
minds of all interested in the history of the wherry for it was
Aylsham that saw the birth and construction of the *Gipsy*. This
wherry was built by Eliza Wright and launched in 1875. She followed the normal pattern of trading until 1885. Then she was
bought by Henry M. Doughty of Theberton Hall, Suffolk who
converted her to a pleasure wherry. On 18 August 1888 she was
towed across the North Sea and during the next few years she
cruised the waterways of Europe to within ten miles of Austria.
The story of these voyages is recorded in two books published in

1889 and 1893, *Friesland Meres and Through the Netherlands. The voyage of a family in a Norfolk Wherry* and *Our Wherry in Wendish Lands*.

North Walsham & Dilham Canal

The most northerly of the Broadland navigations is the North Walsham & Dilham Canal which follows the course of the River Ant from near Dilham to a basin immediately east of Antingham Ponds. The river was already navigable to Dilham when in 1810 the possibility of extending navigation to North Walsham was being investigated. During 1811 three plans were prepared, one by William Youard in January, and two by John Millington of Hammersmith, the first in January and the second in September. Following the latter a meeting was held on 14 September at the King's Arms in North Walsham and it was resolved that application should be made to Parliament for leave to bring in a Bill to make 'a cut or canal for boats . . . from the River Ant . . . at or near a place called Wayford Bridge near Dilham to the towns of North Walsham and Antingham'. The Bill was read the first time on 18 February 1812 and despite opposition from the inhabitants of Dilham and Worstead, who feared local economic collapse if transport facilities were improved to and from North Walsham, it received the royal assent on 5 May 1812.[32]

The Act empowered the raising of £33,000 plus a further £10,000 by mortgage of the rates and dues if the original capital were insufficient. In fact, 586 £50 shares totalling £29,300, had been issued by 1824. Authorized tolls included 1d per mile for passengers; ½d per mile for cattle, horses, and asses; and 6d a score for sheep, swine, and other beasts. Actual construction does not appear to have started for some years as final authority to begin work was not given until a meeting of the proprietors on 15 December 1824.

This delay was probably influenced by the proprietors having to face a claim for damages for possible loss of trade entered by Isaac Harris Lewis, the owner and occupier of a private staithe at Dilham. The case was heard before a jury at the

Quarter Sessions in April 1825. It was alleged that the 'making of the canal would materially operate to the diminution of the trade at present carried on by him'. Lewis's staithe was situated on a short branch at the head of the then navigable portion of the River Ant at Dilham and his concern was that the new canal would leave the existing navigation about a mile below his staithe. It was clear that much of his trade derived from the area which was to be traversed by the canal and that four of the five mills between Dilham and Antingham employed Lewis to carry their corn and flour to Yarmouth. Evidence was also given that Lewis was a dealer in other bulky articles such as coal, marl, oilcake, etc, and when the canal was built people would be able to obtain their requirements nearer their homes and therefore with cheaper carriage. It appeared that Lewis received about £200 pa from the staithe and wanted compensation. At the end of the hearing 'the Jury (who were very respectable) after a deliberation of about twenty minutes, assessed the damages at £1,500'.[33]

Digging began on 5 April 1825 by a labour force of one hundred 'bankers' from Bedfordshire.

We allude to the Canal which is to extend from a point near North Walsham to Dilham completing the line of conveyance to Yarmouth and thus to open a communication along the whole course by water carriage with the sea . . . [It] has been in contemplation 12 years and is under the direction of J. Millington, Esq., engineer. Between eleven and twelve o'clock in the forenoon about sixty of the workmen assembled in the market—from hence they moved forward in regular order, preceded by the committee, with colours flying and a band of music, to Austin Bridge where the first spade of earth was cut by Mr Youard, clerk to the sub-committee, the band playing "God Save the King" and by loud and repeated huzzas from the numerous spectators. After the men had worked for a few minutes they returned to the market in the same order to partake of some barrels of strong beer, which were gratuitously distributed among them.[34]

This canal was John Millington's only venture into canal building although in later years, after he had settled in America, he wrote *Elements of Civil Engineering*, probably the first textbook on the subject published in the United States. This book contains a great deal of information on the practice and problems of canal construction, though it does not refer directly to the North Walsham & Dilham Canal. He died in 1868.

Although the work was under Millington's direction actual construction was carried out by a contractor, Thomas Hughes, who succeeded Millington in 1827 as engineer to the proprietors. Hughes had had experience in canal construction on the Caledonian, Dingwall and Edinburgh & Glasgow Union Canals,[35] as well as civil engineering experience on other harbour and river works.[36]

The line of the canal was not coincidental with the original bed of the river and, therefore, it is a true cut and not strictly a river navigation. Construction was not easy as the land through which it passes is very marshy. In fact, Hughes described it as the worst description of peat, though by puddling he considered that he had been able to make a satisfactory bed and embankments.[37] In slightly more than a year the work was sufficiently advanced to allow the first laden wherries to reach Cubitt's mill on 14 June 1826 and 'Thousands of spectators assembled to witness this interesting scene and the day finished with a plentiful treat to the workmen of Mr Sharpe's strong ale and Barclay's brown stout'.[38] The official opening took place less than three months later on 29 August 1826 with a grand parade of boats traversing the full length of the canal.[39]

The canal's course as constructed ran from Wayford Bridge to Antingham Ponds in a meanderingly north-westerly direction for 8¾ miles. There were six locks sited at Honing, Briggate, Ebridge, Bacton Wood, and two at Swafield, giving a total rise of 58ft.

The terminus of the canal was in a basin adjacent to Antingham mills. Although the Antingham Ponds served as the feeder and reservoir for the canal, the link between the Ponds and the basin was only navigable by shallow draught lighters.

The first bridge over the navigation was, and is known as

Tonnage Bridge for it was here that a wharf and cottage were constructed and the tolls were levied on goods entering and

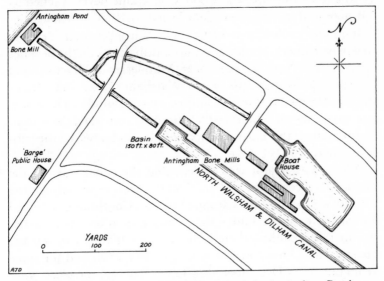

9. The North Walsham & Dilham Canal's basin by Antingham Ponds

leaving the canal. The cottage and wharf have disappeared but the bridge, similar in design to others across the canal, remains.

The vessels generally used were the smaller type of wherry, about 18 to 20 tons with maximum dimensions of 50ft length × 12ft 4ins beam × 3ft draught. Owing to the shallowness of the waterway some vessels were of a type known as slip-keel wherries. In these the cargo would be stowed so that the keel bolts were accessible, thus allowing the keel to be unbolted and removed when the vessel was about to leave deeper water. In order to prevent leakage false bolts were fitted into the keel-bolt holes. Removal and refitting of the keel took place while the vessel was afloat and took about a quarter of an hour. After removal the keel would be towed in the water behind the wherry, so as to keep the timber from drying out and warping. Should this occur the keel would be very difficult to refit. The keel would be replaced after the cargo had been removed so that more sail could be carried when the wherry was travelling light.[40]

The main traffic on the canal was corn, flour, mill offals, coal, feeding cake, manure, and wood. Coal traffic never reached its full potential as the canal dues levied made it, in the earlier years, more profitable to bring the coal from the north east in coastwise colliers, discharge it into waiting carts on the beaches of the north Norfolk coast near Mundesley or Bacton, and transport it overland to North Walsham. Later the canal's share of the coal traffic was limited by the railway. There was one small 12-ton wherry which used to run vegetables from Antingham to the Yarmouth market. It was known as the cabbage wherry.

As early as 1830 it was evident that the canal was not the financial success that had confidently been expected, for the price of a £50 share had dropped to £10. Continuing financial embarrassment persuaded the proprietors to obtain a further Act in 1866 enabling them, among other matters, to sell the navigation.[41] This power was not, in fact, exercised for some years but on 17 December 1885 James Turner, the clerk, gave notice that an application was being made to the Board of Trade for consent to its sale to Edward Press, this being completed at £600 on 16 March 1886. Press, the miller at Bacton Wood mill, also owned and operated several wherries, and so had good reason for acquiring the navigation. The purchase, however, led to a local scandal.

By virtue of the 1866 Act the canal could be sold with the consent of three quarters of the value of the proprietors present at a General Meeting and the purchase price was to be divided among the known shareholders in proportion to their holdings. At the time of the completion of the sale the principal clerk was James Turner, a solicitor of Golden Square, London, and he was entrusted with the purchase money to distribute it to the known holders of 446 shares out of the original 586. After paying out on 55 shares Turner absconded with the balance and the money was never recovered.[42]

In June 1887 the committee considered themselves to be morally, if not legally, bound to reimburse the money from their own pockets but they had second thoughts and made no repayments on the grounds that none of the shareholders was making a claim. Eventually in 1896 they declared a dividend and each of five proprietors, including Edward Press, subscribed £110 17s 7d to make up the sum necessary for the repayments.

Meanwhile on 11 July 1887 the proprietors had appointed Walter Rye, another solicitor, as principal clerk and he later expressed his concern at the 'great irregularities in the management and direction of the Company' which had been going on for years 'amounting to an almost total disregard to the provisions of the Act'. He instanced, among other matters, that although the Act did not permit any person holding any place of profit to serve on the committee, Mr Press, the manager, had so served; and that, although it was required that a treasurer should be appointed and security given by him, no such appointment had been made for years. Mr Rye also pointed out that there was no way under either Act of formally winding up the company. He rightly indicated that the matter could be dealt with as a voluntary winding up under the Companies Act, but if arranged in this way the expense would be out of all proportion to the assets, and furthermore, this method would bring the old irregularities to light and the matter could come before the Courts. In the end the whole subject seems to have been quietly forgotten.[43]

Under the control of Edward Press traffic continued to operate although the $1\frac{3}{8}$ miles above Swafield locks to Antingham were abandoned in 1893. In 1898 400 tons of goods were loaded and discharged on the canal, 5,000 tons were loaded on the canal and despatched to other destinations, and 6,386 tons were brought from elsewhere on to the canal and discharged. By 1906 the trade income was below £400 pa.

On 2 July 1906 Edward Press died and although 'trade had for a long while been decreasing and was now very small' the canal was sold by auction on 11 September 1907 to Mr Percy, one of the directors of the General Estates Company, for £2,550.[44] The General Estates Company were already owners of the freehold ferry rights of the Gorleston ferry and of the tolls of Selby bridge. Another associated company was the Yarmouth

& Gorleston Steamboat Company. This firm continued to own the navigation until 1921 when the concern was purchased by E. G. Cubitt and G. Walker for £1,500. They immediately formed a new company, the North Walsham Canal Co Ltd, and sold the canal to it for the same price.

Meanwhile the canal had been badly damaged in the August 1912 floods when the bank was breached above Bacton Wood lock. Attempts were made during the 1920s to improve the canal works below Swafield locks. This became disused in 1927. The last wherry to use the canal was the *Ella*, owned by Press Bros, which loaded a cargo at Bacton Wood staithe in December 1934. Shortly after this the canal silted up, and the works became derelict. Today the only part of the main line that remains in any way navigable is the stretch from Wayford bridge to the tail of Honing lock. The remains of the canal are still owned by the North Walsham Canal Co Ltd.

CHAPTER VI

The Great Ouse

The history of navigation on the Great Ouse is inextricably bound up with the history of Fen drainage.[1] The complications, however, begin long before Vermuyden's operations in the mid-seventeenth century. In medieval times the main river below Earith took a northerly course, swinging eastwards near March to join the waters of the original River Cam. The combined waters made their outfall at Wisbech, their course, known as the Wellstream, being much along the line later taken by the Wisbech Canal.

During the thirteenth century, presumably in times of flood, part of the water of the Ouse at Earith was forced into the channel of a tributary, known as the Aldreth River, and flowed to join the Cam at Stretham. This channel is today known as the Old West River (which, as it flows eastwards, makes little sense until it is realized that it once flowed in the opposite direction). Later, a new channel was cut from Littleport to Stowbridge, to take the combined waters of the Cam and Ouse to join a stream with its outfall into the Wash at Lynn. As a result, the old course of the Ouse below Earith (it was called the West Water) began to silt up through insufficient flow, as did the water-course between Littleport and Wisbech. After Vermuyden's cutting of the two Bedford rivers, these old courses gradually became extinct.[2]

Part of the old system was used by the Romans; the Car Dyke, from Waterbeach on the Cam to the Witham near Lincoln, coincided for a few miles with the Aldreth River and the West Water.[3] The Danes attacked Ely from the river in 1070; they also penetrated deep into Bedfordshire. Written records, however, are sparse. In 1169 there is mention of a 'passage for boats' at Aldreth, and this is referred to again in 1279.[4] There is evidence of trade between Lynn and Huntingdon towards the end of the thirteenth century. Stone was transported by water from the quarries at Barnack to the great religious foundations in the Fens and at Bury St Edmunds. Cambridge exported grain and received a variety of imports for the growing University and Stourbridge Fair. The effects of the tides could be felt several miles up the Ouse's tributaries and with the wind in the right quarter boats could sail well into the fenland. When the wind failed or was contrary, bow-hauling by men or boys was the rule, sometimes with the aid of a horse. But there were no proper haling ways, obstructions accumulated in the channel and the banks were not kept in repair. By the beginning of the seventeenth century it became clear that action was needed if the Fens were not to become wholly drowned. Local attempts to solve problems of flooding had been tried and failed; petitions accumulated, and in 1600 an Act 'for the recovering of many hundred thousand Acres of marshes, and other Grounds subject commonly to surrounding,' over an area stretching from Cambridgeshire to County Durham, was passed.[5]

This Act enabled those who ventured their capital in drainage enterprise (the 'adventurers') to be recompensed by grants of the land they—or rather their 'undertakers'—had drained. It was followed by various surveys and schemes, some of them encouraged by James I on account of the Crown's holdings in the fenlands. One effort, led by Lord Chief Justice Popham, resulted in 1605 in the cutting of Popham's Eau from the old course of the Nene to Well Creek near Nordelph. But the major operation needed was delayed. Recommendations of a specially appointed Commission of Sewers had little effect, and reports on the rivers in 1618 by Sir Clement Edwards and Richard Atkyns only made clear the differences between drainage and navigation interests.

Until this time it would seem that the Ouse was generally navigable from Huntingdon to Lynn, serving mainly for the export of corn. Pressure was growing for the extension of the navigation to Bedford, a major corn market town. In 1617 a

Plates 13 & 14 King's Lynn: *(above)* King's Lynn: the Alexandra Dock in 1871 from a watercolour by W.F.K. Austin, in the Lynn Museum; *(below)* seagoing ships and inland waterways craft in the Alexandra dock, 1919. The *Teutonic* is in the foreground; behind is a narrow-boat type steam tug and some fen lighters

Alexandra Dock.

Plates 15 & 16 (*above*) Horses towing in the River Cam, from an engraving by J. Walker, 1793. King's College chapel is on the right; *(below)* wooden barge *Charles*, owned by West Norfolk Farmers Manure Co, passing through the tidal gates at Denver, July 1907. The barge was too big for the lock. On board (left to right): Ada Ann Bell, John W. Bell, George Dixon at the tiller (he was drowned off this barge at King's Lynn), Jack Lee, Tom Burrows, John Smith (known as Nelson, being blind in one eye), Sally Smith, Mrs Dixon, three visitors and Maud, George Dixon's daughter

patent was granted to John Gason, of Finchley, empowering him to make various rivers navigable over a 21-year period. However, in February 1618 he gave over his rights in the rivers of Cambridgeshire, Huntingdonshire and Bedfordshire to a Bedfordshire gentleman, Arnold Spencer, and a Westminster vintner, Thomas Girton. In partnership they built six sluices between St Ives and St Neots. Girton withdrew in 1625, and the following year Spencer sold for £740 all rights in the river to John Jackson of St Neots. The first tolls were 1d per ton per sluice, later increased to 1½d and then, ironically after an appeal to the justices of the peace by the traders for a reduction, further increased to 3d. Poetic justice decreed that Jackson's attempt to have them raised again resulted in a reduction to 2½d in 1628.

Spencer was still concerned with the river and, with the Corporation of Bedford, tried, but failed, to obtain an Act to extend the navigation to that town. Nevertheless he persisted, and spent a great deal of money in dredging and improving the river, also obtaining back the six sluices from Jackson in 1638. But he was unable to proceed higher than Great Barford, which became something of an inland port. His ventures proved expensive and he suffered much financial loss. This, together with the onset of civil war, stopped further progress and the condition of the river above St Neots quickly deteriorated. When Spencer died about 1655 his creditors took over the Ouse between St Ives and St Neots and matters became still worse, no positive action being taken until 1674.[6]

By the time things began moving again on the upper river, great changes had taken place below Earith. Discontent over the failure to solve the problem of flooding led in 1630 to Francis, Earl of Bedford, the major landowner in the area, agreeing to drain the area which became known as the Bedford Level. In return he was to have 95,000 acres of reclaimed land, although not all of it for his personal profit. Thirteen other adventurers joined him to form a corporation, obtaining a charter in 1634. Cornelius Vermuyden, the Dutch engineer who had previously drained Hatfield Chase for Charles I, was called in, despite local suspicion of the foreigner. He opened his attack

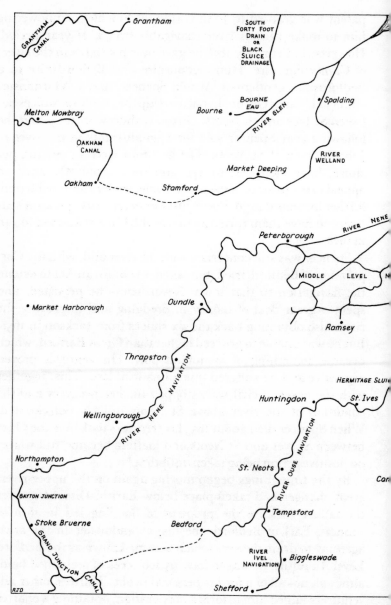

10. The Ouse, Nene, Welland and their Connections

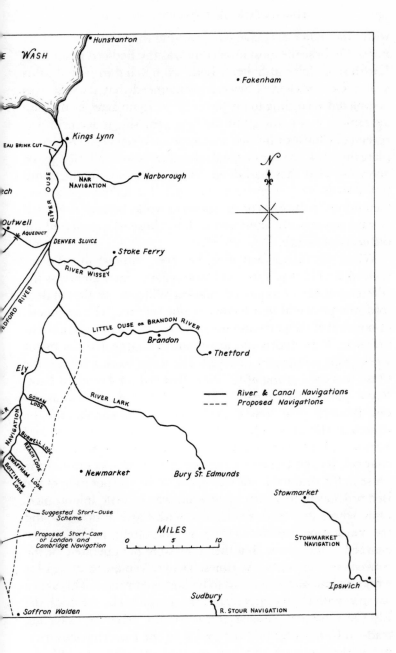

with nine major drainage cuts, varying in length from 2 to 21 miles. Of these the most important was the Bedford River from Earith to a sluice at Salter's Lode, completed in 1637. In this year a Commission of Sewers pronounced that the task was completed according to the terms of the Lynn Law, as the 1630 agreement was known, but the next year this judgement was reversed. Charles I himself was appointed undertaker to complete the work and the original adventurers were allotted 40,000 acres for what they had done. Vermuyden was retained, but political discord intervened and civil war halted operations. Conditions in the Fens deteriorated as works became neglected or were maliciously interfered with by those who preferred the old order of nature.

When the tumult was over, however, interest in the Fens revived, and in 1649 a second Drainage Act (later known as the 'Pretended Act') was passed, making William, 5th Earl of Bedford, the principal in a further major venture. The strenuous opposition of the ports and towns served by the navigation was defeated; Vermuyden was again put in charge and the major works were completed in 1652.[7] The main work affecting the Ouse was the cutting of the New Bedford, or Hundred Foot, River, parallel to the earlier cut which became known as the Old Bedford. The New Bedford became the channel for the waters of the upper Ouse; sluices were built at Denver and Earith, and the river via Ely became little more than a drainage channel. By the General Drainage Act of 1663, control of the Ouse in the drained lands was given to the Corporation of the Bedford Level, to which navigation was of little importance. Only where its interests coincided with those of drainage did the navigation benefit. This was not often; no tolls were charged at the sluices, but then they were not operated for the convenience of boats. At times, Denver remained closed for weeks on end and boats had to be portaged round. This sluice was particularly unpopular; no longer scoured by the tides, the Ely Ouse became choked and silted up, adversely affecting trade to Cambridge and the towns on the eastern tributaries. Below the sluice silt also accumulated and the trade of Lynn was seriously threatened.[8] Only above Earith were there no complaints, as the New Bedford provided a faster and better-conditioned route than the old one. When in 1713, owing to the confluence of exceptional floodwater from the uplands and high spring tides, Denver sluice blew up, the news was greeted with joy and optimism. But the consequence was renewed and repeated flooding, and even further deterioration of the channel below Denver. Between 1748–50, the Corporation replaced the sluice with an improved version including a navigation lock designed by Charles Labelye, but the navigators continued to complain.

Returning to the upper river, we find that in 1674 Samuel Jemmatt, who held a mortgage of the river from Spencer, took over the navigation from Spencer's creditors for £1,200. He leased it to Henry Ashley for £160 a year. Ashley rebuilt some sluices and added others. Energetically he drove ahead, aiming for Bedford, and in 1687 was appointed undertaker to extend the navigation to that town. Within two years it arrived there; Bedford was now linked to the sea, some 74 miles away.[9]

Ashley's son, also called Henry, was equally active. In 1680 he bought out the share of the navigation between St Ives and Great Barford that Samuel Jemmatt had left to his son Nathaniel and did his best to oust John Jemmatt, brother to Nathaniel, from the other half. John held out against the combined Ashleys until a compromise was reached. The younger Ashley also became undertaker for the Lark in 1700. With support from the riverside towns and traders, Ashley junior was enabled by an Act of 1719 to rebuild St Ives staunch and take tolls there of 1d a chaldron of coals, load of timber or grain, or ton of other foods. This was cheaper than what was charged between St Ives and St Neots, where the charge was now 3d for an equivalent weight of goods at each staunch.

When Bedford was reached in 1689, the works on the river between Bedford and St Ives included five staunches and ten sluices. The staunches were of the beam and paddle type, providing a 'flash' to help boats over fords and shallows. The sluices appear to have been pound-locks; they were more costly to construct and their purpose was to help boats through the mill weirs. Tolls for passing sluices were generally higher than at staunches, but passage through the latter was often subject to long delay. Additional works included some small cuts to straighten the channel and the making of haling ways. Despite disputes with millers and landowners—a common feature in river histories—the navigation, with the drive of the Ashleys behind it, began to prosper. The towns it served prospered still more, Bedford in particular developing its waterfront and the coal trade growing in importance. In the riverside towns, notably St Ives, the number of watermen increased, and boatbuilding became a local industry.[10]

In the river's earlier history, the heavily-built, flat-bottomed Humber keels brought coal from the north to Lynn and, until the draining of the mid-seventeenth century, sailed upstream as well. As on the Norfolk wherries, the masts could be lowered to negotiate low bridges. As late as 1845 the Bedford Level Corporation required that railway bridges over their principal waterways should be able to accommodate the keels. After the construction of Denver sluice, however, which restricted the passage of larger vessels, a new type of craft was developed to navigate the shallow waterways. The Fen lighters were about 42ft long, with 10–11ft beam at deck level, narrowing by about a foot at the bottom. Strongly built of elm and oak, they were rounded at bow and stern and rudderless. A lighter could take about 25 tons. They operated in gangs usually of about five, though sometimes many more. The leading lighter in a gang could rig a single square sail but, until the advent of steam, horse-towing was more common; quanting, as on the Norfolk Broads, was resorted to where horse-towing was impractical. For nearly 300 years lighters dominated the waterborne trade of the Great Ouse and its tributaries, the Middle Level and, to a lesser extent, the Nene. Their construction seems hardly to have altered during that period.

In the nineteenth century a house-lighter, which had a cabin for the crew, became a usual component of a gang, and a smaller lighter, or horse-boat, took up the rear position, being used for ferrying the animals across the river when necessary. The owner's name might be painted on the bows of the fore-lighter. All the vessels had a kind of removable bowsprit, that on the second lighter being much longer and used for steering the whole gang.[11] With boundary fences often running down to the water's edge and stiles being preferred to gates, the horses had to be trained to jump about 2½ft without being strangled in mid-air. Any obstacle higher than this the lightermen would demolish. Horses were encouraged 'by a peculiar chant, probably of some antiquity . . . It began with a deep note and then consisted of the constant repetition of a rather higher one, as long as the performer's breath held out. It then finished on a mournful wail on two notes'.[12]

The lightermen developed their own characteristic dress, with 'sleeved waistcoats of blue or red plush with glass buttons', and they wore fur caps. They had a reputation for heavy drinking, which is not surprising in view of the long delays occasioned by waiting for tides or for sufficient depth of water to continue a voyage.[13] There was no shortage of pubs along the Fen waterways, one of the most popular being the Jenyns Arms at Denver, where the 'berthsmen' who took command of vessels using the tidal river, for which they were paid ten shillings a trip, lodged in the taproom.[14] A different class of men looked after the horses; these may have been only casual labourers, working the horses in relays.

By the last quarter of the eighteenth century the navigation of the upper river had passed to Ashley Palmer, grandson of Henry Ashley, and to the Francklin family, via John Jemmatt's grand-daughter who married John Francklin. For many years the income was sufficient to cover costs of maintenance and repair and to yield a reasonable profit. By 1792, however, when Ashley Palmer died the picture was less cheerful. Costs, due to inflation, were rising fast, and increasing traffic, while adding to the income, caused considerable damage. Below St Ives and on the New Bedford, where no tolls were charged, the drainage interest complained bitterly about the damage done to the banks by towing horses and to the sluices by impatient watermen. But a move in 1777 to regulate the navigation failed in Parliament, the volume of protest forcing the Bedford Level Corporation into retreat.[15]

Between Denver and King's Lynn the watermen's chief enemies were the riparian landowners, who were hostile to the use of horses for towing and who tried to levy their own tolls. Not until 1789 was there a measure of reconciliation, when the Haling Act was passed.[16] This set up a body of commissioners with representatives of both landowners and the navigation interest, and laid down haling tolls of 4d a chaldron of coals and 4d a load of anything else, with fines and penalties for evasion. Out of the revenue the landowners were to be compensated for damage caused by horse-towing, and regulations were framed for controlling methods of haling. These measures seem to have been successful, in view of the absence of subsequent complaints.

The Ouse Outfall and the Port of King's Lynn

King's Lynn rapidly developed into a major port when the waters of the Ouse were diverted thither in medieval times, as described earlier. Evidence of its importance in trading with the Continent can be found in its architecture, including the fifteenth-century warehouses of the Hanseatic League. The fleets—narrow tidal channels running through the town—enabled vessels to be loaded and unloaded conveniently. The flow of water widened the estuary and for centuries no real attempt was made to confine the channel. The estuary encroached on the Marshland, to a width in places of over half a mile.

After the drainage of the Fens, whatever was wrong with Lynn harbour was blamed on Vermuyden's works, in particular the construction of Denver sluice. Below Denver silt accumulated and the passage to the sea became progressively more difficult. In 1724 Colonel John Armstrong surveyed the river at the request of the inhabitants of Lynn. His report recommended that 'everything connected with the Great and Little Ouse rivers should be restored to the state, as nearly as possible, in which it was anterior to the execution of the new drainage scheme'. This, he considered, would cleanse the river mouth from the shifting sands which were proving such a hazard.[17] But other engineers reckoned that the channel had been destroyed because the banks were set too far back, the scour hence being insufficient. The great bend in the river immediately above Lynn also diminished the effect of the tides. In his survey in 1766 John Smeaton recommended confining the channel to solve the problem, and rejected the idea that Denver sluice harmed the navigation as it was too distant from the outfall to have much effect. Moreover, the incoming tide drew sand from the bed of the Wash into Lynn harbour, which the ebb was too weak to remove.

During the eighteenth century the condition of the harbour and outfall deteriorated still further. The Kinderleys, father and son, and William Elstobb proposed cutting off the great bend near Lynn by a new straight channel. The case was argued for nearly half a century, until the passing of the Eau Brink Act in 1795. Yet it was not until 1821 that the Eau Brink Cut was opened, following years of pamphlet warfare during which most of the eminent engineers of the time exchanged fire.[18] In view of the hazards of navigation it may seem strange that it was the navigation interest that opposed the Cut, while the Bedford Level Corporation promoted it. The navigators and traders dreaded the imposition of tolls, and King's Lynn, now far less of a major port than it had been in medieval times, feared that the Cut would still further damage the harbour. After the passing of the Act, the exact dimensions of the Cut became a matter for controversy. Eventually, however, all parties accepted an arbitration decision; John Rennie and Thomas Telford were appointed to direct the work for the Eau Brink Commissioners and Lynn corporation respectively, Joliffe & Banks were appointed contractors, and the work was completed in four years. It proved too narrow, and caused a further accumulation of silt in the harbour. On Telford's advice it was enlarged, adding £33,000 to the cost of the enterprise. Telford reported favourably, commenting that the channel between Denver and Lynn had been greatly deepened by the increased scour and that the old channel by the rapid accretion of mud had been converted into valuable pasture. But it had been an expensive operation, costing in all nearly half a million pounds for the 2½ miles of new channel and the other connected works. The opponents of the Cut, the navigation interest, benefited most from it, as trade steadily increased in the immediately subsequent years. It did not, however, as its proponents had hoped, solve the problem of drainage. Throughout the peat Fens, as the peat wastes away so the drains have to be lowered—and as the drains are lowered so the peat wastage is accelerated. Only new methods of cultivation, involving stabilizing the peat upper soil by mixing it with the heavy clay sub-soil, can delay the subsidence. So far more work remained to be done.

Under the Eau Brink Act, commissioners of drainage and of navigation were set up, their powers extending as far up river as St Ives. Both bodies were generally subordinate to the Bedford Level Corporation. The drainage commissioners wielded far more power; their navigation brethren were permitted to make by-laws and construct toll-houses, but dredging, maintenance and the regulation of works came under the drainage banner. Only a quarter of the revenue from the tolls of 4d a ton or chaldron of goods passing through the Cut was allocated to the navigation commissioners. But the interests were not necessarily always in opposition; the construction of Brownshill lock and staunch, primarily to improve navigation above Earith, was contributed to by both bodies.

The River in the Nineteenth Century

By the end of 1800 the main line of the Grand Junction Canal was open,[19] though there was a railroad link at Blisworth until the tunnel was completed in 1805. The threat to the Upper Ouse was obvious. Together with improved highways the canal made coal available at Bedford from collieries much nearer than those supplying the town via the Ouse. The river-borne Bedford coal trade fell by over a quarter between 1790 and 1821. Various proposals were made to link the Ouse with the main canal system. In 1812 John Rennie produced an estimate of £180,807 for a 15-mile canal from Bedford to Fenny Stratford on the Grand Junction Canal, a figure which frightened off would-

be investors. In 1817 a scheme was mooted to link the Upper
Ouse to the terminus of the Newport Pagnell Canal, and there
was also a suggestion to join the Ivel Navigation at Shefford to
the Grand Junction and to the Lee.[20] But, like the London &
Cambridge Junction Canal, all these projects proved abortive.

Great attempts to improve the navigation of the upper river
were made in the early nineteenth century by Sir Thomas
Cullum, who inherited the share of his aunt Susanna, wife of
Ashley Palmer, and by John Francklin. Locks, sluices and
staunches were rebuilt. Cullum, who also inherited the Lark
navigation, spent thousands of pounds (£5,450 on both rivers in
1839), and took over and developed the New Wharf in Bedford
in 1843. His income from the Ouse at this time was about £1,700
a year, while the Francklin share averaged £1,350. One admires
Cullum's optimism, but not his grasp of economic realities. The
prospects for local trade were limited, in view of the pre-
dominantly agricultural nature of the area. Moreover, below St
Ives the condition of the river was deteriorating. Shoals and
shortage of water caused expensive and frustrating delays. In
1849 the New Bedford was reported as having silted up in places
so much that lighters drawing 3ft were sometimes detained for a
week. The Admiralty Inspectors enquiring into the proposed
Norfolk Estuary Bill wondered how it happened

> that the present state of the Hundred-foot river is allowed to
> exist in face of the constant representations which have been
> made during the last 100 years . . . and while we cannot per-
> ceive that any material improvements have been attempted,
> the evils have been augmented by the erection of a dam
> across the Ouse near Bluntisham as recently as 15 years ago,
> a period when it was to be expected such barbarous modes of
> treating tidal rivers had been exploded.[21]

A co-ordinated effort to deal with at least some of the problems, however, was made with the passing of the South Level
Drainage and Navigation Act in 1827.[22] Commissioners
appointed under this Act were empowered to dredge the Cam
below Clayhithe, the lodes—the ancient man-made waterways
connecting the villages on the eastern side of the Cam to the

river—the Lark below Swale's Reach, and the Ouse itself from Hermitage sluice to Littleport bridge. Additionally they were to make a cut from a point below Ely to Sand Hill End, near Littleport, by-passing a meandering curve through Padnal Fen and Burnt Fen. Tolls were to be levied on cargo passing along the Ouse between Littleport bridge and Upware sluice at the entrance to Reach lode, and on the Lark from Prickwillow to Littleport, and rates were also charged for animals passing along the banks. The tolls were mortgaged to Elisha Ambler, who also held the Eau Brink tolls, for £2,560 a year.[23] The South Level works proved expensive, costing initially over £70,000 raised by an Exchequer loan, but they seem to have been done efficiently. But these operations, and the cleansing of the Old West River in 1836, came too late to enable the navigation to prosper. Between 1845 and the end of 1850, railways came by divers routes to Cambridge, and in turn to Ely, St Ives, Huntingdon, King's Lynn, Tempsford and St Neots on the main river, and to Brandon, Thetford, Bury St Edmunds, March, Wisbech and Peterborough on connecting waterways and tributaries. The branch from Bedford to Hitchin on the Great Northern main line was opened in 1857, and from Bedford to Cambridge in 1862.

Let us now look at the Great Ouse from the outfall to Bedford as it was in the 1850s. Following the completion of the Eau Brink Cut, in 1834 Denver sluice was reconstructed according to the design of Sir John Rennie; it remains substantially the same today, with a navigation lock with two sets of gates at each end to enable it to cope with the variation of water level according to the rise and fall of the tides.

The Norfolk Estuary Co, set up in 1846, gave up its ambitious schemes of land reclamation in the Wash, but improved the river below Lynn by the Marsh Cut, two miles long, and a continuation of the channel for a further mile between training walls similar to those constructed for the Nene and Welland. However, an unfortunate side effect was the lowering of the level in Lynn harbour by 3ft and an accumulation of shoals above Lynn. Tolls on the Eau Brink Cut fell to £1,345 in 1854, from over £4,000 5 years earlier. Neither the

Bedford Level Corporation nor King's Lynn showed hostility towards the encroaching railways, the former because of their understandable lack of enthusiasm for navigation and the latter because of the fear that it would lose trade to other waterside towns with facilities for rail interchange. Nevertheless it was essential to try to keep the navigation financially viable and the coal trade from Newcastle was particularly important. By 1855 the rates were reduced to 4s a ton between King's Lynn and Ely, where in addition to the wharf at Annesdale by the Cutter inn, a large interchange dock had been built a few years before beside the newly opened railway station. This dock could accommodate over 200 vessels, which brought agricultural produce for distribution countrywide by rail. Docks were also built at Littleport, Chatteris and Benwick, on a smaller scale. This lessened the dependence of the area, in particular of the isolated pumping stations, on the waterborne coal from Lynn, as coal brought by rail could be offloaded into barges for the final stages of the journey only.

While the river in the Ely area remained busy with short-haul traffic, on the upper Ouse and the Cam receipts fell. Upper Ouse receipts dropped from £7,656 in 1842 to £4,508 in 1851 and continued to decline in succeeding years. After Sir Thomas Cullum's death in 1855, Francklin tried to purchase his share, but rejected Lady Cullum's price of £14,000, including property as well as the tolls. With the Leicester, Bedford & Hitchin Railway enabling coal from the Midlands to compete with Tyneside coal via Lynn, the decline in receipts accelerated. By 1862, tolls fell to less than half the total for 1855. To its owners, the navigation had become a liability.[24]

Various attempts to sell the navigation were made in the next few years, including a public auction in Bedford and advertisement in the local press. In 1869 a purchaser was found: John Kirkham, who paid £1,500 for it, excluding the New Wharf. It was a poor bargain. Trade continued to diminish; navigation above Tempsford stopped after the closing of the Ivel in 1876 and there soon became no point in collecting tolls above St Neots. The deteriorating works were blamed for floods in 1875 and it was recommended that the navigation should be abandoned. In a report, R. B. Grantham proposed the setting up of a drainage authority by Act of Parliament, but there were no funds with which to do so. One of the first acts of the newly formed Huntingdonshire County Council was to join with Bedfordshire and Northamptonshire in putting the matter before the Board of Trade with the hope of setting up a Conservancy Board to take over the drainage, the navigation being declared derelict. Kirkham now tried to sell the navigation by auction, but there were no bidders.

Then came a surprising move by a new company, the Ouse River Canal & Steam Navigation Ltd, which bought the navigation and tried to obtain an Act to link Bedford with the Grand Junction Canal. These proposals were defeated, but a Board of Trade enquiry by Major Marindin was optimistic about the possible increase of trade on the river provided that the necessary and very expensive repairs were executed, which might well prove too much for any single individual. Income produced only £250 a year at this time.

In 1893 the navigation was bought by L. T. Simpson, a stockbroker, for £6,170.[25] He undertook a large-scale restoration programme in the next four years, spending possibly as much as £21,000. He bought lighters and tugs and formed the Ouse Transport Company, which quoted through rates to Bedford from various continental ports. Frederick Howard supported the venture by ordering pig iron from Yorkshire by water for his engineering works at Bedford. Coal and building materials also came up river, while agricultural and market produce went down. Simpson now attempted to raise income by drawing up for Parliamentary approval a new schedule of tolls. The Board of Trade produced a provisional order which Simpson attacked as being inadequate. But his own position proved impossible. The only statutory right to levy tolls was at St Ives Staunch. Above Great Barford, Simpson, as 'undertaker', was entitled to any profits, but between Great Barford and St Ives the river did not come under the terms of the Railway & Canal Traffic Act of 1888 and the seventeenth-century system legally still applied. Bedfordshire and Huntingdonshire County Councils both opposed Simpson, the former maintaining that he had no right

to charge tolls at all and the latter objecting to his attempt to
raise the 1d toll at St Ives and to charge tolls on unloaded boats.
Bedford Corporation, which had just improved its own riverside using materials which had indeed travelled thither by
water, joined the opposition as it desired exclusive rights over
the Ouse within its boundaries. With such strong opposition
and so many legal difficulties, the Bill was dropped.

Then a new enemy attacked—the corporation of Godmanchester. They maintained that they had a right to open the
sluices at Godmanchester, Houghton and Hemingford during
floods. This they did in 1894, damaging two lock-gates, and
Simpson eventually lost a protracted legal action against them.
With tolls down to £150 and enormous costs to meet, Simpson,
on the assumption that the navigation was his own property,
determined to close it, nailed up the lock-gates and removed
part of the sluices. Huntingdonshire County Council now
declared that he had no right to do this as the river was a public
highway and took the case to the Chancery Court in 1898. The
Court decided in favour of the County Council, while at the
same time decreeing that Simpson was under no obligation to
maintain the works. He appealed; the Court of Appeal declared
that the public could pass the locks on payment of a 'reasonable' toll for loaded boats—enough to produce a profit for
Simpson after he had paid for maintaining the works. In 1904
the case went to the Lords, who permitted Simpson to close the
locks. Lord MacNaghten commented that if the navigation was
worth maintaining 'it seems tolerably clear that statutory
powers must be obtained and the navigation placed under a
public body'.

There had been a marked increase in pleasure boating in
recent years, of no benefit to Simpson as the boats passed toll-
free. However in 1906 the River Ouse Locks Committee was
formed to reopen the river for pleasure craft and Simpson
leased to them the locks between Great Barford and Bedford for
a time, nearly 2,000 boats passing through Bedford lock in three
months. The St Ives Transport Company, formed in 1900,
whose rates for water carriage undercut the railways, also
pressed for reopening to Bedford. Simpson, however, now

wanted only to sell, for £10,000 if he could get it. An Ouse Navigation Company was promoted to operate motor barges on the river, but failed to raise enough cash to purchase the navigation. So despite this and other pressures from the various local authorities, the upper Ouse remained closed.

The conclusions of the Royal Commission, printed in 1909, sum up the condition of the river at this time:[26]

> The traffic up to Bedford from King's Lynn, which is alleged to have been considerable and increasing during the time the locks were open, has now altogether come to an end. Below St Ives, various parts of the navigation, including the artificial cuts called the 'Old and New Bedford Rivers', are under the control of various public authorities; and part of it appears to be virtually under no jurisdiction of any kind. There is a small amount of traffic between King's Lynn and St Ives, chiefly conducted by the St Ives Transport Company; but the river is in many places very shallow and choked with weeds and mud, so that barges are often stopped for days, and the use of steam traction, up to St Ives, is impossible.
>
> From King's Lynn to Cambridge . . . past Ely and up the Cam River, the navigation is better, and can be used by craft carrying 60 tons.

The Commission recorded the suggestion that the Ouse and its tributaries should be placed under a single public authority for both navigation and drainage, and that a canal should be cut between Bedford and the Grand Junction. They also referred to the primitive methods of navigation in the Bedford Levels, where 'the local horses towing lighters have to be trained to jump fences on a slackened towing line, as there are no gates in the fences which come to the edge of the bank. The necessity that a horse should have acquired this unusual accomplishment is an effective barrier to the use of horses bringing boats from the Midlands; and even, it is stated, that when a horse trained to Fenland work falls sick, it is difficult for this reason to replace him at short notice.'

The Commission commented in a final paragraph:

> All this eastern side of England closely resembles Holland, where waterways are as numerous and as much used as roads. It is a country eminently suited to purposes of navigation. It is also the part of England where authorities controlling waterways are the most chaotically multiplied, and where least is done by art to make use of the facilities offered by Nature.

It took more than twenty years before the situation on the upper river was redeemed. The Ouse Drainage Board, instituted in 1918, had no powers over navigation, and it was not until the setting up of the Great Ouse Catchment Board, under the 1930 Land Drainage Act, that the problem began to be tackled. Surveys were made, the navigation rights bought for a few pounds from Simpson's executors in 1935, dredging began and work started on rebuilding the locks. By now, of course, it was the pleasure boaters, not the traders, who would reap the benefit.

Below St Ives, the river's recent history has been less dramatic. There was a general decline in trade via Lynn, although local traffic, centred on Ely, continued until after the Second World War. Agricultural produce was moved from farms to railway connections by water; coal for domestic use and the pumping stations came by rail and was finally distributed by boats. Among those operating gangs of lighters in the early twentieth century were E. W. Diver of Isleham, the Appleyards at Ely, Stimson of Chatteris, and the Jacksons at March and Stanground.[27]

With improvements in roads and road transport after the First World War the prospects for commercial water carrying deteriorated still further. The opening in 1925 of a sugarbeet processing factory at Queen Adelaide, near Ely, reversed the trend, as it depended greatly on water transport and operated 6 or 7 tugs and well over a hundred barges. There was another factory at Wissington on the Wissey, which operated similarly but on a smaller scale. The barges collected beet from Fen farms in autumn and winter; during the summer they brought coal to the factory from King's Lynn. This factory continued to be served by water until 1959, since when the annual infestation of the roads near Ely by sugarbeet lorries and tractors has become a local feature. The last survival of commercial traffic on the river was *Shellfen*, the smallest oil tanker in the Shell fleet, a Dutch barge converted to oil carrying. For many years she served the pumping stations in the winter, especially when road transport was impossible, carrying a load of some 4,000 gallons of diesel. Bottisham Lode engine, inaccessible by road, was one that she supplied. In recent years most of the stations were converted to electricity; the demand for her services fell off and she was sold by her owners, the old Ely boat-building firm of Appleyard, Lincoln, in 1974. This leaves only the Great Ouse River Division's maintenance boats as working craft. Otherwise the river, particularly above Denver, is the province of pleasure cruisers.

Below Denver the story is more complicated. For decades, the fact that the tidal reaches were administered by such a multiplicity of authorities made progress towards improvement difficult if not impossible. The Bedford Level Corporation, the Ouse Banks Commission, the Denver Sluice Commissioners, the Ouse Outfall Board, the King's Lynn Conservancy Board and the Norfolk Estuary Company were all involved in 1913.[28] With no overall controlling or co-ordinating authority, no major dredging programme could take place. Conditions in the approaches to Lynn were also getting worse and it became clear that the training walls were beginning to prove inadequate. They were eventually repaired by the King's Lynn Conservancy Board in 1930; two years later the eastern wall was reconstructed by the Catchment Board and further extensions were carried out in 1937. More recently the western wall has been lengthened and turned to head north east, in order to stabilize the position of the channel. A barrier wall was constructed to shut off the previous course of the channel. These walls, of brushwood and stone arranged in a sandwich pattern and resting on a mattress of reed, brushwood and willow, concentrate the tidal ebb and flow and increase the scouring effect, deepening the channel more effectively and cheaply than by dredging.

In 1865 the King's Lynn Docks & Railway Co was formed, continuing to administer the docks until 1948. Alexandra Dock (282,000sqft) was opened in 1869, and Bentinck Dock (400,000sqft) in 1883 across part of the old Fisher Fleet. There was a slow but steady increase in trade, with the total cargo tonnage reaching over 600,000 in 1907 and 1908. Not until 1959 did the figure again top 600,000, by which time the docks were under the control of the British Transport Commission, being transferred to the British Transport Docks Board in 1963. Nationalisation saw a modernization programme put into effect and the area of water and dockside accommodation is more than adequate for the shipping using the port. In the 1960s cargo handled ranged between 630,000 and 894,000 tons a year, with timber and petroleum the principal imports. Exports, however, form only between one-sixth and one-tenth of the total cargo handled.[29] In the longer term, the future of King's Lynn as a port seems to depend on three factors: further development of trade with Common Market countries, governmental attitude towards an integrated transport policy, and the estuary storage schemes for the Wash with the possibility—though it may be a remote one—of the construction of a barrage.

Elsewhere on the river the pre-occupation in recent years has been with the problem of flood control. There was widespread flooding of the Fens in 1937 and 1947 and extensive tidal flooding in 1953. The non-navigable Cut-Off Channel, completed in 1964, skirts round the Fens and carries excess water from the upper reaches of the eastern tributaries to the Relief Channel close to Denver sluice, which continues to King's Lynn. This has been the major work, but improvements are also in hand elsewhere. The Great Ouse Restoration Society, a voluntary organization founded in 1951, has since its inception raised a total of £22,500 towards the reopening of the navigation to Bedford. One by one the locks on the upper river have been rebuilt; in 1976 Great Barford and Willington locks were reopened, and work is in hand over the last few miles. To the River Authority (now absorbed by the Anglian Water Authority), the restoring of navigation is only part of a flood relief and drainage scheme extending as high up the river as Newport Pagnell. And this brings the story back to where it began, to the tangled interests of navigation and drainage. But now the days of commercial traffic are over there can be no arguing as to where the priorities lie.

CHAPTER VII

Ouse Tributaries

✦

River Ivel

The Ivel, flowing past Hitchin and through Biggleswade to the Great Ouse at Tempsford, with branches to Baldock and Shefford, was a tempting prospect for the navigation enthusiasts of Bedfordshire and Hertfordshire in the mid-eighteenth century. A proposal to make the river and its branches navigable appeared in or about 1755; it was estimated that the works would cost £19,185, to include a total of 20 locks and 16 staunches, making new cuts, scouring the river, building bridges, laying out haling ways and purchasing all materials. On a 'moderate computation' 8,500 tons of coal and other goods were anticipated, producing an income of £1,558 a year. Coal brought up the Great Ouse cost 12s a chaldron to be carried by land from Tempsford to Hitchin and 9s to Baldock and Shefford; water carriage would cut these rates by nearly half.[1]

A less ambitious plan appeared in 1756 'for making the River Ivel navigable from Tempsford to Biggleswade Mill'. The estimate for this was £4,000; four locks were costed at £360 each and four staunches at £140 each; £500 was included 'to sundry works which may be unforeseen'.[2] Moves were made to promote a Parliamentary Bill but were met with a lack of enthusiasm in the Hitchin district where the gentry were accused by one of the promoters of having 'thrown so much cold water into the Ivel by refusing to subscribe I fear it will freeze it up for ever. It is talked here and by the Great Ouse too, that the Hitchin people oppose it. Are these things true?' queried the writer, Newdigate Poynting. 'If so, 'tis strange, 'tis wondrous strange.'[3] Nevertheless a petition for the navigation was presented to Parliament in February 1757 and a committee was appointed to examine it.[4]

Langley Edwards, who surveyed the Nar in 1757 and worked on several of the Fen waterways, had made the original survey of the Ivel and gave evidence to the committee. He said that all that was required was a depth of 3ft for barges of 20 tons burden. A charge of 3d for each barge passing a lock was proposed, this to be paid to the millers in compensation for loss of water, but he did not anticipate gangs of barges passing more than once a week. Evidence was given on the savings in the cost of coal, one witness remarking that the poor farmers who then carried the coal by cart from Tempsford would be better employed cultivating their land.[5] There was little dispute and the Act 'for making the River Ivel and the Branches thereof navigable' received the royal assent on 17 May 1757.[6]

The Act named some 500 commissioners, but only five were needed to make a quorum. Edwards and Thomas Yeoman were appointed surveyors and Uriah Clearson, bricklayer, and William Wooton, carpenter, both of Harrold, were contracted with to build the locks and staunches.[7] The plans show pound-locks 110ft × 12ft with V-gates without balance beams, being opened and shut by chains, and arched at the sides like the locks on the Louth Navigation. Chains also operated the paddles in the oaken lock-gates. Locks were built at Tempsford, Blunham, South Mills, Sandy and Biggleswade North, the last not being included in the original prospectus and apparently made as a turf-walled structure 160ft long × 50ft wide.[8] The funds raised proved insufficient to complete the navigation as described in the Act; the river was opened to Biggleswade in 1758 at a cost of something over £6,000 and there, for the time being, it stopped. The first tolls were received in October of that year—£9 9s 11½d for the month. For the first three full years of operation, toll receipts were £278 in 1759, £381 in 1760 and £357 in 1761.[9] In 1762 the debt of the navigation amounted to £6,871; tolls levelled off to average about £350 a year and in 1780 it became possible to begin paying off the debt, at the rate of £15 per cent to every creditor.[10] Coal, of course, was the main traffic, the tolls being 1s 6d a ton, but while Biggleswade remained the head of navigation the income potential was limited and it was clearly going to take many years before the proprietors would be in a position to contemplate extending the navigation as originally planned.

A suggestion that the Ivel Navigation be linked by a canal to the Lee at Hertford was heavily criticized by the proposers of a scheme for a London—Norwich and King's Lynn canal in 1785, and seems to have been pursued no further.[11] Viscount Torrington mentioned the 'frequent navigation' of the Ivel in 1794;[12] certainly by this time receipts were increasing. Benjamin Bevan, an engineer of the Grand Junction Canal, was called in by the commissioners to make a survey of the river from Biggleswade to Shefford; he produced a detailed report and an estimate of £8,000, including the construction of seven more locks able to take one lighter at a time.[13] On further consideration, however, the commissioners felt that the time was not yet ripe, and the matter of the extension fell into abeyance for another ten years.

In 1817, one of the commissioners, William Wilshere, looked carefully at the state of local trade and noted that Shefford was less busy than formerly. Reckoning that extending the navigation to Shefford would bring in merely £100 a year, half the estimated annual cost of repairs, he proposed at a meeting of the commissioners that it would not at present 'be a proper application of the fund in hand to extend the navigation . . .', and this was carried by 16 votes to 2. Sir George Osborn, who wanted to see Bevan's proposals put into effect, subsequently had his motion negatived[14].

The next move came in 1819 when the commissioners met to consider a report by Sir John Jackson with an engineer's estimate for making the river navigable from Biggleswade to Langford Bridge. The engineer was Francis Giles and the estimate was £11,000; Giles also quoted £32,000 for continuing to Hitchin and £36,000 to Baldock.[15] The matter lay under consideration for a further two years; Giles then produced an estimate of £14,000 for continuing the navigation to Shefford and, despite Wilshere's attempt to delay matters by asking for further information, the commissioners carried a motion by 5 votes to 3 for

beginning the work immediately.[16] A loan of £6,000 was applied
for, on the security of a mortgage of the tolls. It was then discovered that Giles had underestimated by quoting for an extension only as far as Clifton Common and an extra £1,700 had to
be added to the original figure.[17] Giles had worked under
Rennie, and the extension to Shefford seems to have been his
first independent waterway undertaking. A few years later he
produced a report and estimate for a proposed Hants & Berks
Junction Canal; a critic of the scheme—which came to
naught—described him as 'visibly panting with all the ardour
of a novice to 'flesh his maiden sword'—or rather, to mud his
maiden spade in this Canal . . .'.[18] Nevertheless, despite the
lukewarm attitude of some of the commissioners and the unwil-
lingness of certain local landowners to sell or even to negotiate,
work on the extension began and the river was open to Shefford
by the end of 1823. While work was in progress, Giles and a few
commissioners surveyed the old navigation, on which no major
improvements had ever been carried out, and Giles recommended that £3–4,000 be spent at once to put it into a 'proper
and complete state of repair'. Even Mr Astell, chief proponent
of the extension, felt that it would have been wiser had this
survey taken place before the extension was begun.[19]

An interesting point about the Biggleswade—Shefford line
is that the contractors, a firm from Bristol, were paid under
two different scales. From Biggleswade to Langford, where the
branch began, the rate was 5s a yard for a navigation channel
5ft deep × 40ft wide. From Langford to Shefford it was
regarded as a canal, 3½d being paid for each cubic yard cut
plus a bonus of £40 for filling in the old channel. Five locks
were made: at Biggleswade and Holme on the main river and
at Stanford, Clifton and Shefford on the branch.[20] It was estimated that some 4,000 tons of cargo, mainly coal, would be
carried annually on the Shefford line.

A few months after the extension opened, a meeting at Hitchin recommended extending the navigation to that town, for
which £32,000 would be needed. The figures quoted indicate
that in the previous nine years tolls from Tempsford to Biggleswade averaged £1,339 and an additional £1,650 a year was an-

ticipated from 11,000 tons at 3s a ton which, it was thought, would be carried to Hitchin. The proposal also mentioned a plan 'to communicate the Shefford Branch with the Grand Junction Canal and thereby to complete an inland navigation between Lynn and London'.[21] But Shefford was as far as the navigation reached. The commissioners had their debts to pay; lighters and barges, usually travelling in gangs, supplied the towns and villages with coal, iron and timber and brought away agricultural produce. A modest prosperity was achieved, so much so that the commissioners were little disturbed at the prospect of railway competition. Improvements to the river diminished the dangers of flooding; none was reported for 17 years until Shefford was flooded in 1841. Eels caught in traps by the sluices were a local delicacy: Thomas Thomas, an Ivel locksman got into trouble for refusing to allow John Harvey's servants to set eel-pots while illegally fishing for eels himself.[22]

The Ivel valley provided an obvious route for the Great Northern Railway's main line from London to the north. With no opposition from the commissioners, the line was opened in 1850, striking northwards within a mile of the river at Langford, Biggleswade and Sandy. Through Shefford in 1857 came the Bedford—Hitchin branch of the Midland Railway. For a few more years the navigation struggled on with falling receipts, the locks crumbling away and no funds available for their repair.

By 1876 movement on the river had ceased. Seven commissioners attended a meeting called by Samuel Veasey, who had been their clerk for 50 years, and resolved to apply to Parliament for an abandonment Act. This received the royal assent on 13 July of that year: 'whereas owing to the construction of railways parallel to and in the neighbourhood of the Navigation the traffic thereon has practically ceased and the income of the Commissioners is utterly insufficient to maintain the navigation and to pay any interest on their mortgage debt'. To pay the debt the property was sold off and the sluices and locks were transferred to the millers. Several relics of the commercial past of this pleasantly attractive waterway can still be found in the Bedfordshire countryside; the unhurried motorist on B658 east of Broom could well pause to exchange ruminations with the enigmatic pedestalled figure overlooking the lock at Holme.

River Cam

The Cam was a navigation, and Cambridge a major inland port, for centuries before the draining of the Fens and the Act of 1702. The river is formed by the meeting of two streams about three miles south of Cambridge and is navigable, as it has been throughout its known history, from Cambridge to its junction with the Ouse at Popes Corner, a distance of about $13\frac{1}{2}$ miles. Whereas Oxford originated from a ford, Cambridge grew up around a bridge—the Great Bridge, rebuilt several times and now known as Magdalen Bridge. As the colleges developed between the fourteenth and sixteenth centuries so those fronting the road parallel to the river extended their buildings at the rear, westwards, on to marshy riverside fields. The main course of the river was a few hundred yards further to the west before this land was reclaimed; its present course along the Backs is therefore artificial.[23]

There is no lack of references to traffic on the Cam in the Middle Ages, particularly as Lynn increased in importance as a port. Often these references take the form of protests at obstructions to navigation.[24] Corn was the principal cargo downriver, while up came a whole variety of goods to supply both the growing town and university and the great annual fair at Stourbridge Common.[25] In the early seventeenth century, however, it is clear that the Cam was in poor condition, as is shown by surveys carried out in 1605 and 1618.[26] Richard Atkyns in his 1618 report mentions sandbanks in the Cam between Cambridge and Clayhithe, and interference with navigation by watermills. Nevertheless Cambridge strongly opposed the measures for draining the Fens, fearing that 'the river . . . will have its stream dried up'.

That there was some attempt to regulate the use of the river before the passing of the 1702 Act is shown by an order made in 1643 by a parliamentary committee called the Committee of the Association, which decreed that no boats should navigate above the Great Bridge between 8pm and 5am, and that no persons or goods should be carried down without a ticket or certificate from the commissioners or other authorized persons.[27] The construction of Denver sluice, cutting off the tidal waters from the Ouse—Cam link, so altered the character of the river that firmer action than this was needed. Protests mounted, culminating in petitions to Parliament from both town and university in 1697, stating that hitherto the district had been 'well served and supplied with coals, fish, salt, and all sorts of foreign merchandise' from Lynn, but that now, by the construction of the sluice and dam, 'the navigation . . . is manifestly prejudiced and impaired . . . so as smaller boats and vessels cannot pass therein without great difficulties, delays, and danger and excessive charges, and the said navigation is likely to be suddenly and irrecoverably lost'.[28] Two years later the Corporation of Cambridge resolved to petition the Commons for an Act for restoring the navigation of the town.[29] This Act, 'for making the River Cham alias Grant in the County of Cambridge more Navigable from Clay Hithe Ferry to the Queen's Mill in the University and Town of Cambridge' appointed conservators, to a maximum of 11, laid down a schedule of tolls averaging out at a shilling a ton from Cambridge to Clayhithe, with wine topping the list at 4s a ton, and a charge of one penny for each passenger. A collector and treasurer were to be appointed and the tolls were to be mortgaged up to a limit of £2,000 to raise funds for speedy improvement of the navigation. Four sluices were constructed, at Clayhithe, Baitsbite, Chesterton and Jesus Green, tolls being collected at the first and last. But the results did not satisfy the Corporation, who in 1723 again petitioned Parliament in similar terms to their previous petition, this time also accusing the Bedford Level adventurers of 'great neglect in scouring out their old sewers, new cuts, drains and outfalls' as a result of which 'the rivers to seawards are very much grown up and stopped for want of freshes . . . and the said navigation in a little time very likely to be lost'.[30] Defoe's vivid description of Stourbridge Fair on his tour of 1722, however, shows that the Corporation may have been overstating their case; having listed the enormous variety of articles sold at the Fair he comments that

> the river Grant, or Cam, which runs close by the N.W. side of
> the fair in its way from Cambridge to Ely, is navigable, and
> that by this means, all heavy goods are brought even to the
> fair-field, by water carriage from London, and other parts;
> first to the port of Lynn, and then in barges up the Ouse, from
> the Ouse into the Cam, and so, as I say, to the very edge of the
> fair.

A few years before this petition and Defoe's visit, Denver
sluice had blown up. Its destruction seems to have made little
difference to the state of navigation; indeed, at low tides there
was sometimes insufficient water to float a barge. But Cambridge opposed its rebuilding. In a Remonstrance to the Bedford Level Corporation in 1745, the Cambridge Corporation
stated that they had been informed 'of a scheme set on foot by
mistaken or ill designing persons for repairing and rebuilding of
Denver Sluice, which former experiences have proved to be per-
nicious and destructive of the general navigation to the said
port'. But by 1750 the sluice was rebuilt; the navigators struggled on.

Toll receipts for the next century give some idea of the success of the struggle.[31] From £432 in 1752 they dropped to the low
figure of £316 ten years later. This was followed by a general up-
ward movement to £887 in 1776. It was another 16 years before
this figure was exceeded; then from 1803 to 1846, apart from two
years, tolls brought in over £1,000 a year, reaching a peak of
£1,995 in 1835. Thereafter there was a general decline. The conservators kept a useful balance in hand and a careful watch on
the river, taking action against boatmen who failed to pay tolls
or who forced their way through the locks.[32] No tolls were
charged at Baitsbite until 1819, and the greater part of the revenue came from Clayhithe. The conservators also owned the
public houses at each sluice, from which they derived a small
rental. It was the publicans who ran the ferries; at Jesus Green,
where the toll-collector's house and the Fort St George inn
stood on an island, the ferry was dashed against the rimers of

the sluice one evening in December 1793 and two women were drowned.[33]

Some indication of the increasing prosperity of the Conservators comes from the fact that in 1823 they contributed £400 to the rebuilding of the Great Bridge, whereas to an earlier rebuilding in 1755 their contribution had been a mere £30.[34] The 1823 iron bridge, designed by Arthur Brown and built under the superintendence of the County Magistrates, is the one still in use at present, having survived a recent move to have it replaced by something more in keeping with this age of prestressed concrete. Just downstream of the bridge, opposite Magdalen College was—and is—Quayside, the last of Cambridge's quays and wharves to survive. Sites of the others, including a corn, flax and salt hithe, were along the present Backs; they were gradually taken over by the colleges and general trade moved to Quayside, while there were other wharves at King's Mill, upstream of the Small Bridge (now Silver Street bridge) and by the mill at Newnham.[35]

In 1829, Charles Humfrey published his *Report on the Present State of the River Cam*, in which he produced an estimate of £5,125 for works, alterations and improvements between Clayhithe and Chesterton. He also recommended the construction of a new sluice at Jesus Green 'upon a much more extended scale and better principle than the very sorry thing which is now there'. Humfrey mentions a town-and-gown problem; the presence of lighters and their crews within 'the sight and hearing of the inmates of Colleges whose apartments are near the River'. To accelerate the progress of the lighters, he repeats an earlier proposal he had made for

> driving some strong piles in situations most convenient for hauling, without being offensive to the sight; to these, stout rings were to be affixed, and a block with pullies, when required, carried a-head in a small boat, and hung on; a towing line was to be passed through this block, and fixed at one end to the prow of a barge, and worked with some simple machinery at the other end, (in the barge): it was to be used in succession, as different gangs might require it; and one

gang being safely lodged in the Mill-pit, the machine in the light boat was then to be taken back, and the same thing repeated with another set of lighters.

He reckoned that this would enable barges to pass the Backs in half an hour instead of half a day, which it took whenever there was a strong current. To prevent 'the lounging and idling which now often takes place under the College walls' and to see that the watermen 'do not moor to the piles, or commit any nuisance' he suggested that a specially appointed person should supervise the passage of each gang, being paid 'a small sum of money for each trip, instead of a salary: for he would then have a direct interest in suffering no one to pass without him, and therefore would not neglect his duty'. The Backs presented another peculiar problem; horses not being allowed passage through the college grounds had to walk up the river. A path had been laid in the river bed, below water level. When the new Jesus lock was built in the mid-1830s, as suggested by Humfrey, a few hundred yards upstream from the old sluice, and the river was deepened, the water level rose further above the path and the horses had to tow half-submerged.[36] But it is clear from engravings by J. Walker (1793) and Ackermann (1815) that the horses got their feet thoroughly wet years before the new lock; possibly the path when covered by water was too risky to be trusted. Further pictorial evidence of traffic on the river in the early nineteenth century comes from I. K. Baldrey's engraving of 1807, showing two lighters by the Small Bridge, one loaded with corn and one with coal—the two principal items carried. The lightermen are wearing blue waistcoats and fur hats; these were the traditional wear during most of the century.[37] Traditional also was the bad language; a tract of 1825 refers to the watermen 'using horrid oaths with every word they utter'.[38]

By the extensions and amendments to the Cam Navigation Act in 1813, the conservators were given extra powers to recover tolls and exact penalties and were also enabled to let the tolls and other revenues for a period not exceeding three years. The South Level Act of 1827, which gave the commissioners control of the river from Bottisham to Popes Corner, also appointed as navigation commissioners the mayor and the vice-chancellor of the University. The conservators removed Chesterton sluice and built locks at Bottisham and Baitsbite; in 1842 they also built for themselves a house still standing at Clayhithe 'in the Tudor style with Dutch gables', with a large room for meetings and banquets.[39] It cost them £880.[40] The year before they had donated £300 towards the rebuilding of the Small Bridge. But the days of such extravagance were soon to end.

In 1845, the Eastern Counties Railway came to Cambridge, forging a direct link with Norwich and London. Toll receipts for the next five years tell the story:[41]

	£		£
1846	1,393	1849	971
1847	805	1850	367
1848	695		

No longer dependent on the trade from Lynn, passage to which might take five days in poor conditions, traders turned away from the river and towards the station, despite its siting a mile from the town centre. In 1862 the E.C.R. became part of the Great Eastern Railway, and in two more decades the Great Northern, Midland, and London & North Western lines also came to Cambridge.

Tolls were altered by an Act of 1851, and by a further Act of 1894 when they were as follows:

Sugar, Vinegar, Soap, Wine and other goods	3d per ton
Litter, straw and hay	3d per ton
Wheat and Barley	6d per score
Oats, Rye and Beans	5d per score
Timber, Lime, Gas Water, Chaff, Mangolds, Tar, Whiting, Slates and Tiles	3d per ton
Bricks	2d per 1,000
Sedge	1d per 100
Sand, Manure, Road Materials and Coal	1d per ton
Turf	1d per 1,000

There was also a ferry charge at Chesterton and a bridge toll at Clayhithe for the horses. The tolls levied by the South Level

Commissioners for the rest of the river were 4d a ton for all goods except coal, coke, other fuel, and road and building materials, which passed for 2d a ton. On this stretch Fen-grown produce within the geographical limits of the 1827 Act carried from Fen lands to the homes of the owners was toll-free, as was manure, but there was a bank charge of 1s a horse hauling lighters, collected by the local authority at Upware. The commissioners' tolls were let for about £300 a year but the conservators, toll receipts were much lower: £99 in 1898, £79 in 1905.[42]

In his evidence to the Royal Commission in 1908, Walter Fuller, then barge manager to Sommerfeld & Thomas Ltd of Lynn, said that he had a steam barge loading 40 tons trading to Cambridge and a wooden barge 76ft long which could only go through Denver sluice when the water made a level. The steamer, *Nancy*, carried general goods, sugar, timber and grain, while other barges took gas water from Cambridge gasworks to Lynn, the ammonia content of the gas water being a valuable ingredient of fertilizer. Some trade in coal continued until about 1920 and bricks came up from Peterborough, Whittlesea and Burwell. Sedge from Wicken was carried in fen boats. Billy Collin, who owned a timberyard in Cambridge which received supplies by the river, bought *Nancy* in 1909, with his £3,000 compensation money when the corporation took over his yard, and ran her until 1914. Another steam vessel, a tug called the *Cutter*, was worked until about 1900 by the Dant family of Chesterton, who ran barges on the river through the nineteenth century. Other boats recorded as using the Cam in these last years of its trading history include *Hearts of Oak* and *Mayflower*, belonging to Colchester & Ball of Burwell, *Bertha* and the steam tug *Bury* owned by E. W. Diver of Isleham, and the motor boat *Progress*, owned by Banhams. The gas water trade continued until shortly before the Second World War, with two steam tugs, *Olga* and *Nellie*, and three barges *Enid*, *Lizzie* and *Eric*. After the war, Banhams bought a Dutch diesel-powered barge, *Nancy II*, but she proved too large for the rivers, having particular difficulty clearing the bridges over the tidal Ouse when the water was high enough for her to float. The attempt to trade with her

Plates 17 & 18 (*above*) Lighters loaded with peat on the Cambridgeshire lodes in 1892. One donkey hauled two boats; (*below*) a fen lighter, possibly *The Black Prince*, salvaged from Roswell Pits, Ely, in 1974 and now at the Cambridge Museum of Industrial Archaeology

Plates 19 & 20 Santon Staunch on the Little Ouse: *(left)* in the 1890s. The man in the boat is spearing eels; *(below)* in 1957

lasted for about $2\frac{1}{2}$ years.[43] Regular passenger-carrying on the Cam is recorded from the mid-eighteenth century, when there was a service between Cambridge and Ely. The boats, carrying both passengers and goods, were not very frequent. In 1825 there was a departure every Saturday for King's Lynn; this particular service stopped in the early 1830s. The latest recorded regular service was between Cambridge, Ely, March and Wisbech, operating in 1839; it is probable that this succumbed to the railway a few years later. As time passed, the Cam developed into a highway for sport and pleasure; rowing became a major university activity and the old Quayside and Mill Pool were transformed into havens for punts. Cabin cruisers now proliferate, despite the fact that the conservators' charges for passing their locks are among the highest in the kingdom.[44] And what is probably the most elegant craft to use the Cam can still be seen on its waters today: the *Viscountess Bury*, $65\frac{1}{2}$ft long, built as a battery-powered launch in 1888. H. C. Banham brought her to the Cam in 1910 and now, after several refits and converted to a 50hp diesel, she is a familiar sight on the river in summer.[45]

The Cambridgeshire Navigable Lodes

Each of them connecting a large village to the River Cam, the Cambridgeshire navigable lodes—Bottisham, Swaffham Bulbeck, Reach, Burwell, Wicken and Soham—have a long history as navigable waterways. Recent research by the Royal Commission on Historical Monuments[46] has generally confirmed the interpretations of Gordon Fowler[47] and there is now enough evidence to say with some certainty that the first three listed above originated in Roman times while Old Burwell Lode and Wicken probably did so. This does not mean that they retain precisely the same course and appearance today as they did during the Roman occupation but rather that they are the descendants of waterways cut for the purposes of both navigation and drainage during those years. By means of the Car Dyke, which the weight of archaeological opinion considers to have been cut by the Romans from the Cam near Waterbeach to the

Witham near Lincoln, a waterway 73 miles long with an original width between 50 and 60ft, the villages at the heads of the
lodes would have been able to trade across the Fens with a very
wide area of the country as far north as York.[48] The section of
the Car Dyke between the Cam and the Great Ouse near Earith
was made between AD 50–60 and was apparently disused by
the end of the second century. Much of the trade would have
been in corn and hides going north and stone and pottery travelling south; much Roman pottery has been found in the course
of the Dyke at Cottenham. Considerable stretches of the Car
Dyke can still be found and are marked on modern OS maps;
the wide ditch on the east side of A10 by the airfield at Waterbeach is part of it, and it can be followed across the fields heading north-westwards to join for a time the Old West River.

Bottisham Lode
Bottisham Lode extends from the Cam a few hundred yards
downstream of Bottisham lock to the village of Lode, itself a
mile from Bottisham. It is about $2\frac{1}{2}$ miles long and, apart from a
bend near Lode village, is now straight but has been re-aligned
probably more than once. It possessed one staunch, of which
only the chamber, 12ft wide, survives, similar in construction to
the staunches on the Little Ouse.[49] The lode is embanked and is
up to 22ft in width.

There is little recorded history of the navigation of this lode.
In 1767 it came under the control of the Swaffham & Bottisham
Drainage Commissioners, who were enabled to charge tolls
and to build staunches,[50] and there are indications of a basin
and wharf by Lode itself, where it obtains its water supply from
Quy Water via the outfall of the mill. It seems likely that it was
disused for several centuries after the departure of the Romans
and may have been used sporadically in the medieval period. It
was in use during the nineteenth century but was not sufficiently wide to take the fen lighters;[51] however, the smaller fen
boats could navigate it and continued to do so until about 1900.
Trade was local and almost entirely in agricultural produce,
tolls being 3d a ton.

Swaffham Bulbeck Lode

The entrance to Swaffham Bulbeck Lode is $1\frac{1}{2}$ miles down the Cam from Bottisham lock. This lode is generally parallel to Bottisham Lode but about a mile longer. It too has been re-aligned and there are traces of its earlier course. The first mention of the lode by name is in 1279,[52] but it seems most unlikely that it carried any significant trade until the eighteenth century. The village of Swaffham Bulbeck is a mile from the end of the lode, but a hamlet originally called Newnham—known today and since the early nineteenth century as Commercial End—developed by the end of the waterway in medieval times. The principal dwelling house in Commercial End, the Merchant's House, dates mainly from the late seventeenth century, and it seems to have had a connection with waterborne trade from the beginning. There are several references to complaints about the condition of the lode in the eighteenth century and the Commissioners of the Bedford Level had the banks strengthened and the channel cleaned many times.[53] About the middle of the eighteenth century a counting-house was built on to the Merchant's House, possibly an indication of increasing business activity. The house passed into the ownership of the firm of Bowyer & Barker, who organized the shipment of grain to Lynn; coal, wine and salt were among the incoming cargoes. Thomas Bowyer took over the property in 1805, adding warehouses and cottages for his employees. There was a wharf at the rear of the house, connected to the end of the lode by a narrow canal; there was also a public wharf $\frac{1}{4}$ mile away on the north side of Cow bridge.

Bowyer died in 1824 and the trade was continued by Henry Giblin. He rebuilt some of the outbuildings and possibly added others, indicating that trading was still profitable. Bills of lading and account books dating from 1793 to the mid-nineteenth century show the extent of the business operations, but these rapidly contracted with the coming of railways, Coprolites were loaded at Commercial End for a time, but in 1877 the Merchant's House, outbuildings and contents began to be sold off.[54]

Commercial End remains as one of the most architecturally

attractive streets (it can hardly be called a village) in the Fenland area. Most of it dates from the eighteenth and early nineteenth centuries, including the malthouse; it is hard to realize
that the *raison d'être* of these fine buildings is the rather insignifi-
cant looking drain heading off towards the Cam, the lower end
of which is used by pleasure cruisers as it provides flood-free
moorings.

Reach Lode
Reach Lode, 3 miles in length, leads from the Cam to the village
of Reach at the termination of the Devil's Dyke. The Dyke, a
massive bank and ditch some $7\frac{1}{2}$ miles long, was thrown up as a
defensive work some time between AD 300 and 600 and originally ran through what is now the green at Reach to meet the
end of the lode, which also formed part of the defensive line.[55]
Reach was a port in Roman times, possibly exporting clunch
among other items, and there is evidence of Roman quays at
Upware, the junction with the Cam.[56] There was a village on
each side of the Dyke—East and West Reach. A fair was established here by the beginning of the thirteenth century and
about this time some 300 yards of the Dyke were levelled, thus
providing a large expanse for the fairground and general commerce. Trade by water now developed considerably; coasting
vessels brought goods to the fair, which became one of the most
important in the east of England. A wide variety of goods is
recorded as being handled at Reach, which traded far more
widely than any of the other inland ports at the heads of the
lodes. There were a large hithe and several wharves and basins,
of which many traces are still evident.

Coasters stopped coming to Reach when the sluice was constructed at Denver, but trade still continued through King's
Lynn and coal imports are reported in the seventeenth century.
Agricultural produce, timber and clunch were principal
exports, while lighters brought in stone, wines and spirits, salt
and building materials. It seems, however, that by the mid-
eighteenth century trade had much declined, although clunch
continued to be exported for another hundred years or there-
abouts.[57]

The Eau Brink Act required the construction in 1821 of a lock on Reach Lode to improve the navigation, and in 1827 Reach and Burwell Lodes came under the control of the South Level Commissioners, who were obliged to keep them in navigable condition 'as far as the navigation of them extends'. Had Rennie's earlier proposals for a London—Cambridge canal succeeded both Reach and Burwell would have been close to its line and the trade in clunch and lime from that area would have been able to develop much further. But the cost of this particular proposal caused its omission from the later plans and the canal itself, of course, was never made. Through the nineteenth century some trading was carried on; peat, used for fuel, and charcoal from the Newmarket area now being among the items carried, and for a time there was some trade in coprolites. Burwell now supplanted Reach as the main lode port, with the establishment there of the fertilizer factory. Vic Jackson took the last cargo of clunch, 525 tons loaded in a gang of lighters, through Stanground sluice to Peterborough in the 1930s; the journey from Reach to Peterborough took him three days.[58] A small trade in peat continued for a few years after that.

Burwell Lode

Burwell Lode branches off from Reach Lode at Pout Hall, ¾ mile from the Cam at Upware. It runs to the western edge of Burwell village and is a comparatively wide 40–45ft waterway. The first mention of Burwell Lode was in 1604, but it is most unlikely that this referred to the present course which was probably cut in the mid-seventeenth century and appears on Moore's map of the Fens, 1695. Traces of an old canal can be found nearby; this was the original Old Lode, as it is sometimes described, which may, like the lodes to the south, date from the Roman period.[59]

At Burwell the lode divides into two branches. One turns south to 'Anchor Straits' and was used by coasters in the earlier years of its history. The other turned north to the 'Weirs'; this was used by lighters. On both branches there are the remains of wharves; the northern branch has some old warehouses. Trade from Burwell in the eighteenth and nineteenth centuries was generally similar to that from Reach, with clunch and charcoal being carried away and coal being brought in.

Burwell took over from Reach as the busiest of the lodes after the opening of T. T. Ball's Burwell Chemical Works in the late 1850s. This developed in the 1890s into Colchester & Ball's Patent Manure Works, a mile westward of the village. By the beginning of the twentieth century, cargoes to and from the works amounted to about 10,000 tons a year.[60] The firm ran its own water transport concern, with three steam tugs and gangs of lighters. When Prentice Bros Ltd took over the business in 1921 they continued to use the lighters for bringing in chemicals from Lynn and distributing fertilizer to the Fenland farms. There was a barge building business in Burwell, owned by Prentice's, which continued building until 1920 and repairing until 1936, when A. V. Jackson bought the lighters. Coal, stone and sugar beet were carried, as well as fertilizer; the barges were also used by the Burwell Brick Co for the conveyance of their repellently coloured product.[61] Tolls on Burwell Lode were 3d a ton, payable to the Burwell Fen Drainage Commissioners, although the South Level Commissioners were responsible for the navigation. But boats to and from the Cam also had to pay 3d a ton for passage through part of Reach Lode, these tolls going to the Swaffham & Bottisham Drainage Commissioners, although again the navigation was the South Level's responsibility.

When Fisons took over the fertilizer factory Vic Jackson continued carrying, bringing silt from Lynn and collecting about 2,000 tons of fertilizer between January and March to distribute around the Fen farms in quantities between 20 and 100 tons.[62] After he retired as a lighterman in 1948, this trade on Burwell Lode ended, although sugarbeet continued to be carried until 1963.

Wicken Lode
Wicken Lode branches off Reach Lode and runs for nearly 1½ miles to about 700 yards from Wicken village. Much of its course is alongside Wicken Sedge Fen, now preserved and administered by the National Trust. The lode is fed by Monk's

Lode and the New River; these waterways are continuous and may have been used for navigation on a small scale in earlier times. Wicken Lode itself is possibly Roman in origin but its present name was first recorded in 1636. It is narrower and shallower than its southern neighbours and it is unlikely that it was used by anything larger than the fen boats.

In the nineteenth and first half of the twentieth century peat was brought up Wicken Lode from Burwell Fen, to be distributed around the farms. Sedge was cut in Wicken Fen and taken by boat to a wharf at the head of the lode. Donkeys were sometimes used for hauling the fen boats. The peat trade continued into the 1940s, when restrictions were placed on further cutting. The lode is still navigable by small, shallow draught vessels.[63]

Soham Lode

The origin of Soham Lode, the longest of the Cambridgeshire lodes, is problematical. Some authorities, by analogy with the other lodes, suggest that it too is Roman, being formed by a diversion of the River Snail at about the same time the Lark was diverted from its old course.[64] But this theory is uncorroborated by evidence, and it seems more likely that the lode as it is today dates from about 1790 when it was cut to take the waters of the Snail into the Ouse instead of into the Lark, to improve drainage in the Soham—Fordham area. The length of the lode to Fordham is about seven miles, but there is no evidence that it was used for navigation above Soham.

A sluice was constructed at the entrance to the lode which had two sets of gates: flood-gates, and another set apparently used to deepen the water in the lode to make navigation possible. Lighters brought corn up to a mill in Soham in the early nineteenth century, and in later years flour was sent to Ely and Chatteris railway depots. Barley, timber and coal were also taken up the lode, the coal traffic increasing when the mill turned from water power to steam.

Railways did not come to the district until comparatively late. Then the opening of the Ely—Newmarket line through Soham in 1879, followed shortly by the construction of a narrow-gauge line into the mill, had a drastic effect on waterborne trade, which probably ended before 1900.[65] In 1906 the lode was described as 'not now navigable'.[66]

River Lark

The course of the Lark is natural from Bury St Edmunds, for some years the head of navigation, to just below Isleham lock. An almost straight cut about four miles long, possibly made in Roman times, took the waters of the Lark to the main river at Prickwillow (the river was referred to as Pryckewillowewayter in 1549) until the diversion of the Ouse in 1830. The lower stretch of the Lark takes part of the course of the pre-diversion Ouse, apart from the last mile, before it joins the present main river two miles south of Littleport.[67]

The Lark may have been used by the Romans for the transport of clunch from pits in the Isleham area, and Barnack stone was carried upriver for the building of the Abbey at Bury St Edmunds. But the first recorded attempt to make the river navigable throughout came in 1635 when Henry Lambe petitioned to make the Lark navigable from Bury St Edmunds to the Ouse. A commission was appointed to examine his proposal and found it feasible; it was agreed that Lambe should commence the work of cleansing the river at his own cost so that it could be used by lighters and similar vessels. However, he had not completed more than a mile of the work before two local landowners, Sir Roger North and Thomas Steward, objected on the grounds of damage to one of Sir Roger's mills. There followed an enquiry by another body of commissioners and two reports were presented, one expressing the hostility of Bury and Thetford and of several owners and occupiers of land and mills along the river, the other generally in favour provided that Lambe made the cost of water carriage markedly less than that of carriage by land. In 1636 the commission was renewed and Lambe submitted his suggested rates: 2s 8d a ton for carriage and 4s a ton for goods to be delivered. These were considerably cheaper than the rates by land. He also agreed to construct bridges and fords and to pay compensation where appropriate.

The commissioners considered the matter again and came out in favour of the work, provided that the navigation below Mildenhall should be free of tolls and that Lambe should pay treble damages for any work that adversely affected the mills. They also set high rates of compensation for land used for towing paths. Lambe found these conditions unacceptable and petitioned against them, having this time the support of his original opponents. In December 1637 all parties concerned were summoned to appear before the King in Council, and the eventual outcome was that four months later Lambe was licensed to make the Lark navigable from Bury to the Ouse for a rent payable to the Crown of £6 13s 4d a year. He was to receive the tolls of all carriage by water between Bury and Mildenhall.[68]

The success of Lambe's venture is not known, but it is certain that the river was unnavigable between Bury and Mildenhall at the end of the century for in 1700 Henry Ashley, the undertaker for the Ouse, was empowered to make the Lark navigable from Long Common, below Mildenhall Mill, to East Gate bridge in Bury, and to improve passage between Worlington and Long Common. Commissioners were appointed and a schedule of tolls laid down, items specified including agricultural produce, timber, deals, coal, groceries, oil, wine, hemp, malt and building materials. A certain quantity of coal was to pass toll-free for the poor of Bury and, at the other end of the social scale, 'gentlemen and persons of quality' were permitted to put pleasure boats on the river without charge.[69]

On the Ouse, Ashley built both staunches and pound-locks, the latter described as 'sluices'. If the same terminology applies to the Lark then he followed the same practice there. In all, fourteen staunches and eleven locks were built, but some, if not all, of them were reconstructed by Sir Thomas Cullum in the early nineteenth century. In any event, in 1716 Ashley received tolls of £475 10s 4d, despite the fact that the navigation was not completed; another £800 was needed to finish the work and it was estimated that this would increase tolls by at least a further £250.[70] There were the usual troubles with millers; in 1720 James Goodwin complained to Ashley that Mr Ralph of Mildenhall was going to be very troublesome and pull up the lower staunch: 'we do not know what put him in this passion' he says. Two years later Goodwin himself was in trouble, being accused by Joshua Palmer, Ashley's son-in-law, of dishonesty and inefficiency.[71]

After Henry Ashley's death a dispute over the ownership of the Lark navigation arose between his sons-in-law until in 1742 the Master of the Rolls allocated this portion of the estate to Joshua and Joanna Palmer. The annual product of the river was reckoned at £267 10s and its condition was reported as poor.[72] For the next forty years trade seems to have pottered along unspectacularly, with just sufficient maintenance being done to keep things going. In 1781 Ashley Palmer, Joshua's son and now owner of the navigation, received a profit of £274; for the next ten years the figures fluctuated between £153 and £642.[73] A move was made in 1790 to connect the Lark at Bury with the Orwell estuary at Mistley by a canal 31 miles long. Rennie surveyed the route and produced an estimate of £75,000; this included a 2,420yd tunnel and a total lockage of 315ft. Attempts were made to raise £35,000 to bring the canal to within seven miles of Bury, excluding the tunnel, but only £5,000 was promised and the project died.[74]

On the death of Ashley Palmer in 1792, his widow Susanna became sole proprietor of the Lark. The receipts from tolls increased but so did the cost of maintenance and the resultant profits remained much as they had been under her husband's ownership. In 1807, for example, tolls brought in £1,348, but the profits were only £408. Shoals at Freckenham began to hinder the passage of boats, and although the trade in coal up to Bury was well maintained, 9,513 chaldrons being carried in 1816, it was becoming apparent that a large investment programme was needed if the river was to remain a viable concern for long. A hopeful offer of the navigation to the Duke of Norfolk for £12,000 was rejected in 1817.[75] Another problem was that the commissioners appointed under the Act of 1700 seemed never to have taken note of their responsibilities and no reappointments had been made. A new Act was therefore obtained in 1817 appointing new commissioners with powers to raise the tolls to pay for the expenses of improving the navigation.[76] A revised schedule of tonnage rates was included in the Act. These rates applied only to the river between Mildenhall and Bury: coal was charged at 4s 2d a Lynn chaldron, most agricultural produce at 2s 7½d a load, groceries at 3s 3½d a ton and wine or oil at 5s ½d. This brought some immediate increase in revenue but for the time being no action was taken to improve the river apart from the building of a lock and staunch near Isleham under the Eau Brink Act in 1821. During the 1820s it was reported as being unnavigable at low water, with obstructions in the channel. In good conditions the journey from Lynn took two or three days; in bad conditions, six or seven. Sometimes an extra lighter was needed at Prickwillow, so that some of the cargo could be unloaded from the rest of the gang to lessen their draught for the journey upstream. Watermen who did not have a spare lighter had to offload some cargo at Prickwillow and return for it later. Two extra staunches were recommended, one near Worlington and the other at Freckenham Gravel.[77] For many years nearly all the trade had travelled up river, with a gang of lighters struggling up to Bury about every day of the week.[78] A small amount of agricultural produce went down to Lynn, but this was to cease altogether a few years later.

Susanna Palmer left the Lark navigation, as well as the share of the upper Ouse which she also owned, to her nephew Sir Thomas Cullum. In the early 1830s he began an expensive and extensive programme of restoration. By this time the South Level Commissioners, formed by the Act of 1827, had taken over as part of their responsibility the stretch of the Lark from Swale's Reach, near Isleham, to the Ouse, and they altered the course of the lowest section to make a junction with the new cut of 1830, introducing tolls both for boats and for the movement of livestock along the banks. But all this happened too late. Cullum rebuilt the locks and staunches, with the exception of Isleham lock added many years later by the South Level Commissioners, and trade in coal and general merchandise from Lynn increased. In 1846, however, the railway freight line between Ipswich and Bury St Edmunds was opened by the Eastern Union and coal prices in Bury immediately began to fall.[79] The town turned its back on Lynn, and the navigation went into a speedy decline.

Ten years later an attempt to revive the Lark trade was made by the Bury St Edmunds Navigation Co, which stated in its prospectus that the Lark had been under the control of the E.U.R. for the past seven years, that trade had been neglected and down traffic had ceased entirely. The river between Fornham and Bury was no longer navigable. The company proposed to reopen the river to Bury railway station, and sought to raise £20,000 by an issue of 2,000 shares of £10 each.[80] The shares were not taken up, and within a few years the navigation between Mildenhall and Bury was in ruins.[81]

Under the Railway & Canal Traffic Act of 1888 the Lark was one of only two river navigations—the other being the Arun—for which warrants of abandonment were issued. However, the year 1890 saw a temporary change in its fortunes when the Eastern Counties Navigation & Transport Co Ltd was formed, with Lord Francis Hervey as chairman and the Marquis of Bristol as vice-chairman. This company bought the river from Lee Brook to Bury and commenced an ambitious restoration scheme, including making navigable the short Tuddenham Mill stream which was dredged, straightened and on which a staunch was built. On the main river the company removed three staunches, repaired the others and converted one to a pound-lock. But, according to Walter Fuller, its traffic manager and secretary, the company spent all its capital, and loans in addition, on the repairs. It took four years to complete the work. The river was reopened to Bury in September 1894, but it was too late; in December of that year the company, its resources exhausted, went into liquidation. After 1894 the river above Icklingham ceased to be used.[82]

The receiver sold the navigation to Parker Brothers of Mildenhall, who carried on a little trade at rates of up to 1d a ton, with a minimum of 2s 6d a boat at Mildenhall.[83] It is probable that highway materials were both the earliest and the last cargoes carried on the river. Gravel from Isleham was carried in the early 1920s, but within a few years all traffic ceased. The river above Lee Brook continued in private ownership, being taken over from Parker Brothers by William Parker in 1928, until the formation of the Great Ouse Catchment Board. In recent years two locks have been rebuilt, at Barton Mills and Icklingham, but any prospect of full restoration has been dimmed by the lowering of the A11 over the river at Barton Mills. It is still possible to navigate through Isleham lock up to Judes Ferry. Restoration to Mildenhall is not out of the question and there are many stretches on the upper river worth trying by canoe, with the remains of several staunches and locks to examine.

The Little Ouse

Among the ordinances made by the Commissioners of Sewers for the hundred of Clakclos in 1575 was 'that Rebech river . . . extending from Redmercote, unto the great river of Ouse in Southerey, be made in breadth 40 feet, until it come within three furlongs of Ouse, and then 30 . . .'.[84] In subsequent years the Rebech river has been known as Brandon Creek, Brandon River and the Little Ouse. The present channel of the river below Crosswater Staunch is artificial and may date from the Roman period; two courses existed in the early seventeenth century, and the presence of Barnack stone in Thetford, used for the Priory built in the twelfth century, would indicate that the river was the line of supply at that time.[85]

That the Little Ouse was to some extent navigable before 1660 is shown also by Badeslade;[86] there are further references to its being navigable to Thetford in 1664.[87] However the condition of the upper river cannot have been satisfactory, in view of the wording of an Act of 1669–70, by which the mayor, burgesses and commonalty of Thetford were empowered 'under the superintendence and control of certain commissioners, to make this river navigable from a place called Whitehouse, beneath Brandon Ferry, to Thetford . . .' and to receive tolls of 6d a ton on all merchandise.[88] But the corporation was then 'not at all in a condition to execute the work', and it was undertaken by the Rt Hon Henry, Earl of Arlington, to whom in 1677 the tolls were assigned. His daughter Isabella, who married the Duke of Grafton, inherited the tolls, but after her husband's death she relinquished her right and interest to the Corporation of Thetford in 1696.[89]

The bequest may have been generous but it brought complications with it. Conditions on the river deteriorated, and in 1742 the corporation had to construct a staunch below Thetford to maintain a navigable level. A petition in 1750 from the corporation, local landowners, farmers, principal inhabitants, merchants and navigators, stated that all the original commissioners were now dead and that no new ones had been appointed; as a result disputes had arisen over haling ways and other matters which could only be settled by costly lawsuits. An Act to appoint new commissioners was requested and, following an enquiry which confirmed that there were no commissioners extant and that there was evidence of lighters being detained unless fees were paid for haling, it received the royal assent in 1751. The Act did no more than appoint new commissioners, but this enabled some progress to be made. The corporation set to work and built seven staunches: Thetford, Thetford Middle, Turfpool, Croxton, Santon, Brandon and Sheepwash. There was also the lowest of all, Crosswater, near the junction with Lakenheath Lode, but this was probably installed later.[90] However, according to Samuel Wells, 'it was in later times discovered that the inhabitants of the town of Brandon, and persons carrying goods to and from thence, had all along received the benefit and advantage of the navigation of the river from Whitehouse up to Brandon, and paid no toll, although the boats passing between these places could not often get to Brandon without the assistance of the sluices and staunches erected between Thetford and Brandon'. So in 1789 a further Act was obtained which vested the tolls in the corporation of Thetford who were appointed the undertakers for 'making, improving and completing the navigation' with powers to use the tolls as they decided. In place of the old flat rate of 6d, a more complicated table of rates was drawn up with differentials for types of cargo and distances carried. The commissioners could borrow £10,000 on security of the tolls to improve the navigation.[91]

Improvement did not come immediately, however. The

navigation is described as being 'mismanaged and neglected till 1827, when it was put into the hands of a superintendent, and a debt of £4,200 incurred in improving it'. Between 1827 and 1835 the seven early staunches were all rebuilt;[92] indeed in 1833 Thetford received an income of £955 from the navigation, out of the town's total income for the year of £1,054.[93] However, the corporation as a whole benefited far less after the Municipal Reform Act of 1835; henceforth tolls went into a separate navigation account, while the corporation received only the rates. Nevertheless, a need for economy was evident; in 1843 it was recommended that the town, which owned a dredging machine with small boat attached, 'the great lighter, the fore boat, the third boat' and a small rowing boat for use in weed-cutting, should sell the 'fore boat' and the 'third boat' and hire when necessary, to save money. An offer of £30 was rejected as too low. In the same year William Aldridge, who was superintendent of the navigation as well as toll collector, was given two months' notice, and John Chambers Roe was appointed in his stead at a salary of £80.[94] One of his first duties was to observe the building of a railway bridge over the river; the Norwich—Brandon line opened in 1845, on the same day as the Newport—Brandon extension of the Eastern Counties Railway.[95]

This same year, 1845, saw the highest tolls recorded—£1,728 including the carriage of over 15,000 tons of coal. They fell sharply to £741 in 1846 when tolls were reduced to compete with the railway, and three years later were down to £439, with coal down to just over 9,000 tons. Then in 1850 the tolls were put up to be let; at the same time it was agreed that repairs to the navigation be done by tender and that John Roe be given notice to quit. The highest offer for the tolls was £275; the corporation asked for £300 but this was refused. After some negotiation, George Godfrey of Thetford, who with his wife and J. W. and G. Gill ran a weekly vessel to Lynn and owned boats and a wharf, took over the tolls for £100 a year, on condition that he kept the navigation 'in good and substantial repair', for a period of three years.[96] John Farrant, who had succeeded Roe as superintendent, decided to emigrate, but was refused a grant of £10 by the cash-conscious Thetford Navigation Committee.

The arrangement with Godfrey was renewed in 1854, for £110 a year, and again in 1859 for £160. But in this year a crisis occurred in Thetford affairs, when a cheque for £320 was passed from the navigation to the finance committee at a meeting of the Council.[97] At the next navigation committee meeting, the Mayor, Cornell Fison, protested at this action and later moved that the transfer of funds was illegal and the £320 should be repaid. He quoted the 1810 Act in support, but the motion was lost and a further motion approving the loan being given without security was passed. The next step was an application for an injunction to restrain the payment of the £320, and an interim order was obtained. The council decided not to oppose the injunction.

Alderman Bartlett, who had opposed Fison from the beginning, opened a counter-attack. He proposed a motion that 'in consequence of law proceedings having been taken against the Council to prevent the payment of the surplus funds of the navigation (that navigation being in good and substantial order) it is determined to comply with the letter of the Act of Parliament relating to the navigation, and it is hereby resolved to raise the tolls from their present rate to that set out by the aforesaid Act and further that the Navigation Committee be hereby empowered to enter into or make such arrangements as may be found necessary for collecting the tolls'. This brought an immediate amendment from Cornell Fison and his brother to the effect that the tolls were quite adequate as they were. As the Fisons were boat owners, steam millers and timber sawyers (and later dealers in vitriol and artificial manures) it is not surprising that they resisted Bartlett's move, but they were routed in the voting. Then a further motion was carried asking Mrs Godfrey, now the lessee, to surrender her lease in return for a new one at £250 a year. This motion blamed the Fisons and J. W. Gill for forcing the Council to comply with the 1810 Act and added that 'but for the opposition of the afore-mentioned gang owners the debt upon the Red Lion would have been paid off and that shortly a further heavy balance would have accumulated . . . which would have enabled the Council to keep the navigation in its present excellent state of repair . . .'. Again the

Fisons' opposition was swamped, and Mrs Godfrey accepted the terms.

But all was not over. In December 1859 the council were informed by Mr John Horshor that in consequence of the council's resolution about complying with all the provisions of the 1810 Act concerning tolls, he had been instructed to file a bill in the Court of Chancery for an account of the tolls since 1830 and for repayment with interest and costs out of the borough funds 'all sums misapplied by the Corporation in aid of the Borough Fund or other Borough purposes since that date out of the Navigation . . . and also for restraining the Corporation by injunction from granting any fresh lease of the tolls . . .'. This was heavier artillery, and the town clerk was authorized to take counsel's opinion. The advice received was that the tolls per chaldron should be adjusted to an equivalent charge per ton, and the town clerk applied to Suffolk and Norfolk Quarter Sessions to reduce the tolls by one-fifth, which would have this effect. Then on 4 May 1850, £320 was repaid by the finance committee to the navigation committee, who invested £300 at 3 per cent.

Now the battle was finished, there was time to consider the state of the navigation. A report in 1863 stated that several staunches needed repair, at an estimated total cost of £135. Mrs Godfrey was told that if she paid half this amount within a few weeks she would not have to meet the full cost. When her lease expired, the corporation would themselves put the navigation into good condition and would retain the tolls for this purpose. On the expiration, William Morley was appointed superintendent for three months, at £1 a week, to collect tolls and oversee the repairs. Within a short time of the corporation's taking over, six actions were filed against them for flooding meadows, and a navigation defence committee was formed to cope with this sort of situation.[98]

Annual receipts between 1864–7 averaged £470; for several years coal, coke and seeds continued to come in from Lynn, while flour from Fisons and hurdles went downriver. Charles Burrel & Son, Ltd, were manufacturing small iron vessels at Thetford in the 1880s, which steamed away when their engines and boilers were installed. There was passenger traffic as well about this time; a 25ft paddle-steamer, *Pride of the Ouse*, converted from a ship's jolly-boat, could carry 20 passengers to Cambridge or on trips around the Fen waterways, and 6 passengers could be accommodated on a 17ft screw steamer, *Louise*. Fisons owned a 50ft screw tug, *Speedwell*, which towed gangs of lighters to Lynn. A light was placed on Brandon church tower to guide navigators in bad weather or 'on festive occasions'.[99]

By the 1890s, however, repairs to the river works were urgently required and the navigation ran into debt to the borough treasurer for £14 3s 9d. Now the navigation committee turned to Fisons for help, asking them to pay £50 in advance of tolls to provide cash in hand. An amendment that this was 'unbusinesslike, if not illegal', was lost. For the last few years of the century Fisons' advances continued to keep the navigation going, there being otherwise only a few pounds collected each month. In 1898, when 3,200 tons were carried producing £42 in tolls, the navigation committee declared their inability to pay their rates and asked for a revaluation at 'a mere nominal figure'. They plodded on a little longer, having to terminate the post of superintendent in 1900 but receiving a windfall of £20 16s 8d in 1904 from a final dividend in a bankruptcy proceeding.[100] Henry de Salis in that year described the part of the navigation in Thetford's jurisdiction as being 'in a very indifferent condition, most of the staunches are out of order, and will not hold up the water'.[101] There had been a trade in gravel from pits on Lord Iveagh's estate via Lakenheath Lode, but this was now finished, and evidence before the royal commission stated that the navigation above Crosswater was practically abandoned. The bottom 9½ miles from Wilton Bridge to the Ouse, which had always been an open navigation, were kept free of weed by the Bedford Level Commissioners, while the South Level Commissioners were responsible for Crosswater Staunch. By 1914 all commercial traffic had ceased.[102]

The Great Ouse Catchment Board removed most of the remains of the staunches, those at Thetford and Brandon being replaced by sluices. It is still possible to navigate nearly to Brandon and, with the increasing pressure by pleasure craft on the Great Ouse system, restoration to Thetford, where the river is still maintained in good condition by the corporation, would seem a real possibility when financial conditions permit.

River Wissey

The Wissey is today navigable for small craft from Oxborough Ferry to the Great Ouse (the Ten Mile River) above Denver sluice, a distance of about twelve miles. It is likely that the name derives from the tribal name *Wisse* with the Old English *ea* subjoined—the river of the Wisse. The majority opinion of the authorities is that 'Ouse' and 'Wissey' are etymologically identical and from the absence of early references to the Ouse north of Benwick it may well be that it was the Wissey in its old course, when it joined the Well stream near Welney, that gave its name to Wisbech.[103]

The Domesday Book (1086) mentions that the Wissey was navigable from 'Oxenburgh' to Cambridge and Lynn; there is also evidence that there was a medieval settlement by the river near Oxborough Ferry. Among the ordinances of the Commission of Sewers which met at Lynn in 1575 was 'that the river of Wisse, extending from Whittington to Stokebridge, be cleansed and made in breadth xl feet', and 'that Stokebridge, containing three arches of the wideness of 40 feet, be repaired by the country near adjoining'. There were further ordinances for cleansing and widening the river between Stokebridge and the Great Ouse, in which nine weirs are mentioned.[104] This bridge was first built in the reign of Henry III; it was destroyed by the Abbot of Ely, who was entitled to the profits from the ferry, but the Hundred Court forced him to rebuild it. It was reconstructed in 1803.

The river was navigable to Oxborough Hithe in the mid-eighteenth century, according to Blomefield's *History of Norfolk*. Here there were granaries and coal yards, coal being imported from Newcastle, with boats trading to Cambridge and Lynn. There are also remains of boathouses at Northwold, about a mile above Oxborough Hithe. But, possibly because there was no town of any size at the head of navigation, there are few references to navigation on the Wissey. It was covered by no legislation other than an Act of 1814, which appointed commissioners for draining and preserving certain fen lands in the parishes of Stoke Ferry, Northwold, Wretton, Wereham, West Dereham and others in this part of Norfolk. This Act enabled the commissioners to 'widen, rode, or crab' the Wissey between Stoke Bridge and Hilgay Creek's End at the cost of the owners and occupiers of land lying within the stated boundaries. Tolls could also be levied on persons passing along the north bank of the river, the receipts being used solely for repairing that bank.[105]

In the early nineteenth century there was a wharf at Stoke Ferry which handled coal, corn and malt; this would have served Whitbread's large maltings at Whittington, connected to Stoke Ferry by a turnpike road.[106] Trade was still continuing at Stoke Ferry and Oxborough Hithe in 1858; the exact date of the ending of the coal trade to Stoke Ferry is not known, but it was presumably a few years after the opening of the branch railway line from Denver in 1882. The river was certainly being used, if only occasionally and to a limited extent, at the end of the nineteenth century when J. Coston of Hilgay operated a barge called *Wissey* which is recorded as calling at Cambridge in 1896 and 1898.[107] There was a revival of activity after 1925 with the opening of the sugarbeet factory at Wissington, accessible until after the Second World War only by the river or by the Wissington Light Railway. Coal from Lynn in summer and beet from the Fens in winter were carried by a fleet of three tugs—*Wissington, Littleport* and *Hilgay*—and 24 steel barges. This traffic ended in 1943.[108] A. V. Jackson was also carrying corn from Stoke Ferry in the 1930s.

River Nar

The River Nar is a natural waterway for much of its length. In ancient times the outfall at Lynn consisted only of the combined waters of the Nar and Gay, the Nar flowing westwards to Wiggenhall and then turning northwards. Subsequently the lower stretch was diverted almost due north to meet the Great

Ouse at Lynn.

The Nar was made navigable under an Act of 1751, following a petition from King's Lynn, Swaffham, Narford, Narborough, Castle Acre and other neighbouring towns and villages.[109] Evidence was submitted from John Spelman, a member of a famous Norfolk family, to the effect that he knew the river and that making it navigable from West Acre to King's Lynn would be of the utmost advantage to the inhabitants of the adjacent towns 'as it must greatly increase the Commerce thereof'. It was submitted that the Nar was capable of being made navigable for 'boats, barges and lighters'; the Bill met with no opposition and was quickly passed.[110] Under the Act any nine commissioners could contract to make the river navigable and the undertakers were empowered to remove all annoyances, to set up locks above Setchey bridge and to lay out towing paths. Tolls were to be levied to defray expenses, with a maximum of 2s 6d for every last of wheat, rye, barley, malt or other grain and 1s 6d per chaldron of coals (Winchester measure) or ton of any other goods from Lynn to West Acre. No tolls were chargeable on goods carried not more than a furlong above Setchey bridge, nor on any pleasure boats. There was to be no haling by horses between King's Lynn and Sandringham Eau 'where the tide ebbs and flows', and the watermen were forbidden to carry guns or nets 'to fowl or fish therewith'. The commissioners were permitted to borrow money on the security of the tolls.

The Nar commissioners, who included the mayor of King's Lynn and three common council men of the borough, met in June 1751 and instructed John Aram and Langley Edwards to survey the river and produce an estimate for making it navigable. Their report, which included the canalization of some stretches, the construction of seven staunches and one pen-sluice and the excavation of a large basin at West Acre bridge, was promptly rendered. Matters then fell into abeyance for six years. In May 1757, for some unknown reason, the commissioners were galvanized into activity; a treasurer was appointed and subscriptions advertised for, all tolls to be assigned to the subscribers. Langley Edwards was paid £100 for the survey and for 'putting out the works from King's Lynn to

Westacre for himself and his assistants until the same is completed', he having to find his assistants himself and pay all their and his expenses. It was decided that the river should be made navigable for boats or lighters carrying up to ten tons or eight chaldrons of coal, and the locks should pen only one lighter at a time.

Edwards produced an estimate of £2,500 for the entire works, the main items being the making of new cuts. The staunches were estimated at about £50 each. He was ordered to begin work at the end of September 1757. Edward Everard, merchant of King's Lynn, and Robert Crow, gentleman of Swaffham, agreed to advance £2,600 at 5 per cent in return for the assignment to them of the tolls. These were fixed at the maximum figure allowed by the Act, but were reduced to 1s 6d on grain and 1s on all other goods in June 1758, when several new commissioners were appointed. The agreement with Edwards to make the river navigable for £2,500 was finalized, it being further agreed that Edwards would not receive his £100 unless the navigation was completed for the stated sum on or before Michaelmas Day next.

By October 1758 over £1,900 had been paid out but the river was nowhere near navigable. Edwards was sent for and asked to complete by 1 January 1759. His fellow surveyor, Aram, was paid 10 guineas for his trouble. Edwards had the time limit extended to 15 February, but with a £20-a-week penalty from that date until the work was finished. It transpired that two more staunches were needed, for which the commissioners considered Edwards should be charged. He appealed against this and the commissioners gave him until 3 August to justify his appeal, to complete the works and produce his accounts. The navigation appears to have been completed by that date, although it is not clear who eventually paid for the extra staunches. Ralph Wilson was appointed inspector of works and collector of tolls, at £40 a year.

In 1760 the commissioners were thinking of applying for a new Act to make a cut from the Nar to the Ouse on the shortest direct line and to enable them to raise more money to discharge their debts. For the period between 29 September 1760 and 31

March 1761 the tolls amounted to £59; after salaries and other payments had been made, the profit was £26. However, outstanding debts totalled £912 and it was decided to increase the tolls to the maximum permitted. The clerk was asked to see if the tolls could be let, to save the cost of collection. Further increases were recommended in June 1763, but the commissioners seemed to be losing interest as there was no quorum at the next meeting and no further meetings were minuted.[111]

At some time in the next few years the interest in the navigation was purchased by the Revd Henry Spelman, who soon became dissatisfied with the state of affairs. In 1770 he submitted a petition in which he stated that the commissioners, having borrowed in all £3,500, had vested the tolls in the proprietors and subscribers, of whom he was now the sole representative.[112] He claimed that the sum due to him, with interest added, amounted to £4,718. He accused the commissioners of failing to fulfil their commitments, 'by which the navigation is greatly obstructed and in some parts rendered intirely useless and that to make the same useful to the public it will be necessary to borrow a further sum of money'. As a result, a second Act was obtained, under which £800 was to be spent immediately on repairs.[113] Spelman lent a further £1,345 to cover the cost of the Act and to complete the works, and he agreed that this sum should be added to the outstanding debt with the total figure being treated as capital bearing 5 per cent interest. This Act stated that damage had been done by allowing boats of too great burden to be navigated on the river. The commissioners were required to lay down limits for preventing damage by 'rude and disorderly persons managing or employed on boats'. According to this Act it was intended that the locks should have upper and lower gates and that they should remain empty except when actually in use.

The Nar navigation, as completed and later improved, included in fact only one pound-lock, the chamber of which can be seen beneath the A47 at Narborough. This lock, referred to as a 'pen sluice' is mentioned in Langley Edwards' estimate.[114] From Narborough to King's Lynn is 12 miles; ten staunches were built in the upper five miles, falling a total of 30ft. Nine of

them seem to have been guillotine staunches; the other one—
Upper Bonemill staunch—was fitted with mitre gates at some
time, possibly to prevent the emptying of over 1,000 yards of
river between Narborough Upper and Bonemill Lower
staunches every time a boat used the latter, which would have
prevented the waterwheel at the bonemill from working until
the water level had built up again. Recent measurements of the
remains of the staunches indicate a minimum width of 11ft
2in.[115] Although no evidence of navigation works above Narborough has been found, the construction of the 'pen sluice' and
the reference in Edwards' estimate of a 'new cutt to Westacre
Bridge, two staunches' makes it likely that the navigation did
extend to, or near to, Westacre. There were also two short
branches, one to Wormegay and one to Blackborough Priory,
which may have been navigable for a time.

Coal, timber, corn and malt were the main items of cargo
handled at Narborough. An Act of 1815 for draining and
improving in the parishes of Wormegay, etc, included provision
to deepen, widen and straighten the Nar and appointed commissioners for the work. The sluices, locks and dams were to be
placed under the supervision of a civil engineer and it was
required that oak, not fir, was to be used for repair of the works.
The Act specified that the work was to be completed within
three months after 5 July, and that the navigation was not to be
obstructed without ten days' warning in writing. Compensation was to be paid to whoever received the tolls in respect of
any tolls lost. A plan, dated 1814, by Charles Burcham, civil
engineer and land surveyor, shows some straightening of bends
on the river.[116]

By the mid-nineteenth century the navigation was owned by
the Marriott brothers, maltsters and corn and coal merchants,
who had a wharf at Narborough.[117] They, with some of the
local landowners, resisted the incursion of the railway. An association was formed, which the Marriotts indemnified against
all costs, which claimed that the proposed line, the Lynn &
Dereham, was 'unnecessary and without any promise of
return'. However the carriage of a ton of coal from Lynn by
water at this time cost 5s and a further 5s or 6s was charged for

onward conveyance by road to Swaffham, with nearly as much again for East Dereham. The Marriotts lost their battle; the line from Lynn to Narborough was opened in 1846 and completed to Dereham in 1848.[118] The oft-told story was repeated yet again; trade on the river diminished, and a Bill for Nar Valley Drainage in 1881 contained a paragraph providing that 'the River Nar or some part or parts thereof need not be kept navigable after the passing of the intended Act'. Navigation to Narborough ended in 1884.

The lowest reach of the river was used well into the twentieth century by the steam tugs and barges of the West Norfolk Farmers Manure Company, bringing the ammonia-rich gas water from Cambridge gasworks. This traffic continued until 1932. The Manure Company's works now belong to Fisons. Opposite the factory are doors controlling the water level upstream, permitting flood water to escape but keeping the tides out of the river. Until recently coasters also penetrated a short distance up the Nar to load at a wharf, and this stretch is still used by fishing boats for mooring, although at low tide the river is little more than a muddy ditch.[119]

CHAPTER VIII

The Nene, Middle Level and Wisbech Canal

•••••••••••••••••••••••••••••••••◆•••••••••••••••••••••••••••••••••

The Nene

Rising near Daventry, the Nene flows through Northampton, where it becomes navigable at the junction with the Northampton branch of the Grand Union Canal; thence it wanders north-easterly to Peterborough. Below Peterborough, a southern branch known as the Old Nene leads into the Middle Level, while the main river continues in a series of artificial cuts to Wisbech and on to Crab Hole in the Wash. West of Peterborough is the site of the Roman town of Durobrivae, famous for its potteries; it may be that the Romans used the river for transportation as there are traces here of what may have been a wharf.[1] Above Peterborough, where it enters the Fens, the character of the river changes completely and the same could be said of the history of the river and its administration until recent times.

Northampton to Peterborough
The first of the many Acts relating to the Nene was obtained in 1713, but various proposals and surveys were made before then. The noblemen and gentlemen of Northamptonshire had surveys made in 1567 and 1606, and there were reports by Commissions of Sewers in the mid-seventeenth century. A pamphlet on the subject was printed in 1653, in which the writer estimated that the whole river could be made navigable for about £8,000.[2] This would include 33 locks, 'as many as are the Mills', to take small vessels of 8 or 10-ton burden, unlike earlier proposals for vessels of 20 or 30 tons. An advantage of using

small vessels would be that they could pass through the arches of the bridges at Wellingborough, Irthlingborough, Thrapston, Oundle and other places, which restricted larger craft. The cost of the land carriage of Newcastle coal to Northampton exceeded the price of the coal itself at the nearest waterside, some 30 miles away, and a boat could carry ten chaldrons whereas a cart could carry only one.

The writer gave an instance of the profitability of carriage on the Nene despite the difficulties of navigating the unimproved river:

> In the year 1648 a Boat of 3 Tun laden with Cheese was brought from Peterborow to Higham Ferrers at Michaelmas Faire, the wayes that wet season being unpassable: and though the owner was forced to hire two men to unlade his Boat at every Mill shore and after lift the Boat to the Dam, and laid her again, which he did sixteen times; yet he brought his Cheese at an easier rate, than at the most seasonable time he could have done by land: (viz) under 12d the hundredweight, he having first offered 2s 6d per hundred, as I was informed by one that had it from the man himself (who is worthy to be recommended for his industry) who there sold his Boat for the price he paid for it at Peterborow.

The prophet Isaiah was quoted on the financial question—'The Harvest of the River is her Revenue'—but more practically it was suggested that the money for the work be raised by voluntary contribution, or by assessment on the neighbouring counties, or by appointing undertakers to do the work and to be recompensed from tolls. The writer concluded by saying that he had heard of many rivers being made navigable, 'but never heard of any that have endeavoured to stop them up again, or with the worke again to do, for any pretended inconvenience whatsoever'. On which subsequent history of the Nene makes its own comment!

It was another 60 years, however, before there was any legislation. Then in 1713 an Act was passed 'for making the River Nene or Nen, running from Northampton to Peterborough, navigable'. This Act, which also refers to the river as 'Neene, alias Nine', lists two pages of commissioners, any nine of whom were empowered to appoint 'such Person or Persons to make the river navigable and passable . . . as they shall think fit'. However, the Act enjoined that nothing could be done unless the commissioners (at least nine of them, as is repeated in nearly every clause) could agree with 'some Person or Persons' to make *all* the said river navigable, and no such persons willing to take on the entire task could be found. So for the time being nothing was done, although the 1713 Act provides incidental evidence that six miles of the river, between Peterborough and Alwalton, were in fact navigable at that time and boats would be allowed to use that stretch toll-free.

In 1724 a second Act noted 'that the good Purposes intended . . . have been hitherto disappointed and frustrated', and gave newly appointed commissioners (2½ pages of them this time, with a noticeable lowering of social status) permission to contract to make any part or parts of the river navigable. It now became a practical proposition, and in September 1726 Robert Wright and Thomas Squire contracted to make and complete the navigation from Peterborough to Oundle North bridge at their own expense, to be recompensed by tolls of 1s 6d a ton on all goods conveyed between those places. They completed the work in 1730. In 1736 Thomas Squire agreed to continue the navigation to Thrapston bridge on the same terms, and completed this by the end of the following year. The river from Peterborough to Thrapston was called the Eastern Division of the navigation, and from Thrapston to Northampton was the Western Division.[3]

To develop the Western Division in the same way as the Eastern proved impossible, and it was necessary for the commissioners to obtain a further Act to enable them to borrow money on the security of the tolls to carry out the work. Again the list of commissioners was brought up to date. They were given authority to borrow money, on which up to 4 per cent interest would be paid, the lenders to become the proprietors of the navigation. It was also stipulated that the work must begin at Thrapston and continue upwards to Northampton. The commissioners held their first meeting on 1 June, 1756, a few weeks after the third Nene Act received the royal assent. 27 attended, with Sir Edmund Isham in the chair, one of the largest attendance figures recorded.[4]

The Western Division commissioners could never be accused of being over-hasty. Holden Bowker offered his services as superintendent, but was told to wait; he had given evidence with Thomas Yeoman in favour of the Bill, and Yeoman had surveyed the Thrapston—Northampton line in 1753. The commissioners flirted with proposals from Ferdinando Stratford, the engineer from Gloucester, and from John Squires, who quoted an estimate of 13,000 guineas. In March 1758 a committee was set up to examine and report on plans and proposals, with a limit of £14,500 for expenditure. John Smith jnr, of Attercliffe in Yorkshire, whose father was engineer to the River Don Navigation, put in an estimate, as did a Mr Case. Case's plans were accepted, but he then dissented from his own proposals and to the terms required. Smith tried again, as did Mr Wyman of Higham Ferrers. Yeoman was asked to examine the proposals, and approved them both. Wyman then withdrew 'on account of Mr Smith's cheaper proposals, his Integrity and superior Experience in such affairs'. So at last Smith's estimate was accepted; meticulously detailed, it amounted to £14,070 4s $2\frac{1}{2}$d. For this the commissioners were to get 20 pound-locks, 100ft long × 10ft 6in wide, 20 horse haling bridges, 14 haling gates, 10 'howls for small drains' and a few other items. £61 was included for raising the height of existing bridges. The contract was signed on 22 June 1758.[5]

It took just over three years for the navigation to reach Northampton. To pay Smith, who was both engineer and contractor, frequent calls were made on the subscribers, most of whom paid up promptly. In 1759 the navigation reached Wellingborough, where Smith built wharves. Traders were allowed to use the navigation as it progressed, and a toll of 1s 8d per ton was fixed between Thrapston and Wellingborough. There were frequent disputes with the millers, not surprisingly, as there were 20 mills on the river between Northampton and Thrapston, and no by-laws existed under which the commissioners could act against either millers or boat owners. At a joint meeting with the Eastern Division towards the end of 1759 two sets of by-laws were drawn up, one to apply jointly and one for the Western Division only. These regulated the use of the river and the conditions of trading on it, and provided that millers had to give five days' notice if they wished to hold up or let down water for necessary repairs.[6]

In October 1760 it was reported that since the navigation had been opened to Wellingborough, 'notwithstanding the unusual dryness of the season, many accidental, and more studied and contrived Impediments,' the tolls amounted to £120.[7] Coal from Sunderland was being sold at Wellingborough at 12½d per bushel, taking two days to arrive there from Thrapston.[8] The commissioners' finances were now being helped by various local gentlemen who donated the money for locks: John Spencer, Sir John Langham and Frederic Montagu gave one each 'for the encouragement of trade and navigation' and Spencer Compton gave two. Not to be outdone, Frederic Montagu gave two more. A wharf was constructed at Northampton and tolls for passing the locks between Wellingborough and Northampton were agreed.[9] In July 1761 Smith reported that over £400 had been taken to date on the navigation for tolls and wharfage, and on 7 August the navigation to Northampton was opened. *The Universal Magazine* described the event:

No less than 38 barges laden with coals and other merchandise and adorned with flags and streamers came up with the greatest ease to the public wharf at the south bridge preceded by a band of music, drums, french horns, etc. The principal vessels were filled with as many persons as they were capable of containing (amongst whom were several of distinction) whose loud acclamations were returned from the spectators on both sides of the river, and several cannon were fired on their arrival at the wharf. The most general illuminations that were ever known, bonfires, ringing of bells at all the churches, and every other demonstration of joy concluded the evening without the least rioting or other disturbance; and what is very extraordinary amongst such an immense crowd of people both by land and water, no unfortunate accident happened to anyone.

The celebrations may have had prolonged after-effects, for in September there were insufficient commissioners present (less than nine) for the monthly meeting to be held. A few months later Thomas Yeoman surveyed the works and reported favourably; the commissioners declared 'the said works of the Navigation are well performed' by John Smith.[10]

Tolls on the Western Division rose to over £1,000 in 1766 and climbed to £1,681 in 1769, a year which saw the appointment of 52 new commissioners, many of them clerics who seemed to have had plenty of time to attend the meetings; at the August 1771 meeting there were 15 clergymen out of a total of 32 commissioners present. Their prayers were needed. Toll receipts never reached £1,800; indeed, in 1781 they fell to £734. Bills for repairs, averaging £200 a quarter, featured regularly in the accounts. Martin Lucas, appointed treasurer, toll gatherer, clerk and inspector of works at £100pa in 1771, had his salary reduced in 1782 to £70 as long as the tolls remained below £1,000. Fortunately for him they soon recovered, and in 1786 the commissioners sold off stock in which they had invested in 1762 to pay off a quarter of the loans originally subscribed. Further repayments were made in 1778 and 1789. In the 1790s, however, receipts fell away again, as the following figures show:[11]

	£
1794:	1,466
1795:	1,208 (repairs totalled £1,181 this year)
1796:	1,106
1797:	964
1798:	750
1799:	458—the same figure as the bill for repairs

In 1792 the Leicestershire & Northamptonshire Union Canal (the 'Old Union') was promoted with the intention of joining Leicester, and so the Trent, to the Nene at Northampton, to which the projected Grand Junction Canal subscribers proposed to build a branch from Gayton.[12] However, after much effort, construction of the L & N.U. stopped at Market

Harborough and the link between this canal and the G.J.C. was completed between Foxton and Norton by the specially formed Grand Union company in 1814. Between 1793 and 1800, however, the work on the main line of the G.J.C. proceeded steadily; in October 1800, with a link by railway across Blisworth hill, that line was opened throughout. Authorized in the Grand Junction Act of 1793 was a branch from the main line to Northampton, and this was the direction to which the Nene Western commissioners looked for the salvation of their Division.[13]

Before describing the negotiations with the Grand Junction company, it would be as well to glance at the state of the Eastern Division. This seems to have been run as a more-or-less private venture by the proprietors and in the earlier years minute books as comprehensive as those of the Western Division do not appear to have been kept. From Thrapston to Peterborough there were 14 locks and 8 staunches, and haling ways had been set out. In 1759 Thomas Yeoman reported that the navigation between Waternewton and Wansford was very bad in places and the commissioners seem to have had little or no authority over the proprietors, who had the sole use of the tolls for themselves, their heirs and assigns.[14] Robert Wright conveyed his share of the tolls to Thomas Squire in 1731,[15] and the Eastern Division thenceforth remained in the hands of the Squire family, who were Peterborough merchants and brewers, for many years. That neither the situation nor the navigation was satisfactory (except possibly to the Squire family) is apparent from an Act of 1794, relating to the navigation between Peterborough and Thrapston, which recognised that the powers of the commissioners were insufficient to fulfil the purposes of the previous Acts. The 1794 Act enabled the commissioners to examine witnesses on oath, to appoint a clerk and overseer (to be paid by the proprietors), to ensure that accounts be kept: generally the commissioners were given more power to ensure that the proprietors maintained the navigation. That they had not done this was clear from a clause stating that the river 'is in many Places grown up and decreased in depth, so that Boats and Lighters navigating thereon, for Want of a proper and suf-

Plates 21 & 22   The Nene: *(above) The South View of the Navigation and the town of Northampton*, from a wash drawing by James Blackamore, early 1760s. Coal barges on the river, and the Crown and Anchor Inn over the South Bridge on the left; *(below)* British Transport Waterways narrow boats at Whitworth's mill, Wellingborough, 1962

Plates 23 & 24 (left) The Wisbech Canal, shortly before its closure; *(below)* shipping on the Nene at Wisbech in the 1860s

THE RIVER NENE W

ficient Depth of Water, are frequently stopped'. Several other points were also dealt with, including the customary difficulties with the millers.

Having obtained their Act the commissioners ran temporarily out of enthusiasm, as at the first meeting, at the Talbot in Oundle, there was not even a quorum. The magic number of nine managed to appear at the second meeting and they appointed a host more, including the Duke of Buccleuch and the Earls of Westmoreland and Cardigan. They also appointed a clerk, J. Bramston, and a superintendent, James Golborne, nephew of the engineer John Golborne, who had already reported on the lower Nene and on the Ouse outfall. The proprietors were named as Thomas Squire (Oundle—Thrapston) and Wright Thomas Squire (Peterborough—Oundle); they were ordered to clear gravel near the locks and to make haling ways. It was not until 1801, seven years after called upon to act, that Wright Thomas Squire replied to the many orders and admonitions issued to him. By this time the other portion of the Eastern Division was in the hands of Daniel Yorke. The overseer, Francis Thompson, reported in 1802 that repairs were in progress, and Lord Lilford was prominent in applying pressure. However, there was little trade; nor did the majority of the commissioners, who failed to attend meetings, seem particularly concerned. In 1807, Yorke produced accounts showing that the income from navigation 'is reduced to a very small sum,' and that 'in consequence of a failure of trade on the river the Balance of monies remaining in his hands is insufficient to satisfy the demands made against him,' (by Lord Lilford among others). The commissioners sought counsel's opinion about raising the tolls but were advised against an application. When Francis Thompson died at the end of 1809, having been overseer since 1795 for £20 a year, it transpired that he had received no part of his salary from Yorke since 1806! It was a sick navigation indeed.

The link with the Grand Junction

As work on the Grand Junction Canal progressed during the 1790s so, according to the Nene commissioners, the river trade suffered. In 1796 James Barnes surveyed a Northampton line for the G.J.C. and produced an estimate of £25,349. No action was taken for the time being. Concerned at the delay, in 1800 the Western Division commissioners proposed raising £12,000 towards the branch. Proposals came from the G.J.C. for a railway connection, estimated at £9,000, and then for two lengths of canal with a railway in the middle, to avoid heavy lockage; this was what the £12,000 would have covered. The commissioners were not enthusiastic about the railway element and declared themselves wholly in favour of a water communication. In 1802 they put a statement before the county and town of Northampton in which they asserted that they had earlier realized that the G.J.C. would ruin the Nene navigation unless the two were linked. The G.J.C.C. had accepted this and inserted an appropriate clause in their Bill, and the commissioners had trusted in their good faith. But now the Nene tolls were down to a quarter of the average before the canal was begun and the roads were being ruined by the extra traffic brought on to them by the canal. The G.J.C.C. was called upon to fulfil its obligations.

The canal company replied that they could not make a navigable cut to Northampton, 'it having been ascertained beyond the possibility of doubt that sufficient Water cannot be procured to supply and maintain the same'. In support of their water—rail proposal they quoted a section in the Act (33 Geo III c80), which said that 'Rollers, Inclined Planes Railways Waggon ways or Cranes' shall be 'considered as part or parts of the said Canal or Collateral Cuts in like manner as if such place or places had been made navigable anything herein before contained to the contrary thereof in any wise notwithstanding'. This—if it meant anything at all—meant that a railway was a canal! The commissioners called in Charles Handley, engineer of the Warwick & Napton Canal, & John Snape, a surveyor of many midland canal routes, to prove that a water supply could be provided. In 1803, in some desperation, they accepted that one mile of the link could be by railroad, but offered the G.J.C.C. double rates if the whole link was navigable. Meantime the river works needed repair and tolls remained low, the figures for the period 1801–1804 averaging £488.

The G.J.C.C. began construction of a rail—water link but changed their minds and completed the link entirely by rail in 1805. Nene toll receipts rose a little, averaging £626 for the years 1806–9. But neither the commissioners nor the town of Northampton were satisfied, and when in 1809 a Bill was put forward, with strong G.J.C.C. support, to promote the Grand Union Canal, to join the Old Union with the G.J.C. at Norton, the commissioners opposed it, with the backing of the Eastern Division commissioners who (for once) were consulted. The commissioners reckoned that if this proposal succeeded it would put paid to any hope of the Old Union reviving their plan for a Northampton branch. Concerned at this opposition, the Grand Junction company offered to meet the commissioners, 'with the firmest expectation . . . that a Collateral Cut will be substituted for the Railway'. The commissioners played cautiously and did not withdraw their opposition until the G.J.C.C. formally agreed to make the water communication within three years. The work, however, did not start until 1812; at last, on 1 May 1815 the branch was opened to Northampton, $4\frac{7}{8}$ miles long, with 17 narrow locks falling 107ft to the Nene. Benjamin Bevan superintended the work, which cost something over £35,000.

There was, however, no dramatic increase in tolls on the Nene. The 1816 figure was £759; in 1817 it reached £847. In the following year it was reported that canal boats were causing great damage to the navigation, 'they being not constructed to fit the locks which causes nearly double the ware with the same quantity of goods and also requires very considerably more water to the great Injury of all the Mills'. The commissioners ordered that the G.J.C. boats should not navigate the river, cargoes proceeding downstream having to be transferred to the customary barges. 6d a ton was added to goods and coals as an extra toll for using the river. An indication of the damage was the bill for repairs in 1818: £1,332, well in excess of the toll receipts of £1,045. Tolls continued to average about £1,000 for the next few years.[16]

In 1825 the Western commissioners asked William Thompson, the G.J.C.'s northern district engineer, to survey the river.

He found the locks badly constructed and in poor condition, and recommended that a surveyor be appointed 'that understands something of the management of canals', that carpenters and bricklayers should be employed full-time, a repair yard set up and all materials book-entered. His report was accepted; a committee of management was formed and Joseph Aris appointed surveyor at £100pa. Aris bought a boat for £36, examined the locks on the Eastern Division, and resigned in 1827, being succeeded by Benjamin Bevan junior. Matters improved somewhat for a time. Bevan had the order banning G.J.C. boats from the river rescinded, and from 1827 to 1836 tolls collected at Northampton ranged between £1,300 and £1,800. Only about £200 a year was collected elsewhere on the Division, indicating that there was little traffic apart from that originating from or feeding the G.J.C., although in 1835 a special toll reduction was allowed for the transport of 1,000 tons of stone and 400 tons of timber from Wisbech for the building of Northampton lunatic asylum. In 1838 the poor condition of the river below Peterborough was blamed for a falling-off in through trade; the commissioners complained to the mayor of Wisbech and sent Bevan as observer to a meeting in 1840 to consider Rennie's report on improvements to the lower navigation.[17]

Both the Western and Eastern commissioners assented to the London & Birmingham Railway Company's proposals for a line from Blisworth to Peterborough, having had clauses protecting the navigation inserted in the Bill. The railway obtained its Act in 1843 and the Western Division profited for a time from the carriage of materials for the line. However, when the railway opened in 1845 the Nene trade began to suffer; to compete, tolls on coal and all goods except corn were reduced by half in 1847 and the Eastern Division was urged to do likewise.[18]

The Eastern Division commissioners had tried in 1830 to get a firmer grip on the running of their navigation. They had the river inspected and ordered that by-laws drawn up in 1808 be put into effect. W. T. Squire had sold his interest in the Peterborough—Oundle stretch to Samuel Staniforth, who undertook some improvements at Wansford in 1834, including replacing the staunch by a lock. The commissioners appointed John Siddons as overseer for this length in 1834; he took over responsibility for the whole Division 9 years later. Staniforth was succeeded as proprietor by Thomas Atkinson, who rebuilt many of the staunches but was accused of doing damage by digging holes and making matters at Wansford worse than they were before. Atkinson seemed more concerned with the state of the river than some of his predecessors and protested strongly to the Midland Railway about their bridge above Peterborough for the Syston—Peterborough branch which rendered the navigation 'at all times most dangerous and difficult'. But he was remiss about producing documents and slow in paying bills.[19]

From time to time the commissioners took opinion as to whether they had the powers to act as Commissioners of Sewers and thus take action about problems of drainage. The answer being in the negative, the problems remained—and they were very serious ones. Floods were frequent and extensive. On 12 December 1848, a public meeting of landed proprietors was held at the George Hotel, Northampton, to hear a report on the subject by the Revd Charles Henry Hartshorne.[20] He described the current situation as follows:

> For the last several weeks the whole portion of the lowlands adjoining the river from Kislingbury to Peterborough, and a great portion of the valley from Northampton upwards, to the north-east, has been subjected to a perpetual overflow and impounding of the waters. The superficial breadth of water thus standing out of the Nene . . . has varied from one to two miles, covering . . . from 8,000 to 10,000 acres.

The lands near the river were only of use to farmers for half the year, and the annual loss was estimated at between £6,000 and £10,000. The river flooded more quickly than previously because local drainage works had brought excess water into the river more speedily but nothing had been done to carry off this increase. Hartshorne also referred to the unhealthiness of Northampton: 'one of six places in England which presents the lowest proportion of persons living to one death'. A letter from Dr A. Robertson, included with the report, referred to 'miasmata' caused by continual floods, and the common Northamptonshire diseases of 'scrofula . . . disorders of the alimentary canal and of the liver, and also rheumatics, acute and chronic . . . aggravated certainly, if not altogether caused, by the continual cold and damp'. Hartshorne referred to the 1633 Commission of Sewers, which had ordered the river to be cleansed and scoured, obstructions to be removed and the river widened 'to its ancient breadth'. Surveys in the early nineteenth century had revealed far greater height of water at the mills than this commission had permitted, and a survey by John Siddons and his son George in 1848 condemned the effect of the staunches in particular for holding up the water. The millers were also much to blame for putting flash boards on the weirs and using other methods to increase the height of water above their mills, until every mill acted like a lock. But 'there can be no dispute', concluded Hartshorne, 'as to where the great obstruction lies in carrying away the waters of the Nene. Mr Yeoman, in 1769, Mr Utting, in 1771, Sir John Rennie, in 1836, and Mr Robert Stephenson, in 1847 (confirmed at a public meeting at Wisbeach, in 1847) have all agreed that no permanent good can be accomplished until the impediments at Wisbeach are entirely removed'.

The meeting elected a committee on Nene drainage, including the Marquis of Northampton, Lords Fitzwilliam, Spencer, Aboyne and Lilford, Hartshorne, Tycho Wing, Atkinson and Yorke of the Eastern Division, and several others. The committee quickly organized its forces, bringing in representatives of the Bedford Level Corporation, the corporation of Wisbech and the interested railway companies. The engineer James Rendel was asked to survey the river and make a report.and in 1851 a figure of £120,000 was quoted as necessary for the proposed works below Peterborough. The Wisbech representatives wanted to defer action and withdrew from the committee when this was refused. Peterborough, however, promised support and £1,000, and with the assent of the Eastern and Western commissioners the Nene Valley Drainage and Improvement Act was passed in 1852.[21]

From Peterborough to the Wash

It is now necessary to look at the history of the Nene below Peterborough. After the diversion of the waters of the Great Ouse to Lynn, the Wisbech outfall rapidly decayed. The original northern branch of the Nene took a wandering course north-eastward of Peterborough, passing close to Crowland and Tydd St Giles, to meet the combined outfall at Tydd Gote. A southern branch took roughly the direction of what is now called the Old Nene to join Well Creek. In the 1470s (he ceased to be Bishop of Ely in 1476) Bishop Morton constructed his leám from Peterborough through Guyhirne to Wisbech, a straight cut, 40ft wide by 4ft deep for navigation and for providing an outlet for the upland waters. In 1570, Morton's Leam was enlarged and, according to Dugdale, it was further improved before 1631.

From the late sixteenth century, Commissions of Sewers had been concerned about the Nene outfall. A new cut had been made during that century, but in 1621 a jury declared that it was defective, 'the river silted up and no water passing that way'. A sluice had been begun at the Horseshoe below Wisbech, but work on this stopped in 1615 through lack of funds. In 1631, the 14 Adventurers, headed by the earls of Bedford and Bolingbroke and including Sir Philibert Vernatti, began work on the outfall. They completed the Horseshoe sluice, the top of which formed a new highway between Norfolk and Cambridgeshire, constructed roads, and demolished houses built on the river embankment to enable the outfall to be improved. By 1636 their work was nearly finished, but it was halted by the political disturbances and not completed until about 1649, under the direction of Vermuyden who also improved Morton's Leam. In the interim the conservators built Piccadilly Hall on the Norfolk bank, to match White Hall on the other side: 'This home of toads and reptiles was changed to gardens and quaint mazes, the oozy marsh to odorous woodland, pools to cascades, swamps to bowling greens and pleasant pastures . . . Alas, the Hall! the haunt of moonlight revellers, of it no memory remains.'[22]

A major improvement to the river between Peterborough and

Guyhirne was the cutting of a new leam in 1728 by the Bedford Level Corporation. Called Smith's Leam, after Humphrey Smith, one of the conservators, who directed the work, it was an extension of Hill's Cut at Peterborough, made earlier by Vermuyden. It is the present main channel of the river. There was also an attempt by the North Level commissioners to improve the outfall. The river then ended about four miles below Wisbech: thence there was a tortuous shifting channel through salt marshes, making pilotage essential and navigation for all but small vessels very dangerous and sometimes impossible. Nathaniel Kinderley proposed to cut an entirely new channel; the work began in 1721 with the support of Wisbech corporation, but that body changed its mind, moved to opposition and destroyed the works 'when there remained little to do to complete them, save making a Dam across the Neck of the old Channel, to turn the Water into the New'.[23] There was no further action until 1773, in which year Kinderley's Cut was completed, with an immediate improvement in the depth of water at Wisbech. But the cut was made too short for the improvement to be permanent.

The problems of the Nene below Peterborough were referred to a succession of distinguished engineers in the later eighteenth century. John Smeaton reported on the outfall and the drainage of the North Level in 1768; his estimate for a solution was £20,695. In 1769 Thomas Yeoman recommended a navigable sluice above Guyhirne and a side cut through Wisbech. Langley Edwards reported on the outfall in 1771, and James Golborne on the drainage and navigation between Peterborough and Wisbech in 1783. The situation in the early nineteenth century was that ships carrying up to 100 tons of coal had to transfer their cargoes into barges or lighters at Sutton Washway for carriage up river; likewise grain had to be so transhipped for export. 29,242 tons were handled at Wisbech in 1805, with a gradual increase to 38,995 ten years later.[24]

In 1814 John Rennie made his first report to the Bedford Level Corporation on an outfall cut, which included a somewhat hesitantly expressed recommendation for a straight cut some $3\frac{1}{2}$ miles long by-passing Wisbech on the north side, with the passage through Wisbech controlled by flood-gates and a lock. Wisbech corporation disagreed with his proposals and called on Thomas Telford for his opinion. Telford's report (1821) confirmed Rennie's views on the outfall, but preferred widening and straightening the course of the river through Wisbech, involving the demolition of a number of properties, and constructing a short straight cut below the town to the Horseshoe Corner, where Rennie's by-pass would also have terminated. Telford's scheme was also rejected by Wisbech; for a few more years the situation continued to deteriorate. In 1822 Telford and Sir John Rennie were asked for revised plans; Wisbech continued to show suspicion, if not hostility, but on the basis of these plans an Act was obtained in 1827. An Act was also obtained for the construction of the Cross Keys bridge across Sutton Wash. Wisbech came into line at last, agreeing to pay £30,000 towards the expenses of the new cut. Lands benefiting from the improved drainage were to be taxed to finance the undertaking, but navigation of the cut was to be free.[25]

The Act appointed commissioners for the Nene Outfall, of whom William George Adam, the Duke of Bedford's agent, was the first chairman. Telford and Rennie were appointed engineers for the cut, and Telford for Cross Keys Bridge. Joliffe & Banks were the contractors, and quoted £110,000 for the new channel. Work soon began; during construction the contractors found it necessary to alter the line, which they did for no extra cost, the revised line coinciding with that originally proposed by Telford and Rennie but rejected as too expensive. The channel was opened in 1830; at first, the tides deposited silt in the new channel, but when the old one was dammed the tidal scour proved greater than had been anticipated. Vast quantities of stone, some from Wansford and some from Yorkshire, were needed to stabilize the banks.[26]

In 1831 the channel was reported as completed, two years earlier than the Act required. The commissioners praised everybody, especially the contractors, the resident engineer, William Swansborough, and John Pear, who superintended the stoning of the banks. Joliffe & Banks presented their account for £149,259 12s 1d. There were complaints about the flow of water at the bridge, which hindered navigation until it was replaced in 1850. Otherwise all was well—except that the commissioners had to borrow £145,000 on mortgage of taxes and had insufficient funds for salaries or maintenance.[27]

One further improvement below Wisbech was Woodhouse Marsh Cut, known as Paupers' Cut as one of its purposes was to employ labourers thrown on the Poor Rate. The other was to align the river above Kinderley's Cut. Work was done in fits and starts between 1827–9; then it was left unfinished, having cost between £2–3,000. In 1830 Wisbech corporation decided to finish it. The contractor spent £1,000 and then abandoned work 'in despair', being apparently unable to waterproof the dam cutting off the old channel. In 1832 another effort was made, when stone from Wansford en route for the outfall was diverted to be used for the dam. A storm blew up and the superintendent went home. A few workmen, however, stayed on, working furiously: within two hours the dam was completed and the water forced into the new channel—which two vessels navigated at once.[28]

11. Telford and Rennie certify the completion of the Nene's New Outfall Cut in 1834

Total expenditure, including land purchase and engineers' fees, on the Outfall Cut was £200,716. The lower part of it was called Tycho Wing's Channel, in honour of that gentleman, vice-chairman of the commissioners and an agent of the Duke of Bedford, who was one of its chief proponents. Its effect on the prosperity of Wisbech is clear from the figures of tonnage handled at the port:[29]

1830:	63,180
1835:	92,844

1840:   109,885
1845:   159,678

There was further development at Sutton Bridge, as the hamlet which grew up by the new bridge was called. The embankment, nearly two miles long, across the old Sutton Washway carried a turnpike road, which was realigned when the first oak bridge with movable centre span of iron was replaced by the iron bridge designed by Robert Stephenson and erected about 100ft to the south in 1850. The present bridge, built as a road and rail swing bridge in the 1890s by the Midland and Great Northern railway companies, stands a further 100ft to the south. The railway track was replaced by a second carriageway in 1963.[30]

The improved outfall and the increase of trade at Wisbech drew attention to the condition of the river in the town itself. In 1836 Sir John Rennie recommended the removal of the stone bridge and the adjoining houses in order to double the sectional area of the river. He proposed improvements to permit vessels drawing 7ft to navigate up to Peterborough, and a back cut in Wisbech to avoid the S-bend which the Nene took through the town. Robert Stephenson and the Eastern Counties Railway, which opened its Wisbech branch in 1847, also supported the back cut, and there were proposals for new docks and the conversion of the existing channel into a locked harbour. The back cut scheme was abandoned during parliamentary proceedings, at about the same time as 40ft of the river wall on South Brink fell into the water.[31] There was a packet twice weekly to and from Peterborough[32] and communication to Lynn was possible via the Wisbech Canal, but the port's prosperity was being threatened by the development of railways. In 1851 the corporation agreed to the proposed Nene Valley Bill for Drainage and Improvement, although fearing that the navigation interest would be subordinated to drainage and that the six commissioners they were allowed would be too few to carry sufficient weight.[33]

Drainage & Navigation

The 1852 Act[34] appointed incorporated commissioners with

wide powers to control and improve the river; it divided the river into two Divisions, the upper from Kislingbury to Bevis Hall, above Wisbech, and the lower from thence to the Nor-folk—Cambridge boundary. Then it stipulated three naviga-tion divisions: Northampton—Thrapston, Thrapston—Peterborough, and Peterborough—Bevis Hall. The com-missioners were elected to represent three districts—there is no need to go further to show the possibilities for chaos and confu-sion. Rendel was appointed engineer, and until his death in 1856 he struggled with what proved a mostly impossible task. George Day, solicitor to the promoters of the Bill, gave a gra-phic account of the navigation of the river in 1852. Between Northampton and Peterborough there were 33 watermills, 11 staunches and 34 locks, the staunches providing dangers and delays and being very difficult to work. Every waterman had to pay 4s 6d a ton to use the river and to undergo 'this laborious, and I will say, not merely Chinese but positively barbarous mode of proceeding. The watermen . . . have to borrow from each other the horses, to enable them to drag along through these staunches . . . but now the water is so little used they can seldom find any parties to borrow from . . .'. Between Peter-borough and Wisbech the navigation 'was in a most wretched state' with boats drawing 3ft constantly detained by shoals at Dog-in-a-Doublet (where the Thorney River left the Nene to supply the Duke of Bedford's estate at Thorney with fresh water). A waterman said he had cooked his meal on the river bed while so detained. To get up to Peterborough when there was insufficient water they had to 'sink a boat or two across the river, and they then put tarpaulin in front; stuff it by the sides, put the deck-boards here and there, and get two or three poor little boys, naked, to go into the river and stuff up the sides, that the water may not escape. They then get water from Wood-stone Stanch, hold it up between that point and the stanch at Peterborough, and so get on to the town.'[35]

The commissioners paid £3,769 for the old Western naviga-tion and £3,750 to Atkinson for what seems to have been the whole Eastern Division.[36] Rendel began a major dredging and embanking programme, estimated to cost £124,800. George

Siddons, of the old Eastern Division, was appointed superintendent of the navigation at £150pa. An amending Act was needed in 1854 to raise money and the commissioners were permitted to borrow up to £325,000 on mortgage of all receipts. Wisbech was also required to increase its contribution. A new swinging bridge was to be built in the town, replacing the elegant but narrow stone bridge that formed a bottleneck for both traffic going over it and water passing underneath. The new iron bridge, made by Armstrong & Co of Newcastle, took three years to construct; it had a tower of corrugated iron on the south side housing the machinery which operated by hydraulic pressure. It was tested once, a week before the official opening, and swung but, in the words of F. J. Gardiner, historian of Wisbech, 'it is doubtful whether any other attempt was made to swing this ponderous and ugly structure'. In later years the machinery and balancing portion of the bridge were removed.

In the mid-1850s bitter disputes arose between Wisbech corporation and the incorporated commissioners, the corporation alleging that the commissioners were not doing the works in the order prescribed by the Act and were favouring the upper division. Matters came to a head soon after John Fowler succeeded Rendel as engineer. Two dams were built across the river above Wisbech, one at Waldersea, the other at Guyhirne, the first with two openings and the other with only one, a draw-door 13ft wide. Below the new bridge in the town a submerged weir was made, with a pair of check-gates, to contract the flow of water to what it was in the time of the previous bridge. This weir was notorious as the 'throttle'; Fowler placed it there as a temporary measure to save the banks above it and guard against floods. These obstructions caused a great accumulation of silt below the bridge; they were said to threaten the trade of the port and to increase the danger of flooding should there be a wet season. Arguments raged and tempers rose; one Wisbech councillor expressed the locally popular view that they should 'clear away the dams and then put all the lawyers and engineers into a boat on the river and send them to the bottom'. The commissioners as a whole, and the Bedford interest in particular

which had a vested interest in the exclusion of salt water from
the Thorney estates and was headed by the Duke's agent,
Robert Mein, were attacked by Wisbech, the corporation peti-
tioning the Admiralty to order the removal of the dams and
throttle. The Admiralty report criticized the commissioners for
failing to observe the provisions of the Act, but said that the
dams and throttle should remain until precautions against
floods were taken or the lower division works were completed. If
the works were not completed, Wisbech corporation should
bring proof of obstruction before two magistrates, under clause
145 of the Act.

In January 1859, this was done. The case was heard on 22 and
27 January; Mr Webster QC, for the commissioners, blamed
providence for the present state of things, went through the 1852
Act, spoke for 4½ hours and 'concluded, having exhausted, if not
the subject, at least all interest in it'. The magistrates ordered
the removal of the dam at Waldersea at the commissioners'
expense. Within a couple of hours of the verdict, groups of men
were seen heading towards Waldersea and during the night the
greater part of the dam was destroyed. Various persons were
later brought before the magistrates for feloniously removing
the dam; many of them said they had been paid by collecting a
few shillings placed on a table in the New Bell, but no one knew
who put it there. The defendants were bound over. The commissioners pursued the case into the Court of Chancery, where
they lost it. An order was made for the removal of Guyhirne
dam, and the remains of Waldersea. Then, following an accident involving a gang of lighters, the throttle was removed on
the advice of the engineer Thomas Page. The Battle of the
Dams was over: the commissioners had lost.[37]

The River since 1862

Almost £200,000 was raised and spent in obtaining the Acts of
1852 and 1854 and performing the works under them. None of
this went on the river above Peterborough. As for the rest, it was
said in 1881 that 'notwithstanding the large expenditure of
money, considerable portions of the banks and bed of the River
from Peterborough downwards to Dog-in-a-Doublet bridge (a

distance of little more than 5 miles) are in the same condition as they were before the Act of 1852, or probably in a worse state'.[38] After the fiasco of the dams there was little the incorporated commissioners could do, especially as they found the financial situation impossible. So a further Act[39]—known as the Nene Valley Act—was obtained in 1862, which halted the works, dissolved the incorporated commission, and set up separate navigation commissioners for the third division. Whatever they may have intended to do to improve the river was frustrated by a perpetual injunction obtained by the Duke of Bedford in 1865, restraining the commissioners from placing a staunch or dam in the Nene near Dog-in-a-Doublet and from interfering with the shoal or hard called Northey Gravel, which, together with a sluice, kept the salt water out of the Thorney River.

Some idea of the pattern of trade at this time can be gained from the Peterborough toll collector's account book for 1863, which shows 275 vessels paying toll at Peterborough in six months, of which 144 came from Whittlesea, 25 from Wansford, 2 from King's Lynn, 2 from Brandon, 1 from Oundle and 1 from Wisbech. Tolls for that year were £745; the highest figure in the next 50 years was £898 in 1897 and the lowest £175 in 1909. With little money to spend, and little to spend it on as major improvements were out of the question, the commissioners had no more to do than argue with railway companies about bridges and the abstraction of water.

In 1880, however, they presented a memorial to the Board of Trade and the Duke of Bedford for the removal of the injunction. At this time work was in progress on a large dock at Sutton Bridge, designed to enclose 13 acres of water, entered by a lock 200ft long × 50ft wide. The Sutton Bridge Dock Company had the Marquis of Huntly as chairman and directors representing the Great Northern Railway and English Bros, a large firm of timber merchants. The dock was intended to cope with ships too big to reach Wisbech, and also to draw off Wisbech trade. Three coal staithes were planned and railway sidings constructed. On 14 May 1881, English Bros' *Garland* entered the dock with a cargo of pitch pine from Norway, while a band played 'Rule Britannia'. Other vessels used the dock in the next few weeks, but on 9 June 1881, 20 days before the planned official opening, the silt on the sides of the lock began to subside. This soon led to movement of silt from under the basin, and within a few days most of the west side of the dock wall collapsed. Repairs were estimated to cost up to £160,000, about the same amount as had been spent. The money was not forthcoming, and golf is now played on the site of the basin.[40] Needless to say, the Nene third district commissioners did not succeed with their memorial.

In the second district matters flourished no better. The commissioners borrowed large sums of money from Lord Overstone on the security of the taxes of drained lands, the loan amounting in 1880 to £59,000. Between 1862 and 1880 tolls produced an average of £360pa, while taxes brought in about £3,760pa. The cost of repairs ranged between £700 and £2,000 a year. Navigation was more of a liability than anything else, but George Siddons carried on as surveyor, doing whatever he could to keep the river open. In 1880 his son John joined him as deputy, without expense to the commissioners, taking over from his father a few years later. In 1892 John Siddons reported to the commissioners on the reduction of traffic. It was five years since the last coal boat called at West Biddles & Co at Northampton, as a siding had been opened at Billing and the coal was taken by rail; previously there had been a trade of 500 tons per annum. He proposed reducing the tolls from Wellingborough to Northampton from 6d a ton to 4d, to compete with the railway. The timber trade from Wisbech to Northampton had stopped, the Elton gravel pits had closed and there was little traffic in stone. The lighter trade to Peterborough from Yarwell, Waternewton and Cotterstock had been discontinued. It sometimes took a day for a boat to pass from a staunch to the lock above. The old watermills were closing down, losing their trade to the steam roller mills at Wellingborough and Peterborough. W. Cornwell's gang of lighters had been carried away in floods and stranded in a meadow. It was a gloomy picture.[41]

Having studied the evidence, the royal commission of 1909 concluded that 'The Nene, from Northampton to Wisbech is navigable with difficulty, where the water is sufficient, by barges of the smallest size; but sometimes navigation even by such barges is for weeks impracticable in some parts of the river'. Below Peterborough it was described as 'virtually derelict'. Of the second district the chairman of the commissioners said: 'You see we must dredge to maintain the drainage, and if we have a dredger we must have proper locks for working that dredger, and, therefore, we must maintain the locks simply for the purpose of maintaining the dredger. At the same time, the river is open for navigation, if navigation would only come.' A little did come; about 7,000 tons a year to Whitworth's mill at Wellingborough in canal boats off the G.J.C., but in 1920 it took a small motor launch a week to cover the 65 miles from Peterborough to Northampton, it having to be dragged overland in places. Lighters with stone fought their way downstream from Wansford into the third district from time to time.

Following the Land Drainage Act of 1930 the Nene Catchment Board took over the river, although the commissioners continued in existence for several more years. The Board found the river 'in unparalleled decay and dilapidation'. The locks and sluices were beyond repair and the river through Wisbech was in very poor condition. Under its energetic chairman, George Dallas, the Board rebuilt all the locks, some of them to replace the staunches which were all removed. A large sluice and lock was built at Dog-in-a-Doublet (as had been suggested in the nineteenth century by various engineers, and opposed by as many), to separate the salt and fresh water and to conserve water in drought. An alternative method of fresh water supply was arranged for Thorney, the Thorney River being closed to navigation, and the Northey Gravels dynamited, giving the river a depth of 10ft. At Wisbech, both banks were piled for two miles and the Board built a new quay for the corporation. In all it was a remarkable achievement on the part of the Board and H. W. Clark, its engineer, proved by the fact that in the floods of 1947, in the words of a government report, 'the new works stood the test of the great flood splendidly. There was no inundation of any consequence from the River Nene.'[42]

With the Catchment Board's improvements to the upper river, some regular traffic returned. From the late 1930s until

1969, Whitworth's mill at Wellingborough was supplied with foreign wheat via London Docks, Brentford and the Grand Union Canal, carried in narrow boats belonging to the Grand Union Carrying Company, the North Road Canal Company, Fellows, Morton & Clayton, and Willow Wren. British Transport Waterways took over the trade after nationalization, and then Willow Wren continued it until they ran into financial difficulties. The annual average was some 7,500 tons.[43] At Wansford, the Nene Barge & Lighter Company was founded in 1946, buying lighters and a tug from A.V. Jackson. This was (and is) a quarrying company, and used the lighters to transport stone for the Catchment Board and the later River Authority. It still runs one steel motor barge, with a capacity of 65 tons, which carries stone to Guyhirne and the lighthouses at the Outfall once or twice a week.

On the lower river, the Thames barges *Thyra, Alan* and *Pudge* traded to Cadge & Colman's mill at Peterborough with wheat between 1953 and 1965. *Thyra* was the most frequent visitor; she traded from the Thames and the Humber to Peterborough until she was sold in 1966. The annual tonnage averaged 4,800. Peterborough, however, has not yet been developed into the inland port that has been envisaged from time to time and there is now no commercial river traffic. The port of Wisbech can take ships up to 240ft in length and drawing 14ft (in spring tides) and handles in all over 300 vessels a year; imports, mainly of petroleum, timber and potash, greatly exceeding exports, and averaging 174,000 tons over the years 1969–73.[44]

Pleasure traffic on the river has increased greatly in recent years, but not to the same extent as on the Great Ouse. Scenically the Nene is a very pleasant river between Northampton and Peterborough, though the guillotine gates make for hard work. Many of the old mills still survive, converted to other uses: Billing mill is now a museum and Barnwell is a restaurant. The river is now in the jurisdiction of the Welland & Nene River Division of the Anglian Water Authority.

Middle Level Navigations

In Vermuyden's *Discourse Touching the Draining of the Great*

Fennes, published in 1642, he laid out the principles and programme he intended to pursue. He proposed to divide the
Great Level into three parts:

1. The one from Glean [Glen] to Morton's Leam.
2. From Morton's Leam to Bedford River.
3. From Bedford River southwards, being the remainder of
   the Level.

These became known as the North, Middle and South
Levels, and were later to have their own commissioners
appointed to them.[45]

Little was done until the 'Pretended Act' of 1649. Then under
Vermuyden's direction work recommenced in the Middle
Level; within two years several major works were completed,
including the New Bedford (or Hundred Foot) River, parallel
to the Old Bedford, cut by Vermuyden in 1631, the Forty Foot
(or Vermuyden's) from Ramsey to the Old Bedford at Welches
Dam, the Sixteen Foot from Well Creek to the Forty Foot, to
drain the area around Chatteris, and several other shorter
drains. Popham's Eau was restored, and Bevill's Leam, cut in
1631, was extended by the Twenty Foot River to join the Old
Nene a mile from the junction with Popham's Eau. In addition
to Vermuyden's cuts, the Level included the channels of Well
Creek, most of which was an old natural waterway, the Old
Nene (some 26 miles of it), and King's Dyke and Whittlesey
Dyke, old artificial waterways from Stanground to the Old
Nene at Flood's Ferry. Access from the Nene was via a sluice at
Stanground and from the Ouse through a sluice at Salter's
Lode at the end of Well Creek. Another sluice at Welches Dam
led to the Old Bedford. In later years a further connection was
made with the Nene with the opening of the Wisbech Canal.[46]

Care was taken to regulate the water levels in the Middle
Level for the convenience of navigation, although details showing the extent of its usage, especially in earlier years, are lack-
ing. There were four meres in the Level; Whittlesey, Ramsey,
Ugg and Benwick. Whittlesey Mere, by far the largest, was,
although sometimes dangerous, popular for pleasure boating.

Celia Fiennes described it in 1697:

> . . . is 3 miles broad and six miles long, in the midst is a little island where a great store of Wildfowle breeds, there is no coming near it in a mile or two, the ground is all wett and marshy but there are severall little Channells runs into it by which boats people go up to this place; when you enter the mouth of the Mer it looks formidable and its often very dangerous by reason of sudden winds that will rise like Hurricanes in the Mer, but at other times people boat it round the Mer with pleasure.

In 1754 an Act was obtained for improving and preserving the navigation 'from Salter's Load Sluice to Standground Sluice . . . and from Flood's Ferry . . . to Ramsey High Load . . . and also the Navigation from Old Bedford Sluice . . . to the River Nene . . .'[47] This Act appointed commissioners for managing the navigation as detailed in the title, empowered to levy tolls of 3d a ton, or equivalent, on goods entering the system at any of the sluices. The only exemptions were for pleasure boats, and manures and compost, malt dust, pigeons' dung and oil cake, unless it was made of linseed. Agricultural produce moved through the Middle Level towards Lynn, and coal, timber and groceries came back in return.

The third Earl of Orford's *Journal of the Voyage round the Fens in 1774*[48] gives a graphic picture of the Middle Level and connecting waterways at that time. The 'Fleet' of which he was 'Admiral' consisted of four 'Sail of the Line', three tenders, a bumketch and a victualler; however, the whole lot could be towed by a fen horse called the Hippopotamus when there was insufficient wind for sailing. Bridges too low for the fleet were jacked up or removed by carpenters; a demand by a fenman near March for fourpence for hauling on the bank was treated with contempt. The party fished, observed the wildlife and agriculture, took trips ashore and enjoyed sailing races on Whittlesey Mere, where they met Lord Sandwich, then First Lord of the Admiralty. Lord Orford commented on the handsome girls of Ramsey and the ugly women of Upwell, Outwell and March, ascribing this to the settlement in the area of a colony of Dutch at the time of the Revolution, 'which accounted for the squat shape, flat nose, round unmeaning face which prevails among the inhabitants'. But the *Journal* mentions only one gang of lighters, which delayed their exit from Salter's Lode, in the 22 days of the expedition. That there was no great commercial use of the system at this time is corroborated by the figure for 1776 of 25 passages a year up the Old Bedford and Well Creek by lighter gangs, with an average toll of £4 a voyage.[49]

The opening of the Wisbech Canal in 1796, along the line of the old Wellstream, in effect restored a missing element in the Ouse—Nene system. The canal joined Well Creek at Outwell, where the Old Nene also joins the Creek (although the Old Nene from Marmont Priory lock to Outwell is sometimes regarded as part of Well Creek). The eastern part of Well Creek, approaching Salter's Lode, takes the line of an early sixteenth-century drainage channel, the New Podyke. With the opening of the canal, the pattern of the navigations between Ouse and Nene was almost completed, although further drainage channels were cut in the nineteenth century.

The 1754 Act, although it legally established the Middle Level as a navigable system, left many problems behind it, one in particular being a clause restricting the use of a relief cut called Tong's Drain until an order in writing had been signed by ten commissioners; this ensured that flood relief could not be given until the damage had been done. Moreover there was inadequate provision for fund-raising for drainage works. In 1810 the Middle Level Act[50] was obtained; this transferred control of the waterways from the Bedford Level Corporation to commissioners who were, by statute, local landowners. Funds were provided by levying a rate on all land subject to taxation under the Eau Brink Acts. Between 1824 and 1837 the sluices and bridges at Stanground, Salter's Lode, Welches Dam and the northern end of the Old Bedford were rebuilt under the superintendence of Mr Dyson.[51] Further nineteenth-century Acts gave the commissioners additional powers, but in practice the Middle Level ceased to be part of the Bedford Level Corporation after 1810, although it was not fully incorporated into a separate commission until 1862.

The principal towns and villages in the Middle Level area are March, on the Old Nene, Whittlesey, the twin villages of Upwell and Outwell, Ramsey, Chatteris and Benwick. March was a small port in Tudor times, with 8 boats working in the coal and grain trades.[52] Before the first railway arrived—the Ely—Peterborough line in 1846—the river was of great import-ance to the town's trade. But March quickly developed into a major railway centre with branch lines to Wisbech and St Ives, previously served by waterborne traffic, and in 1867 a line was opened to Spalding and thence to the north of England. By 1921, nearly a quarter of the working male population in March was employed by the railway, perhaps the highest proportion in the country.[53] As they drew traffic off the waterways the rail-ways benefited the Middle Level commissioners; fewer boats meant less damage to the banks, and livestock were no longer walked along the tops of the banks but travelled by train. On the security of the banks depended the security of the farmland from flooding.

Of the other towns and villages, Whittlesey made use of its Dyke and connecting navigations for transport of agricultural produce and, in the late nineteenth and early twentieth cen-turies, the export of bricks—sometimes loaded into the lighters while still hot with consequent risk of melting the pitch on the timbers. At Benwick, Chatteris, Outwell and Holme, railway transhipment depots were set up, to serve as collecting points for agricultural produce from the fenland farms. Fuel for the many pumping stations, both coal and oil, was delivered to these depots by rail and taken onwards by lighter; many farms and pumping stations were indeed only accessible by water until well into this century. The depot at Outwell continued to be used until the early 1950s, but the others were closed before the Second World War.

Under the Middle Level Act of 1844,[54] only obtained after much discussion and argument, Marmont Priory sluice was built to enable vessels of 4ft draught to navigate into and through Upwell and Outwell, and the Middle Level Drain, of which two miles were navigable, was cut from the north end of the Sixteen Foot River to the Eau Brink Cut near St Germans. This scheme, the work of James Walker, gave relief to Salter's Lode and improved conditions generally. As a result, in 1851 it proved possible to drain Whittlesey Mere, putting an end to a long history of boat outings, regattas, and skating matches in winter. The draining of the mere caused considerable subsidence in the adjacent district; between 1848 and 1932 the peat soil in Holme Fen subsided 10ft 8in, measured by the well known Holme Post sunk into the ground in 1848, and it has continued to shrink since.

The Middle Level Drain burst its banks in 1862, flooding about 9 square miles. There were recurring difficulties with this drain—the principal outfall for the Middle Level waters—until the opening of a new pumping station and sluice at St Germans in 1934.[55] In 1862 also the Middle Level commission was finally divorced from the Bedford Level Corporation and incorporated into a separate commission, now with full legal status and responsibility. There was a further Act in 1874, under which the commissioners promulgated by-laws for the navigation, several being framed to protect the locks and sluices from misuse. Navigation between the hours of 10am and 4pm on Sundays and Christmas Day was forbidden and no steam-powered boats were permitted without permission from the commissioners beforehand.[56]

The figures for 1888 show that 44,034 tons were carried on the Middle Level, producing tolls of £733 and a profit of £216 to the commissioners.[57] The 1898 figures give a total of 42,640 tons: this was made up of 2,049 tons of internal traffic, 24,044 tons loaded on the system, 10,057 tons discharged on the system and 6,490 tons of through traffic. By 1905 the total was down to 12,770 tons and the books showed a loss of £702 on the year.[58] The reason for this falling-off was given in a reply by Alderman J. A. Herbert before the Royal Commission on Canals & Waterways:

> The real reason of that is that one of the great railway companies for a number of years 'went one better' than the other railway companies; that is, they paid for the collection of a

very large amount of hay and straw traffic; and, ultimately, when it was found out by the other companies the whole thing collapsed; they all agreed not to do it; and a very large percentage of that hay and straw from that district is not now carried. It was carried to Peterborough to be put on rail at Peterborough.

The poor condition of the Wisbech Canal and the Nene also affected Middle Level traffic, and the commissioners, as A.H. Plowright, engineer to the Nene third district, said in evidence, 'do not encourage navigation to any great extent'. The principal commodities that were being carried included agricultural produce, coal, bricks, highway materials and non-perishable cargoes generally as required. About 40 pumping stations were receiving coal from the Outwell depot at this period.[59] Other freights that continued well into the twentieth century included peat, dug from the Fens and distributed to all the major centres in and around the Middle Level, and later sugarbeet, the last traffic to endure.

The life of a lighterman working through the Middle Level was not an easy one and was made more complicated by the restrictions imposed by the Old Bedford tidal sluice which could only be worked through for about 20 minutes each tide when the water each side made a level. Unloading goods was especially difficult; the high banks of the rivers meant that everything had to be wheelbarrowed to the top. It was not all work, however; at times, chapel congregations visited each other by water. In her book *Fenland Chronicle*, Sybil Marshall, whose father was a lighterman for a time, records the memories of Mrs Edwards, a keen chapelgoer:

One of our members had a little harmonium and he would bring this and put it in the barge. The men erected seats made of planks, resting on gallon beer barrels borrowed from a pub, all around the outside of the boat, and the children sat in the bottom. Then away we went, pulled by a slow and lazy old horse on the towpath, singing all the way . . . I like to think about them evenings, singing, on the barge. I thought it were beautiful then, and I still think so now. The village we went to most was Home. Soon after the trips I remember, the chapel there were pulled down or had big alterations done to it, and while it were rebuilding, they had a floating church made on a big barge, as went up and down the waterways round the district. I know several people alive today as were christened on it when they were babies.

The horses may have been slow, but they knew their job. To start a gang of lighters, a horse would lean on the rope, then pause, then lean again, and so get them moving. A new horse would lunge at it and either stop himself breathing or else fall over. Experienced horses knew exactly when to slacken off the rope before jumping an obstacle on the towpath; they also knew when not to jump and would hop onto the last lighter or the horseboat when approaching an unsurmountable barrier and scramble up the bank again when the boats were through. They also knew the pubs where the lightermen customarily called, and would stop automatically at them, although these became fewer and fewer as traffic diminished.

Throughout the twentieth century trade was progressively lost to railways and then to roads. By the 1920s there was only a handful of regular carriers, of whom Vic, admiral of Jackson's Navy, was the last to give up. He used horses until 1930 and then turned to steam tugs for towing. When he stopped in 1948 there was only the regular sugarbeet traffic to Ely left; this continued for another ten years in the factory's own boats. The little tanker _Shellfen_ carried on supplying oil to pumping stations until 1971, her skipper, Ted Appleyard, having to get out and push her through Well Creek one Christmastime.[60] The Creek itself fell into disuse, but was reopened in 1975 by the Middle Level commissioners with the support of the Well Creek Trust and the Inland Waterways Association. Although pleasure cruising in the Middle Level is something of an acquired taste, it still provides the essential link between the Ouse and Nene. It is hoped that the conflicting interests of drainage, angling (the system is heavily fished) and navigation can be reconciled and that as much of it as is practicable will be kept open for boats.

Wisbech Canal

The Wisbech Canal was conceived in the late eighteenth century as a link between Wisbech and the Old River Nene at Outwell. From here there were alternative routes: south west into the Middle Level Navigations, or south east via Well Creek and Salter's Lode into the Great Ouse below Denver. The principal object was to strengthen the trading importance of Wisbech in relation to Lynn; as the Hon and Revd Charles Lindsay, who became chairman of the canal company, wrote to Lord Hardwicke on 27 July 1792, commenting on the Eau Brink proposals:

> . . . I think it highly probable that in the event of a successful application to Parliament in the present instance the country near Wisbech will not be satisfied without the opening of the old river between Wisbech and Outwell, but this will be a general good and Cambridge in particular would have reason to rejoice of it since a very large supply of oats would be furnished from this country which à six miles land carriage at present greatly interrupts.[61]

A survey was made by John Watté an engineer who had carried out other surveys of fen drainage and cost estimates of the proposals were prepared. After a successful preliminary meeting at Wisbech on 15 October 1792, Charles Lindsay took the chair at a more formal meeting at the Rose and Crown, Wisbech, on 30 October.[62] Although this meeting was intended to be a local gathering, news had travelled fast. To the surprise of the organizers, 'a very great company arrived from Derby, Leicester, Uppingham, Huntingdon, Bedford, etc, whose object seemed mere speculation in shares, others appeared to have trade for their object'. After some difficulty, the local interest succeeded in fighting off what amounted to a takeover bid but had to agree to giving the visitors preference over all other 'strangers' in the event of a subscription being raised. A committee was appointed, consisting of equal numbers of 'strangers and people at home'.[63] The meeting agreed not to oppose or interfere with the Eau Brink proposals. The Corporation of the Bedford Level were to be approached for permission to open up the old river—

the Well Stream, on the course of which the canal was to be constructed. The Bishop of Ely was asked for support. Jonathan Peckover, the local banker, was appointed treasurer, and James Bellamy, solicitor, the clerk to the company.

In due course subscriptions were collected and a parliamentary petition was presented on behalf of the burgesses of Wisbech and others on 24 February 1794.[64] It pointed out that the old river had been filled in and buildings erected upon it and on both sides of it. The petition alleged that Well Creek was in a defective state and therefore this too should have parliamentary authority for its improvement. Supporting petitions were submitted by the merchants and traders of Cambridge and by the University. At the committee stage, evidence was given that the old river had been navigable by small vessels and James Golborne and John Watté testified that the levels and surveys showed that a canal could be constructed. The latter also pointed out that the navigation from Salter's Lode sluice to Stanground sluice was filling up.[65] The Bill had an uneventful passage through both Houses and received the royal assent on 9 May 1794.

The Act provided that the proprietors would be a corporation known as the Wisbech Canal Company. Commissioners were also nominated in the Act, and their meetings were to be held within ten miles of the canal, each commissioner being paid 7s 6d for every attendance. Power was given to raise £14,000 in shares of £105 and a further £6,000 by loans. Any advances made by the proprietors were to receive 5 per cent interest. Authority was given for the demolition of the houses built on the bed of the old river. A complicated and comprehensive schedule of tolls was set out, with power to lease the tolls if desired. An unusual clause was inserted that grain boats going to Lynn or Wisbech were not to be stopped because of any dispute over quantity. A further charge for 'cranage'—the use of the company's crane—of 6d could be levied on goods other than coals. In addition, a toll of 3d was to be paid by all vessels passing into or out of the canal at Outwell in order to provide funds for maintaining the River Nene. For the same purpose, the canal company was empowered to lend money at 5 per cent. Eventually a fund of £800 was to be invested in public stocks for the preservation of the Nene.

The canal was to be 5¼ miles long with a lock at each end and a pair of gates across Popham's Eau to maintain water in the navigation. Provision was to be made for spaces or openings for turning, lying or passing boats. It was intended that the locks should be 100ft long × 14ft deep with a wooden bridge over each. Construction was planned for the summer of 1794, but it was soon realized that the programme was impracticable and the construction of Outwell lock was postponed until 1795. At the same time it was decided to shorten the Wisbech lock to 85ft.

It soon became clear that the original estimate of £14,000 was inadequate, and a further £3,000 had to be raised. Some reductions were made in the proposed tolls to attract trade. By the end of 1795 the Outwell lock, described as a 'pen sluice', was completed and tolls began to be taken at Wisbech from 1 January 1796. Outwell lock was opened by 9 January. For the first four months of operation, tolls at Wisbech produced £127 and at Outwell £7 10s; however, the Outwell figures quickly improved, totalling £341 for the year ending 1 May 1797 as against the Wisbech figure of £212. £81 was taken at Salter's Lode from vessels using Well Creek, which was administered by trustees appointed by the canal company and the Nene commissioners.[66]

The Wisbech Canal cost altogether £16,557 to construct. The problems of its operation became apparent in the very early days when mention was made of the silt being carried into the canal by the waters of the Nene when the Wisbech lock was being used. The throwing of rubbish into the canal by the local inhabitants also caused difficulties. In 1798 the Wisbech lock was damaged by ice and cost £400 to repair. The Company was having trouble with Watté accusing him of miscalculation and negligence and 'that extraordinary expenses were incurred thereby'; they threatened him with legal action but could not provide sufficient evidence for a firm case. Thomas West was appointed engineer and for some years gave the company satisfaction; in 1803 he was rewarded with a gratuity of 5 guineas as his fees were so moderate.[67]

For the years 1798–1800 Wisbech tolls averaged £354 and Outwell tolls £392. Traffic from a wide area was using the canal as a series of penalties imposed at the end of 1798 indicates when Thomas Carter of Ely and Richard Sirdall of Narborough, both watermen, and Sprignell Brown, merchant of Peterborough, were all fined for giving false accounts of the lading of their gangs of lighters navigating through the Wisbech Canal and thereby defrauding the canal company.[68] A few years later there was serious trouble with another lighterman, Thomas Taylor, who was accused of breaking Outwell lock, assaulting the lockkeeper and refusing to pay tolls; he was eventually sentenced to 14 days' imprisonment and fined £2.[69]

In 1807, 'the continued Accretion of silt at the doors of Wisbech sluice' was described as the 'greatest evil' facing the canal company. Tolls, which had risen to a total of over £1,200 in each of the three previous years, in that year dropped to £958, falling in the following year to only £693 when navigation was suspended for a time for scouring of the bottom and repairs to Wisbech lock. Trade gradually recovered in the next decade, although there was a heavy bill for repairs amounting to £1,670 in 1815, following which West was censured for not attending meetings nor producing reports on the defects at Outwell. The repair bill meant that no dividend could be paid in 1817, just after the shareholders had begun to receive the first returns on their investment.[70]

The next 20 years were difficult ones for the canal. A reduction in trade generally combined with the deteriorating condition of the Wisbech end of the waterway brought toll receipts down from £903 in 1818 to £338 in 1822. It was also claimed that the high rates charged by the company were forcing trade from Lynn away from the canal and on to the longer but cheaper route via the Old Nene to Peterborough. Some reductions were made, resulting in a small improvement in receipts for a few years; by 1825 they crawled back over the £600 mark. Shortage of water was becoming a major problem. Dependent on the Nene for its water supply, it was only by the admission of the tides that the navigation could be kept open. The tides carried more silt into the canal, and a stage was reached when only the spring tides could reach the level of the canal—which could therefore only be filled once a fortnight.

New doors were installed at Wisbech lock in 1829 at a cost of £962; again, dividends ceased to be paid. Toll receipts had fallen again to below £300; indeed, in 1831 the company let the tolls for three years to William Sallabank for £280pa. It soon became apparent that the money spent on the new doors had been spent in vain; an entirely new lock was needed, and in 1833 a contract was signed with J. & W. Gathergood for £1,900.[71] But an exceptionally high tide in January 1834 caused great damage to the recently completed new lock and yet more money had to be raised for repairs.

In 1841 began a period of relative prosperity for the Wisbech Canal. The toll on coal was reduced by 2d a ton; this produced an immediate increase in tonnage carried from 3,534 in 1840 to 7,350 in 1841. Receipts rose from £592 to £717. In 1848, perhaps the canal's most successful year of operation, 29,562 tons of coal were carried, receipts totalled £1,589 and a dividend of $5\frac{3}{4}$ per cent was paid.[72]

Haulage on the canal was principally by horses, although in later years steam power was occasionally used. The maximum length of vessels was limited, except when the levels in the river and the canal coincided, by Wisbech lock, rebuilt to 50ft × 13ft. Outwell lock was 97ft × 11ft 6in, though in practice the beam was limited to 10ft 10in. The maximum draught when the canal was full was 3ft 6in. A passenger service operated for a few years preceding 1883—Whybrow's Packet, run by Mr Whybrow of Nordelph. The fare was 2d from Wisbech to Outwell.[73]

The second half of the nineteenth century saw a steady decline in the canal's profitability, as well as continued deterioration in its condition. Railway competition began with the opening of the Wisbech to Magdalen Road branch of the East Anglian Railway in 1848, a line later taken over by the Great Eastern and forming part of a through route from March to King's Lynn. Gradually the coal traffic deserted the canal. In 1883 the Wisbech & Upwell Tramway was opened to Outwell, being completed to Upwell in the following year. This was constructed parallel to the canal for most of its length.[74] In the year the tramway opened, the canal tolls were £412; by 1893 they had fallen to £279 and by 1896 to £164.[75] On the grounds that the traffic was diminishing and that receipts were insufficient to provide for maintenance or yield any profit, the canal company sought in 1903 to obtain a Bill to provide for the closing and sale of the canal. They submitted figures showing their total receipts for 1902 as £86, of which £46 came from tolls. But the borough of Wisbech and other local authorities petitioned against the Bill, declaring that 'the Wisbech Canal has been allowed to become silted through a want of dredging', but that they were not convinced 'that the loss of traffic is due to permanent causes'. They thought that the local authorities should be given the opportunity to consider whether they should take over the canal. They also profited from being able to carry highway materials on the canal free of charge. The Bill was withdrawn, and the company laboured on.[76]

For the last 20 years of trading, the figures tell a sad tale. Only once, in 1911, did tolls top £100. In 1917 they were £9 4s 6d, and in subsequent years as follows:

	£	s	d		£	s	d
1918:	3	11	3	1921:	4	10	0
1919:	3	2	6	1922:		12	6
1920:		17	6				

Vic Jackson took the last load through for Ellis & Everard in 1922: 18 tons of straw.[77] Then on 14 June 1926 on the application of the Isle of Ely County Council a warrant of abandonment was issued by the Ministry of Transport on the grounds that for at least three years previously the canal had not been used.[78]

Under the Wisbech Corporation Act of 1944 the ownership of the canal bed was vested in the corporation.[79] A road has been built on the bed of the canal in the centre of Wisbech. Most of the line of the canal is still discernible beside the Wisbech—Outwell road. Part of Outwell basin has now been cleared with the reopening of Well Creek, which was unnavigable from 1969–75, but the Outwell end of the canal has disappeared beneath the gardens of bungalows.

CHAPTER IX

Welland, Glen
and Bourne Eau

✦

The Welland

'Weland, having its rise near Sibertoft in Northamptonshire, and taken in some petty streamlets, cometh at length to Market Deping, and S James Deping, where it entereth the fens, and burdeneth them with all the water and downfalls of part of Northampton, Leicester, Rutland, and Lincoln shires; whence passing to Croyland bridge, it divideth itself into two branches; the one leading by South Ea towards Wisbeche, the other in a most slow course, to Spalding and Surflet, where receiving the water of Glen, it goeth on to Fosse dyke stow, and so into Boston deep.'

So Dugdale[1] described the Welland, although it no longer flows under the triangular bridge at Crowland and there is no connection with the old South Ea. Work on the Welland, to relieve the Fens of the burden of all the 'water and downfalls' began at a very early date; in the reign of William the Conqueror, Richard de Rulos, Lord of Deeping Fen, is said to have 'excluded the river Welland by a very strong embankment, because every year it had, by its continual inundations, overflowed nearly all the meadows adjoining', and out of the reclaimed land he made 'fertile fields and desirable land' and a pleasure garden.[2] Like that of the other Fenland rivers, the history of the Welland is in great part the story of the battle against floods.

The Stamford Canal
Stamford was the head of navigation on the Welland, which is

Plates 25 & 26   (above) Vic Jackson's gang held up at March on the Middle Level, 1937; (below) the Chain Bridge, Spalding, 1828, from a watercolour by Hilkiah Burgess. This bridge was replaced by Albert Bridge in 1844

Plates 27 & 28 (left) The River Glen, looking E.N.E. from Surfleet towards the junction with the Welland at the top of the picture; (below) *Mistley*, of London, aground in the Welland near Spalding. She was one of the last vessels of any size to call at Spalding

the subject of one of the earlier Acts concerning navigation: 13 Elizabeth I cap 1, 'An Act for making the River of Welland, in the county of Lincoln, navigable from Stamford to the Sea'. This Act gives evidence of the importance of the river in previous years. The preamble states that the prosperity of Stamford had been 'advanced by the navigation of the river Welland' but this had now 'gone to great ruin and decay, from the prejudice done to the navigation, by the erection of mills between Deeping and Stamford, and the consequent diversion of the stream of the river from its ancient course'. The Act gave authority to restore the navigation in either the old channel or the new—the latter presumably meaning the cuts made for the mills. The amount of trade done on the river before 1571 cannot be determined, but Stamford had certainly been a very prosperous town in the fifteenth century, a good part of the prosperity depending on the wool and cloth trade for which the Welland provided the outlet to the sea. This trade was in decline before the Act was obtained; it is unlikely that the six or seven watermills between Stamford and Market Deeping would have been allowed to interfere with a flourishing navigation.[3]

The 1571 Act brought no immediate result. However it came out of abeyance in 1620, when a Commission of Sewers met in Stamford and granted the corporation leave to make a new cut $9\frac{1}{2}$ miles long from a point between the east side of the town and a cut made at Hudd's Mill to rejoin the river at Market Deeping. Locks and sluices were to be constructed, and the estimated cost was £2,000. Tolls could be levied to reimburse the corporation. A grant of James I in 1623 confirmed the commission's proposals, authorizing a toll of 3d at each lock as soon as the undertaking was completed.

It took far longer to finish the work than was anticipated. A promise to have the navigation open by 1627 was not fulfilled. The corporation searched for an undertaker; in 1636 David Cecil came forward, but neither with him nor with two subsequent volunteers could terms be agreed.[4] Not until 1664 was the work put in hand, when Daniel Wigmore, a Stamford alderman, took on the responsibility. Making the canal, with its 12 locks, cost him about £5,000; in repayment he was granted a lease of the tolls for 80 years for a nominal rent of 12d a year.[5] The exact date of opening cannot be established, but it was certainly in use some years before Richard Blome commented on it in 1673 when he referred to the thriving malt trade at Stamford which almost certainly arose from the carrying of barley by water. The Stamford Canal, as this cut is sometimes known, was by far the longest locked canal in the country when it was made.[6]

The rights in the canal passed from Daniel Wigmore to his son-in-law Charles Halford, who petitioned parliament in 1695 against a tax on sea coal. By this time, the rent had been increased to £100 a year. Halford claimed that he was receiving between £400 and £500 a year from tolls on sea coal, 3,000 chaldrons being carried to Stamford in that year. His petition was unsuccessful; in 1706 he tried again, protesting that the tax had reduced the traffic to only 500 chaldrons. Other cargoes carried included agricultural produce and malt from Stamford, timber and groceries, and stone and slates from Ketton and Collyweston quarries. Loads were carried generally in gangs of four lighters of 7ft beam, each taking 7–14 tons. According to W. H. Wheeler,[7] vessels of more than 15 tons burden could not use the canal, certainly in its later history. It took three or four days to cover the 50 miles to the mouth of the Witham, near Boston, where goods were transhipped to or from sea-going vessels.

The tolls remained in private hands for nearly all the canal's existence, passing from Halford to gentlemen named Feast, Edward Buckley and Thomas Smith, whose heirs still retained it in 1830. Unfortunately no trading figures appear to have survived. None of the various projects to link Stamford to the main canal system in the late eighteenth and early nineteenth centuries came to fruition; in 1809–10, lines from Oakham to Stamford and Market Harborough to Stamford were surveyed by Hamilton Fulton and Benjamin Bevan respectively, but the Bills for both, introduced in 1811, were defeated.[8] In his report, Bevan commented that there were several shallows and fords between Deeping and Stamford, but that the navigation could be restored to good order, mainly by deepening it, and that it could be incorporated into his proposed line.[9] The promoters of the Harborough-Stamford scheme agreed to take in the improvement of the Welland as far down as Spalding; their proposition also included a branch between Deeping and Peterborough

Perhaps there were some repairs to the navigation, because in 1836 it was described as much promoting the trade of Stamford as it was navigable for boats and small lighters.[10] It was still being used for imports from London in 1844,[11] but the following year Henry Tebbett, a Stamford grocer, giving evidence on the Act for closing the Oakham Canal, said that although the cheapest way to get goods from London was by sea and up the Welland it was so uncertain that he would not use it.[12] Some coal was still arriving by water; in 1846, however, the Midland Railway arrived in the town from Peterborough, and a link was made to Melton Mowbray in 1848. With Stamford now having access to cheap coal from the Midlands, the trade in sea coal ended. In 1856 the Great Northern branch line from Essendine was opened. The canal was now leaking and the locks in poor condition. All traffic ended in April 1863. The corporation failed to sell off the line by auction as their title was disputed, but by 1868 they had disposed of what they could. Much of the course of the canal can still be traced, including substantial remains of a lock approximately 6oft × 12ft at Deeping Gate,[13] a mile below Market Deeping bridge, and Stamford still has a Wharf Road with seventeenth-century warehouse buildings.

The Middle River
The succession of villages known as the Deepings—Market Deeping, Deeping Gate and Deeping St James—grew up in medieval times facing the Welland which acted as a frontier and as a route for traffic and trade. With neighbouring towns, Market Deeping petitioned Elizabeth I, pointing out that the banks of the Welland and Glen had decayed and the fens were lost. They requested that the fens be drained and proposed Thomas Lovell as the undertaker. Lovell spent about £12,000 on the task, receiving in return some 15,000 acres of reclaimed land, but his works were destroyed by 'lewd people' in the early troubled years of the seventeenth century. Further attempts

came to nothing, until in 1632 the Earl of Bedford with his group of fellow Adventurers was given the concession for draining Deeping Fen, South Fen and Croyland. The works included the widening and deepening of the Welland from Deeping St James through Spalding to the outfall and the construction of various drains, including Vernatt's Drain from Pode Hole to the river 1½ miles below Spalding, named after Sir Philibert Vernatti, one of the Adventurers. In 1637 the work was declared complete; however, without going into detail of the long history of the drainage of the south Lincolnshire fens, it would be more accurate to say that the turning point was not reached until the opening of Pode Hole pumping station in 1827 with two large steam beam engines.[14]

Two miles below Deeping St James the Welland makes a right-angled turn to run north-eastward to within ¾ mile of Crowland, whence it heads north to Spalding. The streets of Crowland were once waterways, meeting under the steep and narrow triangular bridge. From Crowland until the seventeenth century a branch of the Welland led past the abbey and eventually into the Nene; Edward IV is said to have voyaged from Crowland Abbey to Fotheringhay in 1468. The monastic history of Crowland dates back to the landing of Guthlac on what was then an island in 699; the present abbey is the fourth, of which only the north aisle is complete.

In the reign of Henry III the then Abbot of Crowland was asked by the king to make a road from the abbey to Spalding. He protested about the difficulty and expense 'because it could not be made otherwise than upon the brink of the river Welland, where there was so much water in winter time that it covered the ground an ell and a half in depth, and in a tempestuous wind two ells, at which time the ground on the side of the river was often broken by bargemen and mariners . . .'[15] He eventually built the road, receiving tolls for 7 years to pay for it. In the same reign the inhabitants of Spalding denied any obligation to repair the river, as they claimed it was an arm of the sea. Spalding, therefore, was used to shipping, much of it to and from Stamford, and regarded itself as a port long before the river improvements in the seventeenth century. These improve-

ments, and the construction of the Stamford Canal, gave the
town added commercial impetus. It was called the Port of
Spalding a Boston; it had no custom house, but its own customer and comptroller. The customer's seal, granted in the
reign of Charles I, bore a portcullis and the inscription 'sigil:
officii: port: spalden'.[16] In 1695, the merchants petitioned to
have Spalding made a free port, but the matter was not pursued. At this time there were several quays and storehouses.
The chief exports included oats, coleseed, rape and line oil,
wool and hides, while imports comprised stone, slates, timber,
coals, salt, sugar, groceries, pitch, tar, resin, glass and beeswax.
French wines, sweet Spanish wines and sack came via Lynn,
and the first imports of tea, chocolate and coffee arrived about
this time. Boats also used the Westlode, an old drainage channel, bringing passengers and goods from the area of Bourne.
John Grundy's map of 1732 shows a landing place at the Gore, a
piece of ground now known as the Sheep Market.[17]

Under the Deeping Fen Act of 1664, the Earl of Manchester
and others were appointed undertakers for the draining of
Deeping Fen. The Act stipulated that in return for a grant of
10,000 acres of land the undertakers, who were also to be the
trustees, were, in addition to the task of draining, to maintain
the river banks in good condition, to keep the Welland and Glen
clean and free-flowing, and to preserve and maintain the navigation of the Welland from Eàst Deeping to the sea free of toll.
To preserve the banks, owners of horse boats were not allowed
to land any horsemen, horses or cattle on them between
Michaelmas and 1 May, except at five named places, without a
licence. It was found impossible to complete the task as
required, partly owing to the conditions of the outfall and
partly because of 'the unseasonableness of the weather and
other unavoidable accidents'. The trustees rented out their
lands, but many of the owners were unable to pay the rates as
owing to the continued drainage problems the yield fell below
expectations. The trustees took back about half of their acreage
and sold it in 1729 to Captain James Perry for £4,000. Perry had
worked on embanking the Thames and had also published proposals for draining the south Lincolnshire fens. He undertook

various works in the few years before his death in 1735. Most of what he did was replaced or altered in subsequent schemes, but one item that survived for a long time was a lock south of Spalding by the edge of Cowbit Wash. This lock, called Spalding lock in the Deeping Fen Enclosure Act of 1801, was removed in 1813 by the Welland commissioners appointed under that Act.

Writing in 1792, Thomas Hawkes, treasurer to the Deeping Fen Adventurers and agent for Garfit & Claypon's Bank, indicated how much the prosperity of Spalding depended on the Welland and gave an account of the trading activity of the port.[18] The river, he said, 'is the source of much wealth to the Trading part of the Town, and affords a subsistence to many of the lower classes of people. All the corn grown in the Interior parts of this Country is brought up for the use of the inhabitants—and the surplus is sent to London in vessels belonging to Boston &c. The chief of this Trade is in Oats, and some little Coalseed, very little other grain being produced in the neighbourhood.' It is clear from his account that some goods, including coal, for the Deepings and Stamford were transhipped from Spalding barges into lighters:

> Boats coming for coals—when the tides serve they are halled by horses down the river towards the Ships lying in Boston Scalp and receive the coals immediately from out of the North Country ships—at other times they are delivered by the ships into the Spalding Barges, and then landed in the Merchants' Coal yards, from whence they can at all times be put on board the boats and sent upwards.

In addition to coalyards, there were warehouses and deal and timber yards by the river, much of the timber coming down from Market Deeping where there was an annual timber fair. The merchants built fine houses facing the river, many of which still remain. There was one boatbuilder in Spalding when Hawkes wrote his account: Thomas Goodwin, whose various successors carried on the business of building and repairing small craft until at least 1900. The Spalding barges, with their rounded bows and tall masts, were clearly depicted in a series of watercolours painted by Hilkiah Burgess in the

A TABLE

OF THE

RATES, TOLLS, AND DUTIES,

Authorized to be demanded and taken, pursuant to an Act of Parliament passed 3d *June*, 1824, for improving the Outfal of the River *Welland*, for and in respect of Goods, Matters, and Things carried or conveyed along any Part of the new Cut or Channel made or hereafter to be made below the Reservoir.

	PENCE.
For every Chaldron of Coals,	2
For every Last of Oats or Malt,	4
For every Half Last of Wheat, Rye, Barley, Barley Big, Beans, Peas, Cole, Linseed, Hempseed, or Mustard Seed,	4
For every Ton of Iron, Salt, Lead, Rags, Tobacco, Pipe Clay, Pebbles, Cobbles, Reed, Sedge, Hay, Flax, Hemp, or Turves,	4
For every Butt of Currants, Chaldron of Lime, and Chaldron of Grindstones,	4
For every two Pipes, three Hogsheads or Puncheons, eight Barrels or Half-hogsheads of Wine or other Liquors,	4
For every eight Packs of Wool, reckoning ten Tods to the Pack,	4
For every sixteen Kilderkins, thirty-two Firkins or Quarter Barrels, and Bushels of Sand,	4
For every five Hundred Pantiles or Paving Tiles, five Hundred Bricks, twenty Feet of Stone, one Hundred of Battens, and Half a Hundred of Deals,	4
And for every Ton Weight of all other Goods, Wares, and Merchandise,	4
And also for every fifty Feet of Fir Timber, and forty Feet of all other Timber, Calliper Measure, whether floated, carried, or conveyed,	4
And for every Hogshead of Soap, Tallow, Ashes, Barilla, and Whiteing,	2
And for every two Puncheons of Molasses, four Barrels of Rice, and four Casks of Russia Tallow,	2

And for every Quantity of Goods, Articles, or Things less than the respective Quantities before mentioned, there shall be demanded and taken a rateable Part or Proportion of the said several Rates, Tolls, and Duties.

By Order of the Trustees,

Cha. Bonner,

CLERK.

Spalding, 23d *July,* 1824.

Albin, Printer, Bookseller and Stationer, *Spalding.*

12. Welland toll-sheet, 1824

early nineteenth century.[19] Until the railway age there were
three bridges over the river; the lowest of them, the Chain
Bridge, was a double draw bridge 'for the conveniency of admitting the vessels up into the Town'. This was replaced by the
Albert wooden swing bridge in 1844. The High Bridge was the
principal one, a timber structure replacing an older one and
built by the Adventurers in 1634. Their successors rebuilt it in
1838. There was also a footbridge, replaced in 1837 by a cast-
iron suspension bridge which collapsed in 1844; this has since
been replaced twice.[20]

An Act of 1794[21] brought an end to navigation on the Westlode and by 1824 most of the channel was filled in. The main intention of this Act was to improve the Welland outfall and the
drainage of South Holland by cutting a large canal from the
Reservoir below Spalding to take the whole flow of the Welland
out to the Witham near Boston. It appointed three commissioners and set out tonnage rates for water carriage, which
had hitherto been free of charge under the Deeping Fen Act of
1664. These rates, which were high, were reduced under a subsequent Outfall Improvement Act of 1824. The money to make
the cut was not forthcoming owing to the financial crisis occasioned by the French wars, and the improvements were
delayed.

Trade in Spalding fluctuated to some extent according to the
state of the outfall, although this tended to limit the size of vessels using the river rather than the total tonnage carried. In 1802
barges and keels carrying up to 60 tons could use the port, while
in the 1820s 40 tons was the limit. Figures for the period
1829–1835 are as follows:[22]

	vessels in	vessels out	tonnage in	tonnage out
1829	250	143	12,523	7,138
1830	293	176	14,431	8,676
1831	325	187	16,044	9,059
1832	452	209	22,062	10,286
1833	462	282	22,712	13,951
1834	411	226	20,718	11,398
1835	465	232	23,387	10,928

This was not felt to be good enough as, following the enclosure of the Deeping commons, the agricultural productivity of the area was increasing. The merchants wanted the channel improved to take larger vessels, and in 1836 Mr Finch MP obtained leave to bring in a Bill for restoring the river. The Act was passed the next year, and work on the channel below Fosdyke bridge produced satisfactory results. In one week at the beginning of January 1839, 18 vessels carrying coal arrived in the port, and one from London, while 7 left with beans, woad, carrots and potatoes on board.[23] Eventually it was possible for sloops and barges up to 120 tons to sail to Spalding.[24]

The necessity for maintaining the river for drainage purposes enabled commercial navigation to continue for many years after the first railway arrived in Spalding in 1848. There was, nevertheless, a steady decline. In 1888, 11,690 tons were conveyed on the river, bringing a toll revenue of £478.[25] Evidence before the Royal Commission on Canals & Waterways in 1908 stated that there was a traffic in corn and cake and about 2,000 tons of coal annually, the method of traction being by tugs and horses. The river was navigable to Market Deeping only in times of partial flood. Small coastal steamers sometimes used the river, locust beans for Chamberlain's mills and coal from the north-east for the gasworks continuing into the early twentieth century. Two steel motor barges carried corn, hay and straw for G. F. Birch between Spalding and Fosdyke, where they transhipped their freight to ships from Hull. This trade ended by the Second World War, since when it has never revived.[26]

The Outfall

As with the Great Ouse and Nene, the Welland outfall occupied the attention of many of the most eminent civil engineers, as also did the drainage of Deeping Fen. The Deeping Fen Act of 1801 was based on two reports by George Maxwell and Edward Hare, on the second of which William Jessop and John Rennie collaborated.[27] Despite extensive works, including the cutting of the North and South Drove Drains and deepening of the Welland above Spalding and strengthening of its north bank, the Act failed to produce the desired results, partly because Rennie's recommendation for erecting steam engines at Pode Hole was not carried out and the drainage continued to rely on windmills. Thomas Pear and Rennie both reported adversely on the condition of the fen in 1815 and 1818. Neither of their plans was adopted. They reported independently again a few years later, both recommending the use of steam power.[28] This time the Deeping Fen trustees responded and obtained an Act in 1823 authorizing them to erect one or more steam engines at Pode Hole as Rennie had advised. A consolidating Act of 1856 sorted out various complications, many of them financial, and the trustees continued to administer the area, which is that bounded by the Bourne Eau and Glen to the junction with the Welland and by the Welland to Deeping St James, until the formation of the Deeping Fen, Spalding & Pinchbeck Internal Drainage Board in 1939.

Ultimately the proper drainage of the fenland depended on the condition of the outfall. Under the 1794 Act the Welland commissioners were to make a new cut from the Reservoir to Wyberton Road, between Boston and the Scalp, as has already been mentioned; they were also to build a bridge at Fosdyke and this, built of oak with a double drawbridge, was completed in 1815. It was partly rebuilt in 1871 and replaced by the present bridge in 1910–11. The cut, or some part of it, was completed by 1810, when Bevan reported that it had 'materially benefited both the navigation and the drainage'; he considered that the erection of a sea-sluice at the end of a further extension of the cut would, by keeping out the tides, improve matters still more.

In 1835 James Walker was asked to report on improving the river. His chief proposal was to continue to enclose the channel below Fosdyke bridge in a straight line towards a meeting with the Witham outfall at or near Clayhole and embanking the land on both sides of the channel to reclaim some 2,500 acres. His comment on the method is worth recording, as this was adopted:

If the work were done wholly by excavation, the amount would be heavy, but I think this would be useless labour, and that if the proper direction be given, the requisite size of channel will be formed by the current itself, so that the principal expense will be in supporting the sides by long thorn faggots or fascines, successively and progressively applied, as the depth of the new channel may require.

For this item he estimated an expenditure of £13,000; his other proposals, for deepening, dredging and embanking, brought the total to £70,000.[29]

By 1838, fascine work had extended the channel for $1\frac{1}{2}$ miles below Fosdyke bridge, although this was the only action taken to date on Walker's report. The Exchequer Bill Loan commissioners were querying the public value of the work; Walker surveyed progress below the bridge in October and noted that 'already vessels drawing eight feet can, after reaching the new channel, get through it, and up to the bridge, with as much ease and far greater certainty than those of three feet could do in 1835'. The work done had cost £7,026, a fair proportion of the estimate for the whole. He emphasized the necessity of completing the whole project as in previous years 'six weeks were sometimes taken in getting up through the $2\frac{1}{4}$ miles below Fosdyke bridge'.[30]

Fascine training of the channel continued for very many years. C. E. Wheeler described it as consisting of 'barrier walls or banks made of thorn faggots about six feet long and three feet girt, which are laid in the water in courses varying in width in proportion to the depth; and as each course, which is weighted with clay, sinks, others are laid on till the bank is raised to about half-tide level. The branches of the thorns interlaced with one another, and the silt brought up by the tides rapidly deposits amongst and at the back of this fascine work, and thus a solid embankment is formed, of sufficient strength and tenacity to withstand the strongest tidal current'. Writing in 1878, Miller and Skertchley said that the river 'now gives little trouble';[31] Wheeler, however, in 1882 said that the river was still defective and could not carry off the rainfall, that the banks were broken and the fens flooded.[32] The River Welland Outfall Act of 1867 had given the trustees power to raise more money to repair the

walls, which were threatened by the tide working its way behind them, but after leaving the fascine work the channel still
wandered over the sands, shifting its course continually. In 1917
R. F. Grantham reported that the river was little better than
Wheeler had described it 35 years before. And this despite the
operation in 1889–90 of Harrison's Scouring Dredger, steam-
powered and with two hedgehogs, invented by the Superintendent of Works for the Drainage of Deeping Fen.[33]

Work on the outfall was intensified by the Welland Catchment Board, which came into being following the Land Drainage Act of 1930. The warehouses at Fosdyke were destroyed by
fire in 1934, and the board considered that a much more substantial and suitable building should be provided 'to cope with
the anticipated increase in navigation'. Messrs Birch & Son
had been practically the only users of the river in the past 30
years and they wished to lease the new warehouse. Two warehouses were built and leased to Birch and to Lawes Chemical
Company, of Barking, the two firms guaranteeing to bring 8,000
tons of merchandise into the port. Unlike the other fen rivers,
the Welland never developed a sizable port near its outfall and
the dues earned at Fosdyke were sent to the Boston Harbour
Commissioners. Pilots were provided at Fosdyke; in 1937 the
pilotage, tonnage dues and rents, totalling £592, were sufficient
to provide for all expenses at the port. By this year the Board
had spent £91,537 on the outfall works, all raised by loans and
grants.[34]

In 1944, the Board's chief engineer, E. G. Taverner, produced a major scheme for the improvement of the river of
which the most important elements were the diversion of some
of the Glen waters to the Welland, by means of what is known
as the Greatford Cut, and a by-pass or channel around Spalding to diminish the risk of flooding. The estimated cost was
£723,000.[35] This scheme was completed under the Welland
River Board and the by-pass channel—the Coronation Channel—was opened in September 1953. The tide was excluded by
the construction of Fulney lock, a mile below Spalding bridge.
Small pleasure boats were now using the river but the anticipated increase in commercial navigation had not occurred; in

1955–6 the navigation and pilotage income was only £505 and the account was showing a loss of £150. It is worth comparing these figures with the massive £1,486,447 expenditure on various schemes of improvement in progress at the end of 1956.[36] With the shifting sands of the Wash and the shrinking peat inland, expenditure of this order continues. Today the river is navigable for craft drawing no more than 3ft up to the junction with the Folly River, about 20 miles above Fosdyke bridge; larger craft can navigate to Fulney lock. Pilotage is now available from the Boston & Spalding Pilotage Authority in Boston.

The Glen and the Bourne Eau

There is little recorded history of the navigation of either the Glen or the Bourne Eau. Dugdale's comment on the Glen 'the least river of all the rest', is that it 'serveth almost to none other use, but to carry away so much of its own water, with the rill descending from Burne, as can be kept between two defensible banks'.[37] The bottom of the river even then was higher than the fenland through which it passed, so to a great extent the river served as a high-level drain—as it does today.

The Bourne Eau, fed by springs at St Peter's Pool in Bourne, gave its name to this small Lincolnshire town. Bourne was a market town in the sixteenth century with a good trade in corn, which would seem to indicate that the river was used for transport during that time.[38] However, although both rivers were dealt with in various drainage measures, in particular the Black Sluice Act of 1765, following disastrous floods when the banks of both were broken, there was no navigation legislation until the Bourne Eau Act of 1781. The preamble to the Act stated that the navigation had become almost unusable by being choked with mud and other obstructions; it nominated trustees to scour and cleanse the waterway, making it 5ft deep and 30ft wide 'where its present banks will admit of it'. 2s 6d per ton was to be charged on all goods. Principal cargoes down were corn and wool, via the Glen and Welland outfall for transhipment at Boston for the north east. Coal and groceries came up in return. There was a coal wharf in Eastgate, Bourne, in the early nineteenth century.[39]

Some trade is recorded between Spalding and Bourne by Thomas Hawkes, writing in 1792:[40] 'The boats on the Glen carry Coals up to Borne and bring timber &c from there to Spalding . . . it is seen that the Boatmen have generally a freight both upwards and downwards and thereby maintain their Gangs in a pretty constant course of trade when the river is of sufficient depth of water.' There was also a boat for goods and passengers from Bourne every market day—Tuesday—'but these conveyances are not to be depended upon'. There was often either too little water or too much. The installation by the Black Sluice Drainage commissioners of self-acting doors at Tongue End, the junction of the Glen and Bourne Eau, to prevent the Glen flooding back to Bourne, effected some improvement, but there is a long history of flooding caused by breaches in the banks, particularly of the Glen. Between 1821 and 1882 there were eight breaches in the south bank and six in the north. Evidence showed that each $\frac{1}{4}$in of rainfall over the Glen watershed in a wet season was sufficient to make the river rise 9 to 10 inches.[41]

The railway from Spalding to Boston was opened in 1848 and from Spalding to Bourne in 1866, the latter connecting to the Great Northern at Essendine by a branch built by the locally owned Bourne & Essendine Railway Company. The Bourne—Sleaford line was opened in 1872. There was also Lord Willoughby's little single-track line from Little Bytham to Edenham, opened in 1857, with a speed limit of 15mph, which lasted into the 1880s, although horses replaced its two locomotives in its closing years. Coal for Bourne could be collected from Edenham, about two miles distant.[42] All this meant a rapid decline in river traffic, although for a time there was an interchange basin at Surfleet station by the Glen.[43] Boats were still navigating from Bourne in 1857, 'occasionally'.[44] Subsequent construction of a sluice at Tongue End shut off the Bourne Eau as a navigation, and the Bourne Eau Act was repealed in 1962.

The Glen had been navigable for a few miles above Tongue End. Barges and lighters of about 15 tons burden could reach

Kate's bridge, on the Peterborough—Lincoln turnpike road.[45] There is some evidence that craft at one time came up to Greatford, as there are storage buildings and remains of moorings in the grounds of Greatford Hall, but this must have ended when Kate's bridge was reconstructed. When the Bourne Eau fell out of use as a navigation, however, there was little reason left for trade far up the Glen. In 1904 Henry de Salis said that very little trade was done on the river, and although there was a fair depth of water for some distance above Surfleet station, 'no trade has been conducted above that point for many years'. A few barges continued to use the bottom mile or so of the river until the mid-1920s.

Access to the Glen from the Welland is at a point called the Reservoir. The tide is kept out of the Glen by a sluice, with a guillotine gate for navigation that can only be raised—a three-man job—when the water each side makes a level. It is navigable for small craft for $11\frac{1}{2}$ miles to Tongue End, the last place where it is possible to turn, although weed growth may make passage difficult at some times of the year.

CHAPTER X

The South Lincolnshire Navigations

✦✦✦✦✦✦✦✦✦✦✦✦✦✦✦✦✦✦✦✦✦✦✦✦✦✦✦✦✦✦✦✦✦◆✦✦✦✦✦✦✦✦✦✦✦✦✦✦✦✦✦✦✦✦✦✦✦✦✦✦✦✦✦✦

The Fossdyke and Witham

The Canal Age is so positively associated with the eighteenth century that it is difficult at times to recollect that the use of inland water transport has been part of the economic life of the community for centuries. The estuarial portions of rivers, being in effect arms of the sea, are perhaps an exception to this approach, but the idea of artificial navigations and materially improved rivers goes much further back into history than the well-documented period of the last two or three hundred years would suggest. Here in the central part of Lincolnshire we have the continuing example of nearly 2000 years of effort to maintain an efficient, though often inefficient, local transport system.

Lincoln was an important Roman city linked to other Roman centres by great straight highways. But while these were an excellent means of moving troops and of provisioning other localities with day-to-day needs, they could not offer the same efficiency for the bulk transport of goods. Most Roman cities such as London, Colchester, York, Dover, or Newcastle, were accessible to naturally navigable waters, but Lincoln did not have these natural advantages. Furthermore, being at the heart of a good agricultural area, it was called upon to supply the other centres with their needs. The solution the Romans adopted was to cut the Fossdyke leading to the River Trent in the west and to improve the River Witham leading to the east. In this way they were able to turn Lincoln into an inland port. Torksey at the junction of the Fossdyke and the Trent became,

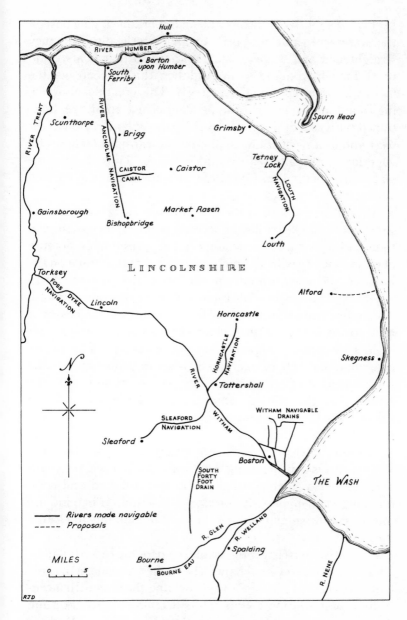

13. The Navigations of Lincolnshire

in effect, a suburb of Lincoln, and an important staging post on the waterway route to York. In an easterly direction they straightened and deepened the Witham so that boats could reach Lincoln from the Wash. And then, thirdly, there was the Car Dyke, referred to in Chapter VII. This great dyke, sweeping round in a wide arc from the Cam near Cambridge, functioned both as a drainage channel for the upland region to the west and as a navigation canal offering transport facilities far superior to the alternative land carriage. Thus these three waterways focused on Lincoln formed the earliest integrated system in the country.

After the departure of the Romans the navigations underwent a period of decay lasting several centuries, though the fact that Torksey retained some importance, presumably because of its association with shipping, may indicate that trade on the Fossdyke did not entirely disappear. Before the Conquest it had 213 resident burgesses while there were still 111 resident in 1086. Thirty-five years later, in 1121, Henry I improved the Fossdyke by scouring out the original channel.[1] Camden suggested that he had cut a new navigation, but in the absence of any other contemporary new navigations it is more probable that the work was that of restoration. This view is reinforced by the record that the King's Monnetari at Nottingham had in Edward the Confessor's time the care of the Fossdyke and the navigation thereon.[2]

Without any permanent organization to maintain the waterway it is not surprising that, from time to time, the channel became so silted up that traffic was impeded and commissions were appointed, eg in 1335, 1365, and 1518, to inquire into its condition and compel the local inhabitants to cleanse the dyke.[3]

Lincoln up to 1369 was the staple town for the east Midlands. This meant that any merchants who wished to trade in the area had to operate in Lincoln, thus providing the king with a centralized organization for his toll collection. It also gave him direct control over the navigations of the Fossdyke and Witham and this royal prerogative continued until James I, finding that the cleansing and maintenance of the Fossdyke was proving too expensive, presented it to Lincoln. By 1660, however, the navigations had once again fallen into decay and traffic had virtually ceased. Some engineering works had earlier been carried out on the Witham, including the erection of a sluice at Boston in 1500, later to become the Grand Sluice, and another at Langrick in 1543; but development on the scale that was to be seen during the construction of the later canals had to wait for another century and more.

The situation had deteriorated to such an extent that in 1671 Lincoln obtained an Act empowering it to improve the navigation between Boston and the Trent.[4] In the event, only the Fossdyke and the 100yd stretch of the Witham between Brayford Pool and the High Bridge was improved. Brayford Pool developed with the erection of wharves and warehouses so that it became the port complex of Lincoln and it was possible for small boats carrying 5 tons of goods to reach the city from Torksey. The improvement was short-lived, for once again in 1717 the Fossdyke was impassable, and in 1735 Torksey waggons laden with hay were seen to pass over the navigation.[5] The income from tolls was quite insufficient to pay for the necessary repairs, let alone improve the navigations. Nevertheless, an average of 1,357 tons pa of coal passed via the Trent and Fossdyke to be unloaded at Lincoln.[6]

In 1724 it was decided to carry out a thorough survey of the Witham as far as Boston, but the report by James Scribo was not presented until 1733.[7] He warned that, unless drastic measures were taken immediately, the navigation would not only fail, but the lands between Lincoln and Boston would be lost for want of draining. Despite several meetings and an application to Parliament nothing developed for some years.

Meanwhile the city had sold a third share of the tolls of the Fossdyke in 1672. This by 1731 was held by Robert Peart, who in turn mortgaged his right to James Humberston for £750. It was now clear that the city had neither the inclination nor the expertise to deal with the problems of the Fossdyke and so they leased the navigation to Richard Ellison, who had been associated with the Don Navigation in Yorkshire, as from 1 January 1741 at a rent of £50 to Lincoln and £25 to Humberston.[8] The average annual tolls for the years prior to this had been slightly in excess of £100, between a minimum in 1733–4 of £66 and a maximum in 1735–6 of £136. Ellison was to maintain a channel throughout the navigation of a depth of 3ft 6in. The work was completed by 1744 and the navigation reopened. His efforts were rewarded, for in 1746 the tolls reached £595 and by 1757 had topped £1,000. Ellison himself died in 1743 and he was succeeded by his son Richard Ellison II whose business ability coupled with the growing utilization of waterways led to the continued prosperity of the Fossdyke, seen in the toll receipts which reached £2,367 in 1789 not long before his death in 1792. By 1811 under Richard Ellison III the tolls were £5,159.

With the Fossdyke at long last proving a viable undertaking a question arose as to the future of the Witham. There, as elsewhere in the eastern counties, the problem was how to reconcile navigation and drainage interests. There was here, also, a third factor: the question of the arrangements between the Fossdyke, including the Lincoln section of the Witham, and the rest of the Witham below Lincoln. The city wanted the Witham navigable from Boston to Stamp End, then on their eastern boundary, but they did not want any interference in their rights by any commissioners who might be appointed to oversee the Witham arrangements. Discussions went on for a number of years until the landowners between Lincoln and Boston ordered a survey by John Grundy, Langley Edwards, and John Smeaton.[9] Their report was presented in 1761 and, on the grounds that the Fossdyke's water level might be affected, it was opposed by Lincoln and towns as far away as Rotherham and Rochdale which were also anxious for trade reasons to protect the Fossdyke. A petition for a Bill based on the 1761 scheme was submitted to Parliament and despite powerful opposition the Act passed on 2 June 1762.[10]

The Act set up two groups of commissioners, one for general and drainage purposes and one for navigation. Under it those sections of the 1671 Act that related to navigation between High Bridge, Lincoln, and Boston were repealed and the new commissioners were given power to make cuts, build locks, and generally improve the river. The navigation commissioners held their first meeting on 18 August 1762 and at the next meeting Langley Edwards was elected surveyor at £25 per annum.[11] Edwards's first job was to put a chain across the river between Stamp End and Washingborough ferry where a toll of sixpence (2½p) would be collected.[12] He was also to prepare plans for a sea-lock and survey the full length of the river. The commissioners also agreed to borrow £6,000 on the credit of the tolls. This was divided into 120 shares of which Boston took thirty and Edwards one.

The division of responsibility between the two groups of commissioners was a narrow one at times. With regard to the Grand Sluice at Boston, essential to the drainage interest, the drainage commissioners were responsible for the sluice itself, but the navigation commissioners gave instructions to Edwards for the lock on the east side of the sluice.[13] The Grand Sluice was opened in 1766 together with the lock alongside and toll collection at the Boston end of the navigation was transferred from Dogdyke to the new lock.[14]

Improvements slowly continued and by 1771 Stamp End, Kirkstead, and Barlings locks were being built. Other work was also needed but once again the commissioners were short of money. The following year they resolved to borrow another £1,200 on the credit of the tolls, though the tolls on the Witham, unlike those on the Fossdyke, were hardly such as would inspire confidence. In 1763–4 they brought in £263, in 1771 they reached £316, by 1782 £498, and not until 1790 did they reach a modest £898. But there was growing optimism. Before the end of the century potential extensions of the navigation by branches from the Witham had been mooted. In 1783 there was a meeting to consider making the Slea navigable to Sleaford, in 1787 the Tattershall Canal, later on to be linked with the Horncastle Navigation, was opened; and earlier still commercial navigation had penetrated the East and West Fen area over a series of drains now known collectively as the Witham Navigable Drains.

This area is to the north of the Witham and access to the drains is now through a lock at Anton's Gowt. The first proposal for a lock here was made in 1779 at a time when funds were short. In fact the lock was not made until 1813, but to enable boats to pass on to the drains land doors were fitted at the open-ing.[15] This way led from the Witham on to Frith Bank Drain, nearly two miles long, and this connects, though not directly in each case, with West Fen Drain, Medlam Drain, Maud Foster Drain, Stone Bridge Drain, Cowbridge Drain and Hobhole Drain. In this system there were four other locks; Cowbridge on the Maud Foster Drain, East Fen on Cowbridge Drain, Lade Bank on Hobhole Drain, and Hagnaby on the West Fen Drain. The completion of these various projects led to the letting of the tolls and in 1810 the rent was £3,000.

Meanwhile what was of more immediate concern to the com-missioners was the situation between Brayford Pool and Stamp End lock. They discovered that the traders who had ware-houses on this section had not been paying tolls, so they placed a boom across the river at High Bridge and demanded tolls from vessels which came from the Fossdyke to discharge below High Bridge but did not pass through Stamp End lock.[16] This was one of the very points which the city had been concerned about when the 1762 bill was before Parliament. Immediately the traders protested:

> Sir. We whose names are hereunto subscribed being the principal Traders below High Bridge think that we have no right to pay any toll for bringing any goods down the town as wod not go through the lock and as the said Lock cannot make any water over Braford Head in the summer season so that our yards are of no use but in the winter when we have a convenience of laying in a stock of goods in a Flood Time when the Lock cannot be stopt. We should have waited on the Honourable Commissioners ourselves but it being our fair it renders it inconvenient. If that you persist in taking the above Toll must be under the necessity of trying it as you have not made your lock according to Act of Parliament but the bearer will give you more particulars and are Your humble servants.
> Hen Bullen, Tho Mackeness, Jas Morris, Samuel King, Thomas Wright. Nat Morris. Edwd Partridge.[17]

The commissioners must have realized the doubtful nature of

their own case because they immediately resolved to suspend collection of tolls until all the particulars were heard at their next meeting on 15 May 1781. On hearing the deputation's case at that meeting they continued the suspension and removed the boom at High Bridge. Another factor in this dispute was that the traders were also paying porterage for having their goods brought under High Bridge in small boats or lighters drawing only a foot of water. There was no through passage for larger boats and consequently no through navigation between the Trent and Boston. Sir Joseph Banks was well aware of this unsatisfactory situation when he was campaigning for the Horncastle Bill. In fact part of the case for the Bill was that there should be a through navigation in Lincoln. In order to support the case William Jessop was commissioned in 1791 to make a survey of the Fossdyke and the Witham and the junction between the two. He suggested two alternatives; either a line via the Sincel Dyke passing round the south side of the city, or to increase the navigation depth under High Bridge, where the passage width was 20ft but the floor of the river under the bridge was of wood with a depth of only 18in below the minimum surface level of the water. He reported that it would be easy to take up the floor, though there would still be the difficulty of the fast-flowing current and no towing path. If the latter were provided the effective width would be reduced and the current would automatically increase.[18]

In the end the city was persuaded that it would be better to forego the porterage dues which they had demanded for passing cargoes under High Bridge and gain from the increased traffic that the High Bridge improvements would bring. The possibility of a canal avoiding the city altogether was too high a price to pay for their rights. The channel under High Bridge was deepened, and by 1795 there was through navigation. Soon afterwards toll receipts started to rise. It is interesting that many years later when Stamp End lock was again being rebuilt, a temporary navigation was provided via the Sincel Dyke and the New South Delph.

By 1802 repairs were again becoming necessary on the Witham, and for advice the commissioners called in John

Rennie. The main issue was Kirkstead lock, built in 1770. He examined it on 1 April 1802 and found that it adjoined a staunch which was in very bad condition. 'I am not at all surprized at his having given way. On the contrary I should have been much surprized had it stood the effects of the flood without failing—matters however being as here described, the question is, how now are they to be remedied. In this I find it difficult to give a satisfactory opinion because not only the construction of the works themselves are bad but they are equally ill placed.'[19] He recommended pulling up the lock entirely and rebuilding it elsewhere. He made a further survey on 5–7 October 1802 and was equally critical. Among various recommendations he suggested that either the navigable drains should be used to reach Boston below the Grand Sluice, or a new cut should be made to the south of, and by-passing, the Grand Sluice and again to Boston Harbour.[20]

He drew up further proposals in 1803 which recommended the demolition of High Bridge and the building of a new one with a clear waterway of 34ft. The total estimate for his proposals, which included a substantial amount for drainage works was £58,400, and for the Fossdyke £12,260.[21] In 1807 he produced revised proposals which included the scrapping of Kirkstead and Barlings locks and the construction of a new lock near Washingborough church. On the basis of these later recommendations the commissioners obtained a new Act in 1808 permitting them to carry out the work and authorizing them to borrow £30,000 on the security of rates and tolls for drainage purposes and £70,000 on the credit of the navigation tolls.[22] Under this Act a company of proprietors were made responsible for the works. New locks were built at Stamp End and Bardney and the old locks scrapped. A new cut was made near Fiskerton and this with the new lock at Bardney disposed of the idea of a lock at Washingborough church. In 1816 Rennie noted that four drains, other than those near Boston, were navigable; Timberland Dike, Carlton Dike, Nocton Delph, and Branston Delph.[23]

The proprietors' problems continued and they were chronically short of money, allegations being made from time to time that there was gross waste of their resources. In order to raise more capital they had recourse to Parliament for new Acts in 1812,[24] 1826,[25] and 1829.[26]

But if things were bad on the Witham they were even worse on the Fossdyke. This navigation was difficult to maintain because of the nature of the ground over which it passed, being sand and, in part, quicksand. In addition the navigation, unlike the Witham, was privately leased. Richard Ellison II was a good business man, but when he died in 1792 he left a two-thirds interest in it to his son Richard (Colonel Ellison) III and one third to his other son Henry, and to their respective male heirs. Henry left the management to Richard who, in his turn, would not spend any money on it if he could avoid it.

In the early 1820s legal opinion was taken on the validity of the leases of 1741; it was found that they were good in law, but that the tolls being levied were not being limited to the sums required to maintain the navigation. There is no doubt that Colonel Ellison found the Fossdyke very profitable, but as he possessed tremendous power in Lincoln little could be effectively done about his lack of concern over the navigation. An attempt was made to reach a compromise, but the anti-Ellison group would not be a party to this. Instead they filed a Bill in Chancery praying that the leases should be declared void and so the compromise was dropped. Meanwhile Richard III died in 1827 and Henry handed over the management to his son-in-law, Humphrey Sibthorp. Sibthorp, also a proprietor of the Witham, realised that improvements ought to be made to the Fossdyke. Apparently Sibthorp got in touch with Isambard Brunel who accepted the invitation to make a survey and report on the Fossdyke.

Brunel went there in 1833 and travelled from Lincoln to Torksey and back, taking soundings and preparing cross-sections of the channel. He also took measurements of all the boats lying in Brayford Pool. Next day he went to Torksey by road and returned on the loaded keel *Industry* drawn by two horses. The passage was reasonable until they were passing under High Bridge and there the keel stuck fast and they were 'obliged to drag her all the way through with the windlass'. He returned a fortnight later to deliver his report,[27] though no positive action appears to have been taken on it. The Chancery case dragged on until 1839 when Henry also was dead; finally the proceedings were abandoned and judgment given that the leases were valid.

Despite the physical and financial problems affecting the two sections of the waterway, traffic continued to develop with the Boston end concerned mainly with imports and exports from coastwise and foreign sources and Lincoln mainly devoted to goods going to or coming from other centres on the inland waterway system. This was a continuation of the trading pattern which had evolved over the centuries. The links which Lincoln had established with the midlands in the mediaeval period continued to have their effects down the years, but it had also developed connections with Yorkshire via the Aire & Calder (opened 1704) and these two areas contributed to the gradual growth of traffic during the later eighteenth century and faster growth during the early nineteenth. This growth was undoubtedly helped by the advent of such new waterway links as the Trent & Mersey (1777), Erewash (1779), and Dearne and Dove (1804) Canals which all used the Trent as a link between themselves and the Fossdyke.

In 1755 because of shortage of corn in Derby large quantities had been bought in Lincoln and sent by boat via the Fossdyke, the Trent, and the Derwent.[28] That market in grain was to expand considerably so that, in 1804 following the opening of the Rochdale Canal with its connection to the eastern counties through the Calder & Hebble, corn was being sent across the Pennines to feed the Lancashire cotton workers.[29] In 1819 over 40,000 tons of corn, much of it harvested in Lincolnshire, were sent over this route. The Yorkshire demand for corn was also met in the 1850s from Lincolnshire via the Aire & Calder; though the share of the Fossdyke and Witham was much less, amounting to some 5,000 tons in 1852, half of which was despatched via Boston.

In the reverse direction the main import to places from Lincoln to Boston was coal and, in the late eighteenth century, this came via the Aire & Calder and then either by coastwise shipping to Boston, or by the Trent and the Fossdyke to Lincoln.[30] The proportions varied between the two routes but in the 1850s about 7,000 tons pa came from Yorkshire pits. In order to help this trade there was a drawback on the transport charges for coal from the Silkstone pits on the Barnsley Canal.[31] However, following the growth of the Nottingham/Derby coalfield a steadily increasing supply from this source was reaching Lincoln in the first half of the nineteenth century, travelling via the Erewash Canal and the Trent to Torksey and then down the Fossdyke to Lincoln.

Despite the problems the receipts for traffic on the Fossdyke continued to increase. In 1818 they passed £6,000 and in 1825 were in excess of £8,000, continuing above that figure for several years. The Witham tolls, too, had increased and for the six months from March to September 1819 they exceeded £4,100 and a dividend of 5 per cent was paid in 1820. These increases reflect the improving agricultural economy of this region. Nevertheless in 1826 it was stated that over £180,000 had been spent on improvements to the Witham and another £40,000 was required. The favourable toll situation had created the climate for a possible extension from the Witham to the Ancholme and Sir John Rennie made a survey. He proposed two alternatives but the scheme never matured.[32] There had been a previous suggestion in 1813 for a canal from the Witham to Wragby on the Lincoln—Louth road but John Rennie's report was not encouraging and nothing more was heard of the idea.[33]

Traffic on the Witham and Fossdyke up to this time had been carried in sailing vessels or horse-drawn barges. There had been occasions when the barges were hauled by men. But in March 1816 the first steam packet, the *Witham*, was launched from Shuttleworth & Robinson's yard on the Sincil Dyke. Before moving to Sincil Dyke Joseph Shuttleworth had operated a boatbuilding yard at Dogdyke. A second steam packet was in service by 28 July 1817. There were, however, teething troubles and in March 1817 'when the *Witham* steam packet was on her voyage to Boston, a few miles down the river the boiler burst; though about 30 passengers were on board no personal injury was sustained'. There was considerable friction between the sailing and steam packets but, as was inevitable, the steam packets survived. In January 1828, during a great flood, the steam packets found themselves in trouble; one managed to bestride a stiff hedge floating in the water with its paddles unable to turn. In 1829 a new type of paddlewheel was invented by a Lincoln man which enabled the boats to travel faster and become more competitive. Speed was limited to 4½mph between Stamp End and Horsley Deeps, otherwise 6mph was accepted. In 1836 iron steam packets appeared and these were clearly more efficient.[34]

The era of the railway was now fast approaching. The first attempts to bring Lincoln on to the railway system were made in the year that Brunel inspected the Fossdyke, though it was not until 3 August 1848 that the first railway reached Lincoln. There had, however, been moves by the Wakefield, Lincoln & Boston Railway to penetrate the territory. In order to lessen possible opposition it entered into agreements with the Witham and Fossdyke proprietors whereby the railway would take over the navigations and allow the proprietors an assured income, before merging with the London & York Railway. Eventually the Great Northern Railway was authorized by its incorporating Act to take over the other two promotions. In doing this the G.N.R. also took over the agreements made with the navigation proprietors, in the one case leasing the Fossdyke Navigation for 894 years at £9,570pa from Richard Ellison IV, and in the other leasing the Witham for 999 years at £10,545pa from the proprietors. The figures were the average of the companies' net profits for the previous three years plus 5 per cent. In the case of the Witham the railway company had further to assume liability for the payment of interest on various mortgages amounting to £24,692.[35] In due course the G.N.R. completed its line along the banks of the Witham to Boston, opening it on 17 October 1848. By 1857 they had redeemed the Witham mortgages.

With the railway and the navigation running parallel almost all the way from Lincoln to Boston an interesting situation developed. The stations on the line were generally near the landing stages where the steam packets regularly called and so there was tremendous competition for the passenger traffic. The railway countered anything the steam packets could do by putting on 4th-class carriages with fares at a halfpenny a mile in 1850 and by 1863 the packet boats were out of business. This was one of the rare examples of a 4th-class being adopted.[36]

The railway also struck a blow at freight traffic, though after 1897 when the Manchester Sheffield & Lincolnshire Railway had become the Great Central, the latter built a large warehouse adjacent to Brayford Pool with a branch dock alongside to provide transhipment facilities. This dock is now quite a swannery. In 1847 19,535 tons of coal passed through the Grand Sluice but in 1854, after the opening of the railway, the total was only 3,780 tons. The wool traffic had disappeared and now it looked as though general merchandise would follow the trend of coal. The overall tonnage on the combined navigation fell from 276,154 in 1848 to 85,134 in 1868. Despite this reduction the G.N.R. still had to maintain the navigation and in 1871 the drainage commissioners required them to deepen Bardney lock by 5ft at a cost of over £5,000.[37] It was clearly in the G.N.R. interest not to let all the traffic disappear. By 1905 the total tonnage had fallen to 18,548 on the Witham, though on the Fossdyke the tonnage was 75,881, out of which 60,342 was consigned to Lincoln. During the First World War the tonnages dropped further, averaging 5,870 on the Witham and 69,611 on the Fossdyke over the years 1913–17.[38] This traffic was mainly agricultural produce and general merchandise.

In 1882 the G.N.R. subleased the navigations to the Great Northern & Great Eastern Joint Committee and after various changes they are now administered by the British Waterways Board. Milestones of the G.N.R. era can still be seen lettered eg GNR . WN Lincoln 9 Miles.

On the south side of Boston a long drain serves a different area of fenland. This is the Black Sluice Drainage and Navigation or the South Forty Foot. It starts at Guthram Gowt just north of the river Glen but does not make a physical connection with that river. It then runs north and then east for 21 miles to join the tidal Witham east of the Grand Sluice. It used to have a sea-lock at the Witham end to prevent the tide entering the drain but this was removed about 1971.[39] The Black Sluice drain, like so many others in this area, at one time carried local commercial and farm traffic, but its purpose was not primarily navigation, and its history is more intimately connected with the drainage of the fens.

One of the Witham Navigable Drains, running south from Revesby Bridge to Boston, is known as the Medlam Drain and from this a short drain, ½ mile long, runs westward to New Bolingbroke. It has been suggested that this was built as a canal by John Parkinson to serve the new town in the early nineteenth century.[40]

Horncastle Navigation

Horncastle is an old market town lying to the north of the river Witham and connected to it by the River Bain. The Bain rises in the Lincolnshire Wolds and flows generally southward without becoming more than a smallish stream in normal times to Horncastle where it is joined by the River Waring. From there the combined waters flow through Kirkby-on-Bain and Tattershall to Dogdyke on the Witham; and it was this lower stretch which was considered in the late eighteenth century as a possible navigation. Already there was a short cut known as Gibson's· or the Tattershall Canal with one lock from the Witham to Tattershall near the line of the Bain. This had been built by John Gibson of Tattershall and John Dyson of Bawtry without parliamentary sanction on the Earl of Fortescue's land in 1786.[41] It served a warehouse at its terminus at Tattershall. Its line was an obvious start for a navigation to Horncastle which would link that town with Lincoln and the Trent in one direction and Boston and the Wash in the other.

A plan was produced by Mr Bullivant in 1791 and a further report dated 30 June 1791 was prepared by William Jessop who considered two possibilities. Firstly, taking the navigation down the Bain to Tattershall, and onwards to the Witham without making use of Gibson's Canal; and secondly, constructing a new canal across country to Kirkstead which would be some miles shorter and bring the junction with the Witham

four miles nearer Lincoln. The estimate for the former was
£12,233 and for the latter £12,544. Jessop was satisfied that even
in dry seasons the water supply would be adequate. In each
plan twelve locks were proposed and these were designed to
take boats 54ft × 14ft 4in and 3ft 6in draught. In the end it was
decided to canalize the Bain. Yet a further plan was prepared in
1792 by surveyors Robert Stickney and Samuel Dickinson
though this incorporated only minor modifications to the earlier proposals.[42]

At a joint meeting between the commissioners of drainage
and navigation on the Witham and the landowners etc interested in the Horncastle and Sleaford navigations in the town
hall, Sleaford, it was agreed that the navigation could be completed through Lincoln between the Fossdyke and the Witham
without injuring the landowners if Jessop's ideas upon lowering
the flow of the High Bridge were adopted. With Lincoln corporation agreeing to pay the cost of deepening the river under
High Bridge and Ellison agreeing to carry out the necessary
work on his part of the Fossdyke affected, only parliamentary
powers were needed. The most expeditious way of getting these
was to include the necessary clauses in the Horncastle Bill.
Thus the Horncastle Act contains clauses which appear super-
ficially to have no relation to the main purpose of the Act.

Parliament was petitioned on 5 March 1792, the petition
being sponsored by Lincoln and Boston corporations as well as
by supporters from Lincoln, Boston and Horncastle. This support indicated the widespread interest the promotion of the
canal was generating. William Jessop gave evidence before the
committee on the anticipated value of the navigation, the Act
being passed on 11 June 1792.[43]

It authorized the purchase for £840 of the Tattershall Canal
with the exception of the warehouse which apparently strad-
dled the canal. Power was given to raise £15,000 in shares not
exceeding £50 with a further £10,000 on the mortgage of the
tolls. Dividends were to be limited to 8 per cent.

The first meeting of the committee was held on 14 June 1792
at the Bull Inn, Horncastle, and among the fifteen members
present was Sir Joseph Banks. It was decided that there should

be a first call of £10 to be paid before 7 July 1792.[44] During the next two months estimates were obtained for various works, including the construction of the locks and the reconstruction of the lock in the Tattershall Canal at a point nearer Tattershall. Negotiations also took place with the Sleaford Navigation to appoint a joint engineer for the two navigations. Henry Eastburn was invited but declined and the appointment went to William Cawley of Mickle Trafford, Cheshire, at a salary of £300 per annum.[45]

One feature of this navigation was that the committee members decided that the bricks should be made locally by makers under direct contract to themselves. On 19 October 1792 they formally instructed their brickmaker to search for clay on the line of the navigation and by the end of November a number of sites had been recommended to them. Their close control, however, was to lead them into difficulties. They specified that the bricks were to be good, hard, merchantable bricks made in a mould to give a brick 10in long × 3in deep × 5in wide. The volume of such a brick is approximately 35 per cent greater than the standard brick of today and even more than the standard eighteenth-century brick. Clearly bricks of these dimensions would require a different technique and it was this factor that the committee overlooked. Some of the bricks can still be found today and they show that the firing must have been uneven.

In October 1793 Cawley resigned and in February 1794 John Dyson, who had been involved in the construction of the Tattershall Canal, was appointed in his place. As the work proceeded the opportunity was taken progressively to open the navigation as far as possible so as to obtain the benefit of the tolls but even this attempt to raise additional capital failed to prevent the growing financial crisis. In September 1794 the A.G.M. of the proprietors gave authority to borrow up to £10,000 so as to complete the works. In 1795, on the grounds that £250 had been received in tolls, despite the unfinished state of the navigation, it was decided to lease the tolls. The lease was not concluded until 26 January 1796 when Thomas Coltman of Hagnaby secured it against a loan of £4,035 with interest. By 1 September 1796 the situation had deteriorated

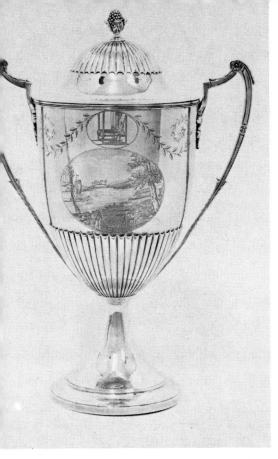

Plates 29 & 30 *(above)* A cup inscribed 'The Gift of the Proprietors of the Sleaford Navigation 6 May 1794' presented to Benjamin Handley on the opening of the navigation; *(below)* Brayford Pool on the Fossdyke at Lincoln in 1858, from a painting by J. W. Carmichael

Plates 31 & 32   *(above)* Discharging grain at Brigg on the Ancholme Navigation; *(below)* the curious construction of Ticklepenny lock on the Louth Canal

still further and the committee appealed to each proprietor for additional loans to tide over the crisis. To this nine responded and averted the possibility of handing over the navigation to the Witham drainage commissioners. By the beginning of 1797 the section to Dalderby Ford had been completed. There the terminus remained while the committee sought means of extending the navigation to Horncastle.

Eventually, after a delay of two years, John Rennie's advice was sought on the possible cost of completion to Horncastle. He reported on 15 October 1799 that on the previous day he had carried out a survey and considered that the navigation between Dalderby and the Witham was in a crooked and imperfect state.[46] He recommended keeping the navigation on the west side of the Bain and making a cut independent of the river 28ft wide at the bottom and 30ft wide at the surface with a depth of $3\frac{1}{2}$ft. His estimate was £8,291 and the committee realized that to raise this additional capital another application to Parliament would have to be made. The winter of 1799–1800, during which the preparations for the Bill were in progress, was a particularly wet and stormy one so that the completed works on the navigation were badly damaged, and the whole future of the undertaking was in jeopardy.

On 10 March 1800 the petition to amend the 1792 Act was presented to the Commons and stated, inter alia, that 'the Petitioners have proceeded in the execution of the Act and completed the greater part of the works and have expended all the money raised or borrowed on the mortgage of the tolls and duties. They have incurred sundry debts and very great arrears of interest payable to the original shareholders and also large sums to proprietors for lands cut for the canal and to enable completion and discharge of debts a further sum is required.' It was then that the petitioners ran into difficulties as the Parliamentary Committee found that standing orders had not been complied with in the presentation of the petition. This was on the grounds that application should not be made to Parliament until after the time limit for giving notices had elapsed. It was noted that, because of the high floods and consequential damage, it was absolutely necessary that the Act should be

amended and some additional rates procured during the present session, otherwise the works would be totally ruined. Nevertheless it was directed that the petition should 'lie on the
table'.[47] It was again reported to the House on 26 May 1800
when the urgency arising from the 'very violent and continued
floods during the whole of the last unseasonable winter' was
again emphasized.[48] It was agreed that the failure to comply
with standing orders could be condoned and the measure
speedily passed through all stages, receiving the royal assent on
9 July 1800.[49] The Act gave the welcome facility to raise £20,000
either by mortgage or annuities and also the power to charge
higher rates. The restriction to a maximum dividend of 8 per
cent was also lifted.

By June 1801 the additional capital had been raised and at a
meeting on 12 November 1801 it was recommended that W.
Walker, one of the shareholders not present at this meeting,
'from his great knowledge of mathematics and numberless
other reasons is a very proper man to superintend the execution
of the works necessary to complete the canal'. Presumably because good progress was being made it was resolved on 1 January 1802 that the treasurer 'do pay and allow each person now
working on the navigation who shall continue and complete
their several contracts one shilling each to spend'.

At long last, and ten years after the passing of the Act, the
navigation was completed to Horncastle, a distance of eleven
miles from the Witham. On 17 September 1802 the formal
opening took place. 'At one o'clock the *Betsey* of Horncastle
and the *Martha* of Dalderby, the property of Messrs Gilliat &
Wilson; and the *British Queen*, the property of Mr Boyers,
entered the different basins of the navigation; they were
hauled in by ropes, amidst the cheers of the surrounding
spectators, and were beautifully decorated with colours.'[50]

When the navigation was complete there were two basins
at Horncastle. A small basin at Tumby, known as Tumby
Cut was extended in 1876, very late in the navigation's history, to serve Swan's granaries. There were eleven locks;
Horncastle, Thornton, Martin, Dalderby, Roughton, Hal-
tham, Kirkby-on Bain, Fulsby Mill, Tumby, Coningsby or

Second and Tattershall. This was one less than the original proposal of 1792. The total fall from Horncastle was 84ft.

Once vessels could navigate through to Horncastle traffic began steadily to increase though it was ten years before surplus profits could be spared to pay a dividend. Nevertheless when dividends started they remained at a reasonable level for the next forty years. Between 1840 and 1855 two rates were paid; the higher for those shareholders who had made an extra subscription after the 1800 Act, and the lower rate for those who had not so advanced their holding.

Table of average annual dividends

	per cent		per cent		per cent
1792–1812	Nil	1845–9	7 and 5	1860–4	3
1813–1839	5	1850–4	6 and 5	1865–9	1
1840–1844	7 and 5	1855–9	3	1870–3	$1\frac{1}{2}$

No further dividends paid.

The first threat of railway competition came in 1845 when the proposed London & York Railway wished to cross the canal by a swing or draw bridge. This proposal was opposed by the committee, as also was the much more serious threat of a Great Northern proposal to build a railway from Tattershall to Horncastle. The threat became closer with the opening on 17 October 1848 of the Boston & Lincoln line along the bank of the Witham although there was a temporary gain to the navigation by goods being transhipped from the railway to boats and vice versa at Dogdyke. In fact when the Horncastle Railway was again promoted in 1853 it was stated that £1,677 had been paid in canal dues by the G.N.R. in 1852 to the Horncastle company, and as the navigation company had £1,700 net available for dividend in that year a good traffic potential showed itself. Despite strong opposition from the navigation the railway company obtained its Act without having to pay any compensation. The navigation suffered in another way because Sir Henry Dymoke, who had successfully opposed the 1846 railway proposal, resigned as president of the Horncastle Canal in 1854 'as he wished to give the proposed railway all the support in his power'. He was chairman of the railway and the extent of his secession is shown by his comment at the opening of the railway when he said: 'It is perfectly absurd and monstrous that they should be trusting now to a canal with an old tug boat when they could get more expeditious and convenient means of communication.' The opening of the railway on 11 August 1855 occasioned the dramatic fall in dividends from 6 per cent in 1855 to $1\frac{1}{2}$ per cent in 1856, and although canal rates were reduced in 1856 to try to regain the lost traffic there was little success. It is interesting to note that descendants of the same families whose members had been instrumental in bringing the navigation into being were some of the sponsors and advocates of the new competitor. Such is progress.

The Horncastle, in common with most waterways, had its problems with staff as well as its faithful servants, such as William Flower. The events leading to Flower's appointment are themselves of interest. In 1819 John Crow was the keeper of Low, or Tattershall Lock. This was the most important lock on the navigation as it was here that the tolls were collected. On 21 October 1819 Crow found himself in trouble for permitting certain oversize boats which damaged the locks to navigate on the canal in spite of a specific prohibition by the committee. At the enquiry it was accepted that the superintendent, Frankland, was the principal offender and he was dismissed. Crow, because he had been 'a deserving servant of the company for so many years was reprimanded and continued in his situation'. Twelve months later Crow was in trouble again for allowing vessels to pass with greater tonnage on board 'then was returned by the parties and paid for to the company by which the company had been defrauded to the amount of £200 and upwards; the great part of which has been since recovered from the boatmen by process'. On this occasion Crow's long service did not save him for he was dismissed.

The vacant post was then advertised and 70 applications were received. From the short list Ben Sharpe of Hull was appointed, but did not last long. On 20 September 1821 he was in trouble because he was frequently intoxicated and particularly on Saturday 8 September 1821 'when desired to attend the Magistrates Office at Horncastle to lodge a complaint against

John Taylor, a boatman, he came so very drunk that the magistrates ordered him out of the room'. He, too, was dismissed. William Flower had been one of the other candidates when Sharpe was appointed. He was approached by the clerk to the company to enquire whether he still wished to have the post. He accepted and was appointed on 18 October 1821.

Flower was apparently a go-ahead sort of man although his acquisition of a horse in 1824 evoked an immediate criticism from the committee. Their displeasure stemmed from the reports that Flower had been hiring out his horse to boatmen. He was informed that he would not be permitted to keep a horse as 'it may form a connection between him and the boatmen which might lead to bad consequences'. By 1838, after 17 years service, he thought he was entitled to a rise in salary so he wrote to the committee:

17 October 1838.

Gentlemen.

I am extremely sorry after the many favours I have received from you during a period of 17 years that I feel myself under the necessity of troubling you with a further call upon your liberality. I have now a family of 9 children. The salary I receive from you is my only income and having no other emolument I find that with the utmost economy I and my wife can use it is very inadequate for the support of ourselves and family and enabling us to educate our children, place them out, and to appear with that decent respectability becoming my situation. I humbly beg therefore that you will take the matter into your consideration and that you will extend your kindness in making such an advance to my salary as you can do with justice. I am fully sensible of the responsibility attached to my office and trust and hope that you will continue to experience from me the same care, diligence, and punctuality which hitherto I have anxiously endeavoured to use and which that responsibility demands.

With my most heartfelt thanks for all you favours

I am, Gentlemen,

Your humble servant,

William Flower.

The result of this application was that Flower was given £10 for the previous year and his salary was raised from £60 to £70 pa as from the current year. This more than 16 per cent rise no doubt made a considerable difference to the Flower household. Flower continued to serve the company until his death in August 1848.

As with most other navigation companies the committee made regular inspections of their property and prior to 1822 they used to hire a boat for the trip down the canal. Because they were 'seldom able to meet with a boat they can use with safety or comfort to themselves' they instructed Thomas Wilkinson, their carpenter, on 8 October 1822 to build a boat for their use. On 13 May 1823 they proudly recorded that they went 'down the canal in the yacht lately built for the company's use' but they ensured that it would not be improperly used by stating that no one, not even a member of the committee, could use the yacht without a written order from the meeting. Two years later they complained that the curtains of the boat were very inconvenient in cold, wet, and windy weather, so they instructed Richard Harrison, who had succeeded Thomas Wilkinson, on the latter's appointment as superintendent, to fit up the boat with glass doors and windows and with a table to write upon. It was apparently expected that the collector at Tattershall Lock would arrange for a meal at the end of the inspection tour and there is a very human note by Mr Smith, the collector, recording the aftermath of the meal on 26 August 1868:

They left us the remaining provisions after their servants, Richard and William Burnett, Robert Graves, and Boatman Porter Dennis and the man helping to cut the weeds had taken their dinners. Given by Mr Gilliat and Mr Cussons the remains of a roast chine of beef, lean part of a hare, fragments of a couple of fowls, one pound of cheese, and three small loaves of bread, ale and porter. They collected among the committee eight shillings and sixpence given to Mrs Smith for potatoes, which I had dug and she had cooked, setting out the lunch and waiting upon them. They got to our house at one and left about three. Mr Cussons bought a couple of ducks and Mary gave him nine eggs and Mr Armstrong three ducks.[51]

In due course the boat, *The Lady Banks* became unfit for further use and was offered for sale in July 1876. The next year they went down the navigation in a hired steam barge.

The main traffic was coal, fertilizer and general cargo to Horncastle and agricultural produce downwards usually to and from Lincoln and Boston, but occasionally vessels made longer journeys as in June 1847 when a boat arrived in Horncastle from St Katherine Dock, London with a general cargo. The coming of the railway was the beginning of the end but traffic still continued during the 1860s and early 1870s though steadily declining. By 1874 it was described as trifling and a further loss was sustained that year by the insolvency of the late treasurer, Mr Gilliat. Nevertheless it was not until 1880 that it was proposed that the concern be wound up, although an offer to purchase the navigation for £4,000 had been made and refused in 1870. The last recorded cargo from Horncastle was 150 quarters of wheat for Boston on 7 May 1878 while the last boat to Horncastle was 31 tons of guano from Boston on 11 May 1878. Coal traffic to Horncastle had ceased in 1876 and the last coal boat on the navigation was one with 17 tons on 11 October 1877 to Kirkby-on-Bain.[52] Even after traffic had ceased meetings continued and an unusual sidelight on the company's activities is recorded in August 1880: 'The stock of swans consists of 13 old birds (including 4 of 1879 which have paired) and 8 young ones, cygnets of 1880, four of one clutch and four of another. The four 1879 birds have got a habit of straying into the Witham and thence into the Sleaford Navigation.'

The last annual general meeting was held on 11 November 1884. On 23 September 1889 R. Toynbee, a member of the firm of solicitors who had latterly acted for the company, wrote to the Board of Trade stating that the 'canal is now a defunct undertaking'.

Today, several of the lock chambers, minus their gates, remain, but the wharves and warehouses at Horncastle have largely disappeared and the canal basins have been reconstructed as drainage channels. The old dry-dock at Horncastle is now the site of a swimming pool. The railway was closed to passenger traffic on 13 September 1954 and to goods traffic on 1 April 1971.

Sleaford Navigation

Situated some 17 miles south of Lincoln and on the main road from that city to Peterborough, Sleaford had long been an important market centre in southern Lincolnshire, but towards the end of the eighteenth century influential local landowners, including Sir Christopher Whitchcote, Bart, of Aswarby and Sir Jenison Gordon of Haverholme Priory, felt that modernization of communications with other parts of the country, and particularly Lincoln and Boston, should be undertaken to stimulate and increase trade. The town lies on the River Slea, which rises in the high lands near Ancaster to the west and flows generally easterly through Sleaford to South Kyme, where its name changes to the Kyme Eau for the remainder of its course to the River Witham at Chapel Hill.

About 1774 there had been a survey for a canal from Sleaford to Grantham, but by 1783 the eyes of those interested had turned in the opposite direction, for then the proposal was that the Slea and the Kyme Eau should be made navigable from Sleaford to the Witham. This was in essence the revival of an old traffic route, as the Kyme Eau had been navigable as far back as the reign of Edward III. In 1375 Gilbert d'Umframville, Earl of Angus, was presented for unlawfully taking toll for the previous 12 years at Holmemylne dyke in Kyme for boats from Boston to Kesteven carrying 'merchandise for the sustenance of men there dwelling'; this merchandise was probably corn, wine, herrings and wool. In his defence before the king he stated that there was 'passage by water across his manor of Kyme, called Kyme Eau, between Dog Dyke and Brent Fen'. This was very suitable for 'ships and boats of those parts' but the channel was silted up and the banks broken so that the navigation was impassable. He had agreed to make the necessary repairs and by letters patent of 26 December 1342 he was granted the right to levy toll.[53]

Over the centuries the navigation had once again fallen into decay and was unusable when on 16 January 1783 a meeting was held in Sleaford to discuss the promotion of a Sleaford Navigation. It was immediately clear that there would be little hope of financial, or even practical, success unless the Witham commissioners could be persuaded to reduce their tolls on traffic using the Witham and passing to or from the Sleaford Navigation. It was, therefore, decided even at this early stage, to seek their consent for such a reduction from 1s 6d to 9d a ton. It was suggested that the increased traffic arising from the proposed navigation would offset the reduction. This suggestion was considered by the Witham commissioners at their meeting on 30 January 1783, where it suffered a very cool reception and generated a tart rejoinder. The commissioners did, however, temper the wind in resolving that when the Sleaford Navigation should be completed they would review the position to benefit the Sleaford without injuring the Witham.

Some special pleading must then have taken place because on 30 July 1783 a further resolution was passed stating that they would not oppose the insertion of a clause in the Sleaford Bill providing for a reduction of Witham tolls.

At a later meeting on 6 November 1783 of the Sleaford committee the members had another discussion on the allocation of the tolls between the Witham and the Sleaford. It was now suggested that a further 6d should be added to the existing 1s 6d Witham toll and that, of the total, 9d should go to the Witham and 1s 3d to the Sleaford. The Witham commissioners considered this on 13 November 1783 and agreed to the new proposals, subject to safeguards against fraudulent evasion. Nevertheless they still had reservations, although they recognized that the traffic on the Sleaford would benefit the Witham, one of their reasons being that under the Witham Act the commissioners were restricted from lowering river tolls until a competent part of the money borrowed was paid off. At this stage, far from the loans being paid off, the interest was considerably in arrear. As there was already traffic on the Kyme Eau from which the Witham was collecting the full toll of 1s 6d they were anxious that this traffic should in no way benefit from the proposed reduction and they, therefore, wanted a point fixed on the Kyme Eau beyond which the reduction, if granted, should be allowed. This point was originally suggested as the southeast corner of Anwick Fen, amended to the Befferies, and finally to Ewerby Clapps.

Following this flurry of activity in 1783–4, the scheme lay relatively dormant for seven years. The next move was in 1791 when William Jessop and John Hudson were commissioned to survey the Slea and the Kyme Eau; their report, including an estimate of the cost of making the river navigable to Sleaford for £9,979, was published on 25 November 1791. Rather strangely Handley of the Sleaford committee submitted the report to the Witham commissioners at their meeting on 6 December 1791 whereas the Sleaford committee themselves did not consider it until 29 December.

At the Witham meeting on 6 December a revised boundary point for the reduction of tolls was substituted for Ewerby Clapps. It was now agreed that boats passing through the lock above Drewry Dyke on the Sleaford Navigation should benefit from the half toll rate.

On 29 December the Sleaford committee meeting at the Angel Inn, Sleaford, decided to adopt the report and apply for an Act immediately. Although there was some objection on the grounds that the making of the navigation might cause land damage, the Bill had a fairly uneventful passage, receiving the royal assent on 11 June 1792.[54] The undertaking's full title was 'The Company of Proprietors of the Sleaford Navigation in the County of Lincoln', the capital being £13,500 in £100 shares. Among the subscribers was Boston corporation who clearly thought that the trade would benefit that port rather than Lincoln. Of the 135 shares issued, apart from ten purchased by non-Lincolnshire residents, 50 per cent were taken up by Sleaford people. It was therefore very definitely a locally-financed scheme.

The first meeting of the proprietors was held almost immediately on 22 June 1792 at the house of Edward Bates in Sleaford.

A committee of six was elected, of whom four were Sleaford residents and the other two were from neighbouring villages. Benjamin Cheales was appointed clerk at a salary of £20 per annum and Benjamin Handley treasurer. At this meeting a sense of pride in proprietorship appeared, a theme which was to run like a thread through the deliberations of the committees right into the final meeting in 1881. On this occasion it was, 'ordered that the device for a seal this day produced and recommended by Sir Joseph Banks, Bart. be adopted and used as the Common Seal and that the thanks of the meeting under the Common Seal be given to Sir J. Banks for the very essential services derived from his support and assistance to this Company and undertaking'. Further meetings were held on 7 May and 28 December 1793 and eventually £16,000 including loans was raised.[55]

The Act authorized the proprietors to take the navigation along the Sleaford millstream to New Sleaford and Old Sleaford, through the south bridge in Sleaford and along the south branch of the millstream to the Castle Causeway. Power was also given to make new cuts where necessary so as to provide a waterway 18ft wide at the bottom and 30ft wide at the top. It was to have a depth of 4ft to Haverholme Mill and from there to the Castle Causeway 5ft. As mentioned later the navigation ceased at the public wharf in Carre Street and was not extended to Castle Causeway. Its length from Sleaford to the Witham was 12¼ miles.

The seven locks, each 60ft × 15ft, had an average fall of 4ft 9in and were named from west to east; Coggleford Mill, Dyers Mill, Corn Mill, Paper Mill, Haverholme, Anwick, and Kyme Lower.

The general toll for the full distance was not to exceed 2s per ton, but this was to be reduced for shorter distances. Lime, limestone, manure, or road material were to pay only half the normal rates. For traffic passing to or from the Witham, the Witham tolls were to be reduced by one half. This was in conformity with the concession allowed to the Horncastle company. It was further laid down that dividends must be limited to 8 per cent and that when they exceeded that figure then, after reserving £1,000 for contingencies, tolls were to be reduced. In fact there was a reduction of tolls in 1802 although a dividend of 8 per cent had not been declared.

Construction was completed in less than two years and the committee announced that the 'Navigation will be open from the river Witham to the Town of Sleaford for the passage of boats barges and other vessels on 6 May' 1794.[56] This announcement brought an immediate public advertisement from John Dyson, the contractor, that 'unless the said Company or Committee do before that time satisfy the Contractors for the Works executed thereon such navigation will not then be opened'.[57] Apart from informing the public that Dyson's 'conduct in the execution of the works for which they contracted will become the Subject of Investigation in a Court of Law as the only proper place where the differences between the parties (after such an advertisement) can be decided upon', the committee decided to ignore the threat and the opening went ahead on 6 May 1794 as planned.[58] The gratitude of the committee on this occasion took the form of a presentation to Benjamin Handley of a beautifully engraved silver cup illustrating, among other details, a scene on a navigation including a keel with sail set and being towed by two horses. Round the base of the cup is engraved the words 'The Gift of the Proprietors of the Sleaford Navigation 6 May 1794'.[59]

As on most Lincolnshire navigations, the tolls were from time to time leased to toll farmers. In 1816 the committee advertised the letting of the tolls but it is not clear whether at this time they were successful, but by 1826 the tolls were held by John Keyworth of Lincoln for £1,010. By 1830 Enoch Blackbourn of Hunslet, Leeds, held them for £1,310. Joshua Bower, also of Hunslet, a glass manufacturer, took them for three years in 1836 for £1,340 per annum, and renewed his lease in 1839 for another three years at the increased figure of £1,590. Difficulties in letting the tolls because of falling receipts caused the committee to revert to collecting the tolls themselves in 1851.[60]

Although a dividend of 2½ per cent was paid in 1795 the income thereafter did not justify a further dividend until 1817 when 3 per cent was paid. This was repeated in 1818 and then there was another gap until 1824. From 1826 there were regular dividends, and in the twenty years after 1836 they remained at

Sleaford Navigation.

An ACCOUNT or SCHEDULE of the feveral GOODS, WARES, and MERCHANDIZES, which are to be taken and confidered as a TON, and to pay TOLL accordingly.

QUALITY.	QUANTITY.	TONS.	QUALITY.	QUANTITY.	TONS.
Coals, - -	1 Chaldron, -	1	1 hatch Reed,	5 Hundred,	1
Oats, - -	10 Quarter, -	1	Grocery, —	2 Hogfheads	1
Barley, -	6 Quarter, -	1	Latten Reed,	250 Bunches,	1
Malt, - -	10 Quarter, -	1	Soap, —	2 Hogfheads,	1
Wheat, -	5 Quarter, -	1	Woad, —	1 Hogfhead,	3 qrs.
Beans, -	5 Quarter, -	1	Spetches, -	8 Packs, —	1
Peas, - -	5 Quarter, -	1	Squares at 9 Inches	250	1
Rape, - -	5 Quarter, -	1	Sheep, —	Twenty,	1
Bark, -	10 Quarter, -	1	Porter, —	6 Barrels,	1
Whole Lime, -	1 Chald. & half	1	Flour, —	8 Sacks, —	1
Sleck'd Lime, -	2 Chaldron,	1	Seed, —	5 Quarter,	1
Potatoes, - -	130 Pecks, —	1	Hay, —	20 Hundred, —	1
Lime Stone, -	4 Hogfheads,	1	Glafs, —	7 Whole Crates	1
Timber, (Oak, Afh, & Elm)	40 Feet, —	1	Hemp Seed, Pofts 4 and half	40 Strike, — 120,	1 1
Fir Timber, -	50 Feet, —	1	Coak, —	100 Strike, —	1
Bricks, -	5 Hundred, —	1	Pavements,	3 Hundred,	1
Flat Tile, -	1 Thoufand,	1	Stone, -	16 Feet Cubic,	1
Pan Tile, -	5 Hundred, —	1	Paving Stone,	10 Superf. Yards.	1
Oil Cakes, about 6lb. and half a Pair.	1 Thoufand,	1 & half			
Larger Cakes in Proportion,					
Wine, - -	2 Pipes, —	1			
Felloes, - -	120 —	1			
Seven Feet Pofts,	Sixty —	1			
Six Feet, Five Feet & half	Eighty, Ninety,	1			
Single Deals, -	Half Hundred	1			
Double Deals,	QuarterHund.	1			
Battens, -	1 Hundred	1			

N. B. ALL other Articles not mentioned in the foregoing Lift to be fubject to 2s. per Ton of 2240 Pounds, to be afcertained either by Weighing or Draught of Water.

B. CHEALES,

Clerk to the Company.

14. Sleaford Navigation table of ton equivalents

over 5 per cent reaching 8 per cent in at least two years. After the period of railway development in Lincolnshire in the 1850s they rapidly diminished until in 1868 no dividend was paid.

In 1827, at the time when the company's fortunes were in the ascendant a proposal was made to extend the navigation west-

		Revenue		(to nearest £)	
	£		£		£
1838	1,441	1865	211	1873	209
1848	1,785	1866	168	1874	159
1853	1,885	1868	257	1875	166
1858	1,057	1870	88	1876	137
1859	386	1871	105	1877	132[61]
1861	234	1872	138		

wards for 3 or 4 miles to Wilsford, and then in 1833 J. Rofe and his son put forward a much more ambitious scheme.[62] This was, in effect, a revival of the 1774 project to form a 16-mile junction canal between Sleaford and Grantham in order to give the Midlands a direct link to Boston and the east coast without transhipment of cargoes, as was necessary for either the Lincoln or the Hull route. Both these proposals, however, remained pipe dreams.

A local trader made an abortive attempt in 1833 to have the navigation extended to Castle Causeway, the limit specified in the original act, but the company took counsel's opinion on their liabilities under the Act and stated: 'The works were then compleated to the East End of the town of Sleaford where a suitable wharf was erected for the use of the Company, but beyond the extremity of this wharf no works were ever erected. This point is a distance of 4 or 500 yards short of the Castle Causeway. There was only £700 left to carry the navigation to Castle Causeway which was barely enough.' Counsel took the view that there was now no residual liability to extend the navigation.[63]

Two further examples of the committee's pride of proprietorship occurred in 1839 and 1841. In 1839 it was ordered that an octagon copper lamp of extended size be placed in the wharf yard, the pillar to be elevated on a block of Bramley Fell stone. In 1841 they purchased from the Butterley Company a 10-ton crane to be fitted alongside the wharf wall at a cost of £300. Included in the contract was the following 'and the words in raised letters cast upon the crane—Sleaford Navigation erected by the Company of Proprietors'.[64]

With the fall in revenue in the 1860s and 1870s the proprietors realised that there was little chance of a successful future for the undertaking, and as early as 30 January 1865 they were considering 'terminating the duties and responsibilities of the Proprietors of this navigation'. As trade continued to decline application was eventually made to Parliament for an Act to enable them to abandon the undertaking; this, the Sleaford Navigation (Abandonment) Act 1878 received the royal assent on 17 June 1878. It provided not only for the dissolution of the company but also for the action to be taken in connection with the locks. Three of them, Corn Mill, Dyers Mill, and Coggleford Mill, were to be filled in in a substantial manner to the height of the banks. The action on the next three locks was conditioned by the fact that for five miles the navigation passed through or bounded the estate of the Hon Murray Hatton of Haverholme Priory. These locks, Anwick, Haverholme, and Paper Mill were, out of the assets of the company, to be put in good and sufficient repair and then handed over with the navigation to the Hon Mr Hatton to be maintained by him or abandoned at his discretion. If he abandoned the navigation then he had to provide sluices at the locks and fill up the lock chambers in a substantial manner. Incidentally, he also had the right to use the towpath on the north-west bank, which was not on his land, between Haverholme and Anwick locks. In return the owner of the towpath had the right to use the navigation between the locks.

The seventh lock, Kyme Lower, $1\frac{3}{4}$ miles from the Witham, had also to be put into good and sufficient repair and then handed over to the general commissioners of the Witham who would, at their discretion, have power to remove the gates, fill in the lock and dispose of the materials. The formal decision notifying the closure took place on 14 May 1881 at the last general meeting of the proprietors when a final dividend of 2.6 per cent was declared. Although this meeting marked the close of an era the committee, true to their tradition, felt the dignity of the occasion as they passed the following resolution: 'In recording the final winding up of the Company this day the Proprietors desire to express their thanks to the committee of management and more especially to Mr Marston, the Chairman, for their valuable services in obtaining the Act for the dissolution of the Company and in winding up the affairs of the Company.'[65]

Despite the legal abandonment of the navigation and the closure of the upper locks, more than half the waterway, the $6\frac{1}{2}$ miles from the Witham to Ewerby Waithe Common, remained navigable until the 1940s when the general commissioners at long last converted Kyme Lower lock into a sluice. This left only the truncated arm from the Witham to the sluice available for pleasure craft, though the old navigation still serves as a drainage channel for the waters of the Slea and for surface drainage. Yet there still remain in Carre Street in Sleaford the navigation office with the arms of the navigation displayed over the door, and the massive stone entrance to the wharf proudly and defiantly inscribed '1792 NAVIGATION WHARF.'

CHAPTER XI

The North Lincolnshire Navigations

◆◆◆

Ancholme Navigation

On the dominant ridge running north from Lincoln and along which the Romans laid down their important military road, Ermine Street, there rises a small stream which flows down the eastern slope into the valley between the ridge on the west and the Lincolnshire Wolds on the east. This stream, the River Ancholme turns suddenly north after about four miles and originally followed a meandering course through the marshland to join the Humber at what is now Ferriby Sluice at South Ferriby some three miles west of Barton-upon-Humber.

Despite its meanders, its silted bed aggravated by the influx of the tides from the Humber, and the generally waterlogged condition of the land on both sides, it was early recognized as offering a means of communication into the northern part of Lincolnshire. The problems of maintaining it were similar to those found elsewhere in the Eastern Counties, for dangers arising from neglect with consequential flooding were ever present. Even before 1287 craft had been able to make some use of the Ancholme mainly, no doubt, in times of flood, for in that year a patent was granted to improve Ancholme to Bishopbridge 'that ships and boats laden with corn and other things might then more commodiously pass with corn and other things from the said river Humber into the parts of Lindsey than they at that time could do and as they had done formerly'.[1]

But despite the need for, and benefits of, adequate transport local criticism was far more vehemently directed against the failure of the Ancholme to drain the marshlands than against its failure as a viable navigation. This dichotomy affected its development and maintenance right down to the present day. For example between 1289 and 1418 there are at least thirteen references in the Patent Rolls, an average of one every ten years, to the need for channels to be scoured owing to the lack of drainage. These reflect the concern of riparian owners to prevent inundation of their lands and to minimize any consequential damage. The references do not always mention navigation, even though the facilities offered by the river would be of benefit to neighbouring farms and estates.

The chronic cycle of concern, improvement, euphoria, and neglect continued over the years until in 1635 power was given to Sir John Monson to construct a new river for drainage purposes.[2] It was at this time that the configuration of the river took the basic form it has today, with most of the meanders eliminated and a straight drainage channel, Dutch in appearance, drawing water from the Ancholme, Rase and other streams directly north from Bishopbridge through Brigg to Ferriby Sluice to drain into the Humber. Although this Patent obviously played a direct part in the ultimate development of navigation on the Ancholme there is no specific reference in it to the works being of advantage for transport purposes. In fact the impression is given that the navigation interest was only continued on sufferance: 'If any new cuts or drains were made or any of the old drains enlarged then there was an obligation to keep the river as useful for the passage of boats as it then was or had been for the seven years last past (excepting in flood times).' It was at this time, too, in the late 1630s, that the first sluice was erected at the outfall of the Ancholme into the Humber (although there was a bridge there as early as 1312) so that better control could be exercised over the tidal deposit of silt in the river on the ebb tides. This sluice had 3 arches and 24 doors but the method of working it for navigation is not indicated.[3]

The river then suffered another period of laissez-faire on the part of those responsible which resulted in progressive deterioration so that in 1724 William Stukeley in his 'Itinerarium curiosum' could write

We pass'd by the spring of old Wintringham and the marsh at the mouth of the Ankham, which is a vast tract of land left by the sea; and came to Ferriby sluice, a stately bridge of three arches with sluices for voydance of the waters into the sea, but now broken down and lying in dismal ruins by the negligence of the undertakers whence travellers are obliged to pass the river in a paltry short boat, commanded by a little old deaf fellow with a long beard. Into this boat you descend by the steep of the river, thro' a deep miry clay full of stones and stakes. Nor is the ascent on the other side any better, both dangerous and difficult. This with the hideous ruins of the bridge (sic) like the picture of hell gates in Milton and the terrible roar of the water passing thro' it, partly represented Virgil's description of Charon's ferry. Nor would a poet wish for a better scene to heighten his fancy were he to paint out the horrors of the confines of hell.

> Hence the way leads to Fereby forlorn
> Where Ankan's oozy flood with hideous roar
> Tears up the sands and sluices ruin'd vaults.
> A squallid Charon the dread ferry ply's,
> In leaky skull, whose furrow'd cheeks lye deep
> With hoary beard insconc'd.

When we had mounted the precipice again from the water and paid our maul to the inexorable ferryman we had several clayey lakes to ride over impassible in winter.

Conditions had become so intolerable by the 1760s that the landlords had the river surveyed by Thomas Yeoman who reported on 17 September 1766: 'Ferriby Sluice had decayed and the Humber water had gone up to Glanford leaving much silt. The New Drain 40ft wide is reduced to 15ft—16ft in some places which is the chief cause of flooding. Above Glanford it is interrupted by Lug Beds, Weeds, and Sands and wholly silted up for the last 5 miles next to Bishop Briggs.'[4]

After having considered this report the landlords petitioned Parliament on 26 January 1767 for leave to bring in a Bill to improve both drainage and navigation up to Bishopbridge. The

Bill passed through the various stages fairly rapidly and on 20 May 1767 the royal assent was given.[5]

The first meeting of the new commissioners was held on 17 June 1767, when John Bennett of Barton-upon-Humber was appointed clerk. Mr Bennett had been responsible for much of the work in connection with obtaining the Act and at this meeting he was awarded £861 for it and his trouble. Despite the Act's recognition of the need for improving navigation the minutes of the commissioners' meetings indicate, from their pronounced bias towards drainage matters, that these were the prime purpose of the legislation. Nevertheless work was done which benefited navigation. A major matter was the construction of a new sluice and lock at Ferriby. The new sluice had three openings but the sills were laid 8ft above the level of low water spring tides. This unfortunate design was to pose problems for the next 77 years as, in times of heavy rainfall, adequate run-off to clear the flooded lowlands could not be obtained. The lock was 70ft × 14ft 9in and was on a separate channel from the drain to the sluice. An adjacent lockhouse was also completed under the direction of Joseph Page, engineer, on 12 September 1769.

During the next ten years it was gradually realized by the commissioners that encouragement of navigation would be generally beneficial although it was alleged that they were being motivated by too much self-interest. Nevertheless it was resolved that Dunderdale, the engineer, should stake out land at Bishopbridge as a coal and general goods wharf.[6] Despite this order the commissioners do not appear to have been in any hurry to acquire the land, though the resignation of Dunderdale and the appointment of Thomas Bradley as engineer on 2 October 1781 may have prolonged the delay. It was not until 20 July 1785 that a meeting was arranged to treat with the proprietors for the purchase of land at Bishopbridge.

In order further to forward their development of Bishopbridge the commissioners, also on 7 April 1778, instructed their engineer to provide a lock at Harlam Hill as that 'would greatly increase the revenue arising from the navigation'.

On 2 July 1781 the commissioners adopted a practice which was to be followed on and off for nearly a century; that of leasing the tolls. On this occasion they leased them to Jona-than and John Goodwin for £402 per annum for eleven years, the leaseholders keeping the lockhouse, locks and bridges over the hauling ways in repair. The commissioners recognized that situations might arise where it would be improper to charge the cost to the lessee and so it was agreed that damage by tides of more than £20 was to be repaired by the commissioners but if less than £20 by the lessees.[7]

On the expiration of Goodwin's lease on 2 July 1792 the commissioners resumed operating the navigation themselves and appointed their own collector. This new situation made them look more critically at the toll rates and one thing they noticed was the varying capacity of the waggons at the various collieries whose coals passed along the navigation: 'Tonnage of coals be taken after the rate of one chaldron for each waggon of Haigh-moor and Flockton Coals; of one chaldron and six bushels each waggon of Sir William's coals; and of one chaldron and 'nine bushels of Parkgate, Flockton, [repeated], Bramlin, and Fenton's coals.' This decision gives an indication of the source of the coal supplies for the Ancholme hinterland. Some of this traffic would have travelled via the Aire & Calder, some by the Don, and the Humber.[8]

The last decade of the eighteenth century saw an intensi-fication of the commissioners' perpetual problem of drainage and the urgent need to find an effective solution prompted them to obtain a comprehensive report and recommendations on the Ancholme level. Instructions were given to Isaac Leatham of Barton, near Malton and he presented his report on 1 and 29 August 1800. The cost of his proposals for both efficient drain-age and an effective navigation startled the commissioners, who regarded £22,975 as excessive for the amount of work involved.

Later in the same year they requested a survey by John Rennie, as a second opinion, which they received on 9 November 1801. Most of his proposals concerned drainage and in particular the construction of catchwater drains but he also proposed widening and deepening the river, providing two new locks, and reconstructing the road bridge at Brigg. The commissioners were even more staggered by his estimate of

£53,921, of which £6,063 was for the improvement of navigation, but Rennie suggested that the work be carried out by stages. He later, however, submitted a modified plan for £25,413 and on this basis the commissioners decided to proceed.

Application was made to Parliament to authorize the work and Rennie gave evidence. There was no opposition and the Act passed on 26 June 1802.[9] Power was granted to construct two locks, at Harlam Hill and Kingerby, to improve the navigation of the river's upper reach. A subsidiary requirement was that the commissioners were to provide mooring posts in oak to be numbered as mile posts at one-mile intervals from Ferriby Sluice.

Tenders for the supply of materials were sought from 'Stone Dealers, Brickmakers and Timber merchants': 4,100cu ft of stone from Bramley near Leeds was required to be delivered by the end of April 1803 to Ferriby Sluice, the new bridge at Brigg and to the locks near Bishopbridge. In addition 150,000 bricks were to be delivered to Ferriby Sluice in May and 170,000 at Brigg bridge in July. No specific date was given for the delivery of 60 loads of soft wood and 50 loads of oak.[10] This prompt ordering of materials was bedevilled by chronic shortage of finance; progress was so slow that it seemed the work would never be finished.

Meanwhile in July 1808 Samuel Porter the engineer died. He was a native of Henley in Arden and prior to his appointment to the Ancholme Navigation, had been for many years engineer to the Stratford-upon-Avon Canal.

In 1824 Rennie's son Sir John Rennie was consulted and he recommended that the works specified by his father should be completed and furthermore the river should be widened and deepened to double its capacity. The sluice at Ferriby as modified by John Rennie senior should be completely reconstructed and the sill laid level with the L.W.O.S.T. instead of 8ft above it. A new entrance lock 20ft wide to take vessels of up to 60 tons should also be constructed.

On the basis of these proposals yet another Act was obtained in 1825[11] and work was resumed in 1826. Fairly good progress was maintained but financial stringency and litigation over the amount of rates each district should pay led to further delays though these mainly affected the drainage works. The financial arrangements caused Rennie some concern for he wrote to the clerk to the commissioners on 26 October 1826.

Dear Sir,

I have just seen Mr Burcham and have had a good deal of conversation about the Ancholme Works and was surprised to find that you have no person to comptrol the accounts and measurements. This should not be. I should therefore recommend that Mr Atkinson should be appointed to assist Mr Bradley in order that everything may be properly carried on and that no money should be paid to the Contractor without it being previously well ascertained that money is due. This will certainly be acceptable to me as well as yourself and request that you will speak to Mr Burcham in order that he may be appointed accordingly.

Believe me Dear Sir,
Very sincerely yours,
John Rennie[12]

It was during the years subsequent to 1826 that some of the structures standing today were erected, including bridges to replace wooden ones with several openings which restricted the flow of water. One of the most interesting is Horkstow bridge. It was originally intended that this should be a cast-iron bridge of 80ft span but before construction started the design was changed for that of the present bridge. This very attractive suspension bridge of 130ft span carries a farm road across the river. The design was accepted at a meeting of the commissioners on 2 December 1834 and it was erected very shortly afterwards. It therefore ranks now as one of the earliest suspension bridges still standing.

The present bridge near Yarborough mills in Brigg is a stone single-segmental arch structure built to Sir John Rennie's design at an estimated cost of £2,524. It replaced an earlier bridge and was completed in 1827, though it has been subsequently widened. A year later in 1828 Brandy Wharf bridge was completed. This, like most of the bridges across the Ancholme, is of iron with stone abutments. There have been a number of reconstructions since this period, eg Snitterby (1872), Hibaldstow (1889) and Cadney (1892) but the series of Ancholme bridges still presents an interesting range of design.

In 1827 too, Harlam Hill lock was re-constructed but the second lock at Kingerby was abandoned. Harlam Hill, 71ft × 16ft 6in, was also built to Sir John Rennie's design and estimate of £2,027. The only major alteration from the original design is the replacement of the upper gates by a guillotine gate. The existing ground-paddle casings are the original ones and are marked and dated 'J. Clayton, Bramley, Yorkshire 1827'. The balance beams for the lower gates are of an unusual, and yet very attractive, design being metal bars light in appearance without the usual massiveness of the normal wooden beams. These works of navigation improvement were completed to Bishopbridge by 18 June 1828.

Sir John Rennie's close control over the details of design is shown in the following letter of 17 March 1831 to William Jessop (son of the waterway engineer and manager of Butterley ironworks) regarding the construction of Brandy Wharf bridge (otherwise known at that time as Brandy Wath bridge):

Dear Sir,

I ought to have answered yours before relative to the construction of the Ancholme Bridge at Brandy Wharf but only saw my way clearly about them a few days since. With regard to casting the Ribs in two pieces I have no objection. With regard to your second question of leaving out the abutting plate in the centre and substituting distance pieces and allowing the ribs to abut against each other I prefer the former plan of enabling all the ribs to act together instead of individually. If, however, you are decidedly of a different opinion I will give way but recollect it must be entirely upon your own responsibility. With regard to the cornice and palisading I thought everything was clear. Of course the palisades are to be wrought iron. You must not put in hand any more than this one bridge until further orders and the sooner it is done the better.

Believe me, very sincerely,

J. Rennie.[13]

Meanwhile the possibility of extending the navigation southwards had been discussed. In 1823 a meeting of owners and occupiers of lands in the neighbourhood of Market Rasen was held at the White Hart inn in that town at which they discussed seeking powers for a canal from the Ancholme to Market Rasen. The Ancholme commissioners were then asked for their help but, after a further meeting on 3 September 1823, the scheme seems to have been dropped.[14] After lying dormant for about five years, it was revived in 1829 in more elaborate form as a plan to extend the Ancholme from Bishopbridge for 14 miles to the Witham at Barlings Eau, some $6\frac{1}{2}$ miles below Lincoln. It was considered that seven locks would be necessary, including one at the junction with the Witham. The estimated cost was £90,000. This scheme was also dropped, but even as late as 1841 and 1844 the idea was being canvassed, with support from Sir John Rennie.[15]

Although there was no extension southwards the Ancholme provided transport northwards for traffic between north Lincolnshire and the East Riding of Yorkshire, in particular the Hull and Beverley areas. The Humber was, however, a formidable barrier between the two communities. A regular service across it had been provided by William Colton, who operated a packet between Hull and Brigg from about 1793. In 1823 he announced that 'for the better accommodation of the public he had commenced running a steam packet every day, except Sundays, which leaves Hull every afternoon at three o'clock and arrives in Brigg in sufficient time in the evening for passengers to take the Lincoln coach'. The return journey was timed to leave Brigg at 7am and reach Hull by 10.30am.[16] Later the ferry was taken over by the Hull, Ferriby Sluice & Brigg Steam Packet Company. This company, formed in October 1856, had 32 shareholders, most of whom were farmers who lived in the area between Brigg and the Humber.[17]

On 4 October 1841 Sir John Rennie attended a meeting of the commissioners to discuss the reconstruction of South Ferriby Sluice. He considered that the work, to include a new lock, should be done as soon as possible. His estimated cost was

15. Seal of the Hull, Ferriby Sluice & Brigg Steam Packet Company

£16,533. The commissioners authorized the expenditure and the work was put in hand almost immediately. Since then, apart from the replacement in 1935 of the swing bridge over the lock by one of similar design to the original, the structure remains as designed by Sir John Rennie. Work started in March 1842 and the formal opening of the new sluice took place on 22 May 1844. It was opened by the Earl of Yarborough and Miss Alice Corbett, and the Earl of Yarborough's brass band attended the function. After the official opening the Earl sailed on the first vessel to pass through the lock, a schooner captained by William Twidale. In accordance with custom a cold collation followed. The total length of the bridge is 41ft 8in and it was designed to take a maximum weight of a loaded waggon and three horses—a total weight of approximately 6 tons. The swing-bridge over the lock, cast at Butterley, continued in use for 90 years without incident but in 1934 it was badly damaged in an accident when a large vessel struck it head on. The present swing-bridge was fabricated by Head Wrightson & Co Ltd in 1935.[18]

An indication of the navigation's prosperity is shown by the rents paid by the toll leaseholders. As previously stated the annual rent was £402 in the 1780s. This had risen to £950 in 1828 and £1,470 in 1836. From 1837–9 it was £1,620; 1840–2 £1,852; 1843–5 £1,857 and finally there was a sudden leap for the years 1846–8 to £3,020. Then the railway came, Brigg station being opened on 1 November 1848 and the line from Brigg to Gainsborough on 2 April 1849. Tolls for 1849 were £1,482 and for 1850 £949. By the end of the 1850s they were again being let, but at the greatly reduced figure of £700 pa. After three decades receipts started rising again and in the 1890s they were averaging £1,000. In the 1930s there was a growing traffic in sugarbeet and in the three years before the Second World War the tolls averaged £1,294 per annum.[19]

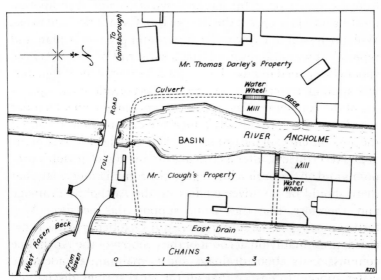

16. The Ancholme Navigation's basin at Bishopbridge, mid-nineteenth century

There is now no commercial traffic up to Bishopbridge, but

at one time it was a very important distribution and collecting centre for both agricultural and domestic goods for the farms and villages lying to the south. There were two corn mills, warehouses, and an inn and some conception of the activity can be gained from the accompanying plan of the area. Today the upper part of the navigation above Harlam Hill lock is rather weedy and shallow, though it is still navigable with difficulty by pleasure craft. This situation, however, could readily be rectified. There is still commercial traffic between Ferriby Sluice and Brigg, and the wide straight channel makes it much easier to traverse than most other commercial navigations. This section is very well maintained.

Caistor Canal

Growing realization of the economic advantages stemming from the post-1767 improvements to the Ancholme navigation led to a proposal in 1792 by a Mr Hall that a canal should be cut from the main river to the market town of Caistor. A promotion meeting on 3 July 1792 at the George Inn, Caistor decided to ask William Jessop to carry out a survey and prepare a plan and report.[20] It was also resolved that a subscription list of £12,000 should be opened in £100 shares. John Turner, a local solicitor, was appointed clerk. Jessop's report was considered at a meeting of the Ancholme Navigation Commissioners on 3 October 1792,[21] but there was clearly a measure of apprehension about the possible effect of the proposed scheme on the drainage of the area. Nevertheless, after a critical examination of Jessop's proposals and on the basis of his report, the commissioners felt that there should be no adverse effect on the Ancholme drainage and, therefore, that they could support the measure. At a further meeting of the subscribers on 31 October 1792 it was decided, presumably on account of the concern of the Ancholme commissioners about drainage and to maintain an adequate water supply, to ensure that all the local springs discharged into the head of the canal.

A parliamentary petition of Lord Middleton and others was presented on 18 February 1793 and on 3 June 1793 an Act was passed for 'Making and Maintaining a Navigable Canal from the River Ancholme, in the Parish of South Kelsey . . . into the Parish of Caistor'.[22] It was to be used for the conveyance of coals, corn, wool and other goods, wares and merchandise to the advantage of Caistor and surrounding districts.

The COMPANY of PROPRIETORS of the CAISTOR CANAL NAVIGATION in the COUNTY of LINCOLN.

THESE are to certify that Thomas Johnson of Caistor in the said County of Lincoln Gentleman *. . . is a Proprietor of* One, One Hundred and Thirty Second *Share of the Caistor Canal Navigation, being No.* 40. *. . . subject to the Raising more Shares of One Hundred Pounds each, not exceeding the Sum of Ten Thousand Pounds, in such additional Shares, and to the Rules, Regulations, and Orders of the said Company: AND that the said* Thomas Johnson *. . . his Executors, Administrators, and Assigns, is and are entitled to the Profits and Advantages of such Share.*

GIVEN under the common Seal of the said Company, the Second *. . . Day of* January *in the Year of our Lord One Thousand Seven Hundred and Ninety-* Five

ENTERED.

17. A share certificate of the Caistor Canal

The proprietors were authorized to raise £15,000 in £100 shares and a further £10,000 in loans. However, only 132 shares were issued. Unfortunately the one share register found records the allocation of only 80 shares, each certificate being dated 2 January 1795. These indicate local support for the navigation, twelve shares being distributed among seven persons living in Caistor. Twenty-six other shares went to Lincolnshire residents, while two shareholders with substantial holdings lived outside the county. Lord Middleton of Wollaton, Nottingham, held twenty shares and Francis Ferrand Foljambe of Aldwark, Rotherham, held ten shares. The latter was the grandson of the

Francis Foljambe who had so vigorously opposed the making of the river Don navigable to Sheffield. F. F. Foljambe was already a commissioner of the Ancholme Navigation, having been appointed from 5 July 1790, and he was chairman of the Caistor promotion meeting on 3 July 1792. In addition to purchasing shares in the company he entered into an agreement with the proprietors on 22 January 1798 to loan the company £4,600 at 5 per cent per annum interest. However, the tolls on the canal were insufficient even to pay the interest, so that, by 1813 £574 3s 6d arrears of interest were outstanding, in addition to the principal. At this time the treasurer reported that he had no money in his hands and owed £60 for repairs already done.[23] As far as can be traced the loan was never repaid.

Apart from merely nominal share transfers, shares were being sold in 1800 for a consideration of £20 each, a figure which reflected the adverse trading situation. On 10 April 1828 at Spalding four shares were offered for sale by auction with the laconic and depressing comment in the sale catalogue: 'No interest has yet been paid.' There is no record of the price paid nor which shareholder was so disposing of his shares.

The canal constructed under the direction of its engineer, Robert Dickenson, left the Ancholme four miles south of Brigg and ran for approximately four miles in an easterly direction—but never reached Caistor. A lane laid out in anticipation of the completion of the canal leads from Caistor town centre to the proposed site of the terminal basin and is to this day known as Navigation Lane. It was intended to serve as the final link in the line of communication between the Ancholme and Caistor. In fact the canal ended in a basin some four miles west of Caistor at Moortown on the Market Rasen—Brigg road (B1434). The vestiges of this basin can still be traced though the lines of some of its boundaries demand the eye of faith. The canal to Moortown seems to have been opened to traffic about 1800 and in 1801 an abortive proposal was made to extend it in a more southerly direction to Market Rasen.

Originally there were five locks (though Priestley states there were six) known in sequence from Moortown as Moor, Mill, Willow, Ings, and Beck End. The total fall was 42ft. Between

Mill and Willow locks lay South Kelsey basin and bridge.

Alford Canal Project

Alford is a small town lying about halfway between Louth and Skegness and about 8 miles inland from Mablethorpe. As with other towns in the eighteenth century lying near the Lincoln-shire coast, it needed improved communications which could best be provided by a waterway. Abortive proposals, based on levels taken by a Mr Featherstone, were made as far back as 1765 for a navigable drain terminating at Trusthorpe, near Mablethorpe, while in 1784 a further report and estimates were prepared by William Jessop and John Hudson, this time with the outfall at Anderby.[24] The cost of building harbour piers and the problem of shifting sands once again caused the proposals to be shelved. In 1807 Joseph Crow made a survey and men-tioned the advantages derived by Horncastle from its canal. He also dwelt on the qualities of Wainfleet Haven for the coasting trade: 'A safe and commodious harbour is there found by nature in which 100 vessels and upwards may ride at ease and in a state of perfect safety.'[25] He estimated construction costs at £33,308. There was little support and his scheme, too, was dropped.

Nearly twenty years later in 1825 W. Tierney Clark made another survey, based largely on Jessop and Hudson's report, on behalf of a local committee in Alford. There was to be a sea-lock at Anderby and another lock about $3\frac{1}{2}$ miles inland lifting the canal to just over 8ft above sea level. The canal would then continue another $1\frac{1}{2}$ miles to a terminal basin. An Act was obtained on 5 May 1826.[26] The authorized capital was £43,000 and the work was to be completed by October 1833.

Despite all this effort and the successful grant of an Act the canal was never built. There appears to have been con-siderable dispute between Clark and Stephen Langton, one of the committee, about the accuracy of the levels, but whether this was the prime cause of the canal not being built or whether it was due to the more mundane failure to raise the finance is difficult to say. Tierney Clark certainly had a high reputation as an engineer, particularly for suspension bridges, and he had also had canal experience as engineer to the Thames & Medway Canal.[27]

Louth Navigation

Louth, lying on the eastern edge of the Lincolnshire Wolds on the small river Lud, overlooks a coastal plain extending some 12 miles to the North Sea. It was this barrier between the town and the coast that had prevented Louth developing its trade beyond the local countryside for which it was the focal point and market town. Nevertheless it had a long and important history demonstrated by the magnificence of its parish church and the traditions which enabled it to have a go-ahead town corporation in the eighteenth century. It was this corporation which realized the potential commercial value to the town of a navigation to link it to the North Sea.

A preliminary survey as to its feasibility was carried out in October 1756 by John Grundy, engineer, of Spalding.[28] He reported that:

> the nearest ports or harbours to Louth are Saltfleet, Tetney, and Grimsby from whence it is supply'd with coals, deals, groceries etc. and to which a great part of the corn, wool and other produce is convey'd by land carriage for Exportation. The country through which this land carriage is performed being mostly flat drowned marshes, the soil a strong clay, and the roads in wet season so deep, founderous, and bad that it is with the greatest difficulty and at an immense expense that this land carriage is effected to the great detriment of Trade and Commerce and to the great hurt and disadvantage of the Landed Interest of all the country adjoining.

A navigation from Tetney Haven to Louth appearing possible, a subscription list was opened on 28 January 1760 to pay for a proper survey and an Act. Louth corporation headed the subscription list with £100 and individuals followed with donations of up to £50 each. The list totalled £850 and it was resolved that these subscribers should have first preference for the shares. For the full survey Sam Towmaw, the town clerk of Louth, sought the help of John Smeaton on 18 February 1760[29] who replied five days later in a rather non-committal way asking for further information. He added a shrewd postscript: 'P.S. Is the expense and practicability the chief point, or the getting the Bill through Parliament on account of an expected opposition?'[30] The town clerk assured Smeaton on 1 March 1760 that little opposition was expected but that John Grundy had carried out a survey and considered 'the making this intended river is very practicable but yet the gentlemen are not willing to proceed till they have Mr Grundy's opinion confirmed by you'. The letter also explained the desirability of getting the Bill into Parliament in the next session.[31]

Smeaton sent a further reply on 11 March 1760 giving very wise counsel on the need to hasten slowly. He also explained how busy he was and that he would not wish them to delay their application because of him. Then he continued:

> I will, however, give you this caution to be very careful of giving public notice as early as possible of your intention to apply to Parliament and in making the gentlemen of your country acquainted with your scheme. Be very careful in applying to the land-owners whose estates lay upon or near the intended navigation, and if possible get the consent of the majority of the principals of those who may be affected by it, for if the least opposition arises, which seldom shows itself till after the petition is presented to the House, they generally hang upon those matters; for upon this footing the Wey Bill was thrown out last year, tho' it is likely to pass this, and the present year the Tamworth petition has been thrown out upon the same footing without ever entering into the merits thereof.
>
> I am Sir
> Your most humble servant.
> J. Smeaton[32]

Eventually on 7 August 1760 Smeaton went through the report with Grundy. Grundy proposed a navigation from

Tetney to Louth and this included straightening the course of
the River Lud by means of cuts, constructing a sea-sluice and a
lock where the river enters the mouth of the Humber, making
bridges and building nine locks. The length was to be slightly
less than $11\frac{1}{2}$ miles. Smeaton confirmed that Tetney Haven was
the proper outfall and it would afford 'communication with the
inland navigations of Yorkshire and the Trent for flat bottomed
barges without going to sea which at some seasons of the year
would be dangerous or impracticable'. Smeaton also submitted
a series of estimates for different canal terminals. That for the
whole distance was:

	Two Barge Canal £	One Barge Canal £	Lighter drawing 2 ft £
Tetney Haven to New Bridge, Louth	15,590	13,686	10,884

After Smeaton's report was received Grundy was asked to ac-
company some of the committee to Lincoln Races 'to wait on
the Noblemen and Gentlemen with the plan'.[33] This method of
approach was apparently successful for few of the landowners
expressed themselves as being lukewarm or hostile. One,
indeed, promised, in the absence of opposition, to obtain the
Act for £150.

Negotiations leading up to the Bill now became more
leisurely; the reports were not printed until September 1761 and
this was only after one of the members of the committee had
been 'desired to correct false spelling etc. in Mr Grundy's
report'.[34] On 6 December 1762 the petition was presented to
Parliament and the Act passed on 24 March 1763.[35] The Act did
not provide for raising money for construction except by borrowing on the credit of the tolls specified in the Act; this condition was to lead to difficulties in the future.

In April five of the commissioners made an order stating that
on 30 May 1763 they would treat with persons willing to lend
money not exceeding £14,000 for putting the navigation into
execution on an absolute assignment of the tolls. No offers were
received despite an extended date being allowed. Twelve

months later they tried again on a different scheme. This time they agreed that £12,000 in transferable shares of £100 would be accepted and those prepared to offer were to attend a meeting on 20 September 1764. Even then the full amount was not subscribed until 13 February 1765. Included among the subscribers was Charles Chaplin, one of the commissioners. He held ten shares.

Construction then began and on 18 May 1767, four years after the passing of the Act, five miles of the canal were opened from Tetney Haven to Fire Beacon Lane. It was another three years before the navigation was completed to Louth. The opening took place in May 1770. Further subscriptions had been found necessary to complete the works and ultimately £27,500 was spent.

The commissioners had been granted powers under the Act to lease or let the tolls from time to time for the best sum for a period not exceeding seven years and in January 1770 Charles Chaplin, the commissioner mentioned above, contracted to take the tolls for seven years at a rent of 4 per cent pa payable to the shareholders and, in addition, to pay all costs and charges and maintain the navigation to the extent of £500pa.[36] If the costs exceeded £500 then the commissioners were to pay the excess. Chaplin was also given the right to renew the lease for a further seven years on expiry at a rent of 6 per cent pa. When the time came for renewal the commissioners advertised the letting but even after two adjourned meetings there had been no offers. The commissioners then negotiated with Chaplin who agreed to take the tolls on revised terms. He proposed to advance all money necessary for the repair of the navigation (the original work had apparently not been done too well); keep the navigation in repair subject to the orders of the commissioners; pay the officers' salaries and all other expenses; pay 5 per cent pa interest half-yearly to the subscribers. In return Chaplin was to have a lease for 99 years. This agreement was clearly *ultra vires*, but its validity was not queried for over 50 years, despite the fact that the commissioners' decision was not unanimous. In 1782 the commissioners reminded Chaplin that he had not been paying the interest regularly; as there was no improvement he was ordered in August 1788 to attend annually at Louth to make the payments.

By 1792 there were complaints that the navigation was not being properly maintained. A survey showed that because of silting, horses had to be used for haulage instead of craft being sailed, and that to obtain sufficient depth it was necessary to raise the water level above the limits which would permit drainage of the neighbouring lands with frequent consequential flooding. Although the commissioners made orders requiring repair work Chaplin ignored these orders and did virtually no maintenance, while complaints from the boatmen of the bad state of the river continued. Soon after this Chaplin died and his son Thomas as executor assumed control. It is possible that he had some doubts as to his title to the navigation as he proposed at a meeting on 13 April 1795 that the money expended by his father should be refunded and he would then relinquish his right to the residue of the 99-year lease.

Although the proposition appears to have been accepted it does not seem to have been implemented because by 1811, when the navigation was again in a bad state, George Chaplin, the son of the late Thomas Chaplin, had at his own expense widened and deepened the river to the satisfaction of the commissioners. In 1814 he spent another £400 on improvements.

Though we do not know the actual tolls during this period, it has been estimated that from an average of £2,000 pa in the late 1770s they rose steadily to about £5,000 pa in the late 1820s. During the whole of this period the interest payable had remained constant at £1,375, ie 5 per cent pa. Chaplin maintained that the navigation had not been a profitable undertaking to his family until the last few years preceding 1828.

The traders of Louth felt that they were being unjustifiably exploited by the Chaplin family and also that the tolls which were laid down in 1763 should now be revised to take account of the increased trade on the navigation. As a result of these criticisms and of doubt about the validity of the 99-year lease of 1777, a further Act was obtained in 1828 which confirmed the residue of the lease to the Chaplin family and also reduced the tolls.[37] There was no doubt that the Chaplin family were in a strongly entrenched position because a number of the commissioners were members of their family and several others were very friendly to them.

The story of this particular lease does not end there. In 1847 two railway Acts were passed. The first was 'an Act to authorise the East Lincolnshire Railway Company to purchase an existing lease of the Louth Navigation';[38] and the second was 'an Act to enable the Great Northern Railway Company to take a lease of or to purchase the East Lincolnshire Railway and Canal'.[39] Thus the navigation became part of the Great Northern empire for the remaining 29 years of the lease. The G.N.R. stated that they agreed to purchase the lease in order to prevent opposition from the existing lessees.

In March 1876 when the lease was about to end, Henry Oakley, general manager of the G.N.R., sent the following canal account to the directors:

	£	s	d
Receipts *Year 1875*	1,807	5	7
Expenses	1,104	7	6
Profit on Working	702	18	1
Interest on Mortgages	1,545	12	0
Net Loss	842	13	11

Oakley then made his recommendation:

If this canal passes into the hands of private owners it will, of course, become a competitor with us for Louth traffic and the tolls which we have purposely kept up to the highest legal rate will no doubt be lowered and the trade on the canal encouraged. By the Act constituting the canal the tolls are to be let by auction every year and the Louth Commissioners are at present considering what course they should take. . . . Though we may be exposed to some little loss by the competition of the canal I think on the whole we had better abstain from interferance and if at the end of a year or two we find that for any reason it is desirable to obtain re-possession of the canal we should no doubt be able to compete for it at the annual auction and give better terms than any outside parties would be able to afford, but for the present it appears to me desirable not to interfere unless application be in the first instance made to us.'

The G.N.R. board minuted this on 17 March 1876: 'Recommendation approved.'[40]

On 5 July 1876 the Louth commissioners wrote to the G.N.R. to say that there would be a meeting on 15 July for accepting tenders and enquiring whether the G.N.R. would apply. Oakley again reported to the board in a way which showed his single-minded business approach to the situation:

I have consulted with Mr Ashley on the point whether it would be more economical to make a loss on the canal for the purpose of securing the traffic on the railway and we were unable to form any estimate of the probable effect of the competitive powers of the canal. Traffic may be sent by it coastwise to Grimsby, to Goole, and to the northern ports but, on the other hand, unless it arises in the immediate vicinity of the canal it must be brought to or carried from Louth by railway as the canal ends at Louth and has no further inland water communication. I think therefore that the competition it can create will not be very damaging and in that view I am not prepared to recommend the Committee to rent that canal on any such terms as £1,000 per annum. . . . The canal in hostile hands would be only effective if the tolls were reduced but in that case the lessee would incur a greater risk as he would have to depend on a large increase of traffic to replace the amount of tolls he would lose by the reduction; and it seems hardly probable that anyone working the canal would adopt such a course.[41]

As a result of Oakley's report the board decided to make no offer for the tolls.

An auction of the tolls was arranged for 8 June 1876, but there were no bidders, so the commissioners took the collection for the time being into their own hands. After three months, during which time £388 had been collected, a lessee was found and the tolls were let for the remainder of the year for £566 making a total of £954. For 1878 and 1879 the lease was for £755, for 1880 £864, and for 1881 £900. In 1882 the leaseholder defaulted after paying only £225 and the collection reverted to the commissioners who collected another £774 a total of £999 for the year. During this year tolls were reduced, but despite this the amounts collected annually continued to be satisfactory until after the turn of the century. Thereafter there was a fairly rapid decline until 1916 when traffic virtually ceased. The following table shows the receipts in selected later years:

Year	£	Year	£	Year	£
1887	1,417	1902	874	1912	453
1898	1,026	1903	659	1913	410
1900	932	1904	553	1914	375
1901	939	1911	470	1915	160
				1916	66

The traditional traffic was the export of corn and wool and the import of coal, but railway competition drove the management committee to seek new sources of traffic. On 20 June 1887 they reported that they were treating with the Aire & Calder Navigation on grain rates. The negotiations were successful and an increased traffic developed in wheat to Leeds and Wakefield. But the hazards of the seaward approach to the navigation, although technically within the Humber estuary, and the absence of inland water connections during wartime conditions undoubtedly hastened the end of regular traffic and the demise of the canal, although it was not formally closed until 1924.

Probably the most interesting feature of the navigation, and one which can still be seen, was the construction of most of the locks. Although Grundy had originally suggested nine locks only eight were constructed and of these six were built to a unique design: Top or Louth, Keddington Church, Ticklepenny, Willows, Salter Fen, and Alvingham. Instead of the

18. Louth basin, 1924

sides being parallel they consisted of four segmental arches in the vertical plane curved into the land. At the springing point of each arch there were wooden land ties. The design indicates an attempt to provide a structure which would withstand more effectively the pressure from the adjacent land. On the other hand, the two remaining locks, Outfen and Tetney Sea Locks, were provided with normal parallel sides. The effectiveness of the arched sides is open to doubt as in 1828 it was recorded that at Alvingham lock the walls were overhanging the foundations by upwards of two feet. The other odd feature about the locks was that no two were exactly the same size. The lengths varied between 85ft 11in at Willows to 88ft 7in at Ticklepenny's and 100ft at Tetney and the widths from 15ft 3in at Top, Keddington Church, and Alvingham, to 19ft at Outfen. The total fall from River Head at Louth to Tetney was 43ft 8in.[42]

The navigation head was very well laid out with wharves and warehouses and there was also a small shipyard and dry-dock. This yard and dock was offered for sale in April 1803[43] and again on 21 January 1808[44] when with other premises it was described as late the estate of John Martin of Louth, victualler and shipbuilder, assigned for the benefit of his creditors. In 1854 a Mr Motley privately built a warehouse lower down the navigation at Austen Fen and this was used as a distribution centre to the surrounding area for groceries, sugar, flour, dried fruit, etc brought up by barge from Hull.[45]

The vessels navigating the canal were sloops and sailing barges carrying between 60 and 120 tons, and latterly these were sometimes of iron as, for instance, the *Industry*, owned by W. Nettleton of Hull, a hay and straw merchant which, in 1911, was shipping shingle to Alvingham. On a return journey to the Norfolk coast to load another cargo of shingle she rammed Biergate swing-bridge, causing damage. After the accident the captain took the vessel out to sea in an unfavourable wind and ran it aground so that it could not be reached for examination.

On 18 September 1895, a time when leisure activities were becoming more popular, a suggestion was put to the commissioners as an idea for raising extra income, but there is no evidence that it was ever acted upon:

North Cotes Rectory
GRIMSBY.

Dear Sir,
    You are perhaps not aware what a popular place for excursionists Tetney Lock is becoming. I think your Canal Company should be up and doing. A pretty little steamboat for pleasure trips to Louth and back would be, I think, a decided success. A few nice boats also for rowing parties would form a profitable investment, and why not let an acre or two of land and make the Tetney Lock Canal Gardens which would make the mouths of Sheffield people water. Houses also are much wanted in which comfortable apartments could be had. There is a general concurrence of feeling that there is nothing nicer than a stroll along the canal to Thoresby Bridge and along the sea bank to the Haven. Please regard this as merely a private communication and believe me.
                        Yours very truly,
                        T. R. Matthews.[46]

    The end came in 1924. An application had been made to the Ministry of Transport in 1920 for an order relieving the commissioners from all liability to maintain the canal, although, at the Louth town council meeting on 8 April 1924, one of the councillors made a strong plea for its retention. The motion was lost as only the proposer and seconder voted for it.[47] The County Council and the Rural District Council agreed, however, to take over and reconstruct the bridges over the canal, although a sum of £1,500 had to be contributed by the commissioners out of the sale of their property. On 5 September 1924 the last annual general meeting was held. The sale of the property took place on 8 October 1924, houses being sold for £60 and £70 each. The total proceeds of the sale, which included most of the property round the River Head at Louth and a smallholding at Fulstow, reached £6,240. In 1927 the residue of the funds was distributed to the mortgagees at the rate of just under $11\frac{1}{2}$ per cent of the amount of the original mortgage. Much of the waterway remains and it is still conceivable that the vision of T. R. Matthews could be realized.

Authors' Notes and
Acknowledgements

◆◆◆ ◆ ◆◆◆

We should like to thank the very many who in various ways have helped to make this book possible but, without doubt, our deepest gratitude must go to Charles Hadfield, who with infinite patience has cajoled, guided, and stimulated the work to completion.

No book of this kind can be written without recourse to the record repositories and therefore we acknowledge our debt to the Archivists and their staffs of the British Transport Historical Records Office (now part of the Public Record Office), of the Public Record Office, both at Chancery Lane and Ashridge, and of the County Record Offices of Essex, West Suffolk, East Suffolk, Cambridgeshire, Norwich and Norfolk, Lincolnshire, Northamptonshire, Huntingdon, Bedfordshire, Hertfordshire, Middlesex and the G.L.C. Our thanks also go to the Librarians and their staffs of the British Museum (Bloomsbury and Colindale), the Wisbech and Fenland Museum, the Guildhall Library, the Hackney, Waltham Forest, Redbridge, Tower Hamlets and New Ham London Borough Libraries, and of Northampton, Cambridge, Lincoln and Thurrock for their readiness to search out relevant material and provide background information. Particularly do we thank the Librarians of the House of Lords and the Institution of Civil Engineers, the officers of the Welland and Nene River Division and the Curator of the Spalding Gentlemen's Society for allowing access to their records.

It is impossible to list all the individuals who have helped us but we feel we must mention Professor A. W. Skempton, Dr M. J. T. Lewis, Dr K. Bascombe, Mr W. D. Miles, engineer to the

Welland & Deepings Internal Drainage Board, Mr Christopher Taylor of the Royal Commission on Historical Monuments, Mr Lee of the Essex River Board, Messrs Davey and Stubbs, Solicitors (Brigg), Messrs Ted Appleyard, C. Arthey, N. Birch, J. S. Bissett (Manager, Great Ouse River Division), Ronald H. Clark (Newcomen Society), T. E. Dagwell (Sleaford), J. L. Gilbert, Geoffrey Gregory and Tony Reynolds of Whitworth's, Wellingborough, Richard Hillier, A. V. Jackson, M. Palmer, C. Page, E. Paget-Tomlinson, Mrs D. Pepper, Miss Lesley Pepper, G. Tonkin, P. White, A. E. Wilson (Bishopbridge), Mrs Margaret Wilson and Ian Wright.

Ronald Russell is happy to acknowledge the generosity of the Trustees of the Leverhulme Research Awards, which materially assisted research into the Nene and Welland, and the especial help of Alan H. Faulkner.

Finally we thank our respective wives and families for their co-operation in the research and for their tolerance and unselfishness in foregoing time when other (and possibly more appealing) things could have been done.

Our thanks are due to the following for photographs and text illustrations: plate 1, *Strand Magazine*; 2, 5, 6, 7, 8, 9, Essex Record Office; 3, John H. Boyes Collection; 4, Redbridge Central Library; 10, East Suffolk Record Office; 11, 12, Norfolk County Council, Norwich Division Libraries; 13, King's Lynn Museum; 14, 16, A. H. Faulkner; 15, Bene't Gallery, Cambridge; 17, Birmingham City Libraries, Sir Benjamin Stone Collection; 18, Cambridge Industrial Archaeology Society; 19, 20, Ronald H. Clark and the Newcomen Society; 21, The Marquess of Northampton and Northampton Public Libraries; 22, Ian L. Wright; 23, 24, Wisbech Museum; 25, A. V. Jackson; 26, 28, Spalding Gentlemen's Society; 27, Aerial Photography Dept, University of Cambridge; 29, Mrs E. V. Graham, South Africa; 30, Usher Gallery, Lincoln; 31, 32, John H. Boyes Photographs. Text illustrations: 4, Waterways Museum; 11, Welland & Nene River Division; 12, Spalding Gentlemen's Society; 14, Charles Hadfield; 17, John H. Boyes Photographs.

Notes

Notes to Chapter II

1. British Museum, Harleian MSS, 391 f.103.
2. B.M. Harleian MSS, 391 f.4. I am indebted to Dr K. Bascombe for drawing my attention to these two documents and providing the translation and interpretation.
3. 3 Henry VI *c*.5.
4. 9 Henry VI *c*.9.
5. 13 Eliz I *c*.18.
6. Lincolns Inn Library, MD 103 f.241.
7. *Address to Their Majesties on the opening of King George Reservoir*, 11 April 1913 (author's collection).
8. 13 Geo II *c*.32.
9. Lee Navigation Minute Books, British Transport Historical Records, now Public Record Office (P.R.O.) Unless otherwise stated the source of information used in this chapter is from these minute books.
10. Smeaton's Report, Bodleian Library Oxford, Gough Maps 17 f.15b.
11. 7 Geo III *c*.51.
12. 19 Geo III *c*.58.
13. *Gentleman's Magazine*, March 1774, p 121.
14. P. R. O. SUPPLY 5/353.
15. This paragraph is based on John Rennie *Reports* Vol. 3 (Institution of Civil Engineers Library).
16. P.R.O., MT 19/122/620.
17. 13 & 14 Vic *c*.109.
18. Essex Record Office, D/DYc 11/2.
19. P.R.O., MT 19/66/275.
20. P.R.O., MT 19/66/276.
21. Winter, *History of Waltham Abbey*, 1888.
22. P.R.O., J 54/69/L42, Lee Conservancy Board v Button, 1877.
23. Select Committee on the Lee Conservancy Bill, 1867–8. Quest. 496/7.
24. Frederic Johnson, *Weldon's Guide to the River Lee*, 1880.
25. 31 & 32 Vic *c*. 154.
26. *Second Report* of the Commissioners appointed to inquire into the

best means of preventing the pollution of rivers (River Lee), 6 May 1867.

27. 320 & 21 Geo V *c*. 192.
28. The previous canal was the Slough Arm, dug in 1882–3. Charles Hadfield, *The Canals of the East Midlands*, 2nd ed., 1970, p. 223. A. H. Faulkner, *The Grand Junction Canal*, 1972, p. 200.
29. 13 Geo II *c*. 32.
30. *The London Chronicle*, 30 November 1758.
31. 32 Geo II *c*.42.
32. 6 Geo III .78.
33. George Duckett, *Ducketiana*, 1869 (B.M.).
34. Hadfield, *East Midlands, op. cit.*
35. Lee Navigation Minute Book, 16 February 1774.
36. Saffron Walden Museum, printed pamphlet, *Facts and Observations in support of the plan for making a canal from Bishop's Stortford in Herts to Brandon River in Norfolk.*
37. City of London Records, Thames & Canal Committee, Jnl 71 f.124.
38. John Phillips, *A Treatise on Inland Navigation*, 1785.
39. E.R.O., D/DBy E33 (newspaper cuttings).
40. John Rennie, *MS Reports*, I, f.81 (Institution of Civil Engineers' Library).
41. *Ibid.*, I, f.89.
42. B.M., Add MSS, 35685 f.142.
43. E.R.O., Q/RUm 1/17.
44. John Rennie, *Reports*, Vol. 6 f.384 (ICE Library).
45. 52 Geo III *c*.141.
46. 54 Geo III *c*.168.
47. B.M. Add MSS 35691 f.6.
48. P.R.O., B 9/14.
49. *Report of Select Committee on River Pollution (River Lee)*, 1886.
50. *Ibid.*
51. Hertfordshire County Record Office, D/EGe 03.
52. Lee Conservancy Board Minute Book, 30 April 1909.
53. *Ibid.*, 14 May 1909.
54. *Ibid.*, 11 April 1913.
55. Herts C.R.O. D/P 21.
56. Information from Mr John Wilkinson, Little Hallingbury Mill.

Notes to Chapter III

1. *Victoria County History of Essex*, V. p. 187.
2. Journals of the House of Commons, 9 March 1736/7.
3. 10 Geo II *c*.33.
4. P.R.O., C 110/164, Goodman v Goodman.
5. E.R.O., D/DHs L1.
6. E.R.O., D/DHs T19.
7. Companies' Registration Office, File 698360.
8. E.R.O., D/DCq E2.

9. E.R.O., Q/RUm 1/14.
10. E.R.O., Q/RUm 1/20.
11. *Chelmsford Chronicle*, 25 September 1818, and E.R.O., Q/RUm 1/25.
12. P.R.O., CREST 2/270.
13. *Ibid.*
14. *Ibid.*
15. E.R.O., Q/RUm 1/27.
16. E.R.O., D/DOp B103.
17. 38 & 39 Vict *c.* 155.
18. E.R.O., D/DU 455/1.
19. 39 & 40 Vict *c.* 182.
20. E.R.O., D/DU 633/9.
21. 43 & 44 Vict *c.* 107.
22. E.R.O., D/DBc E 50.
23. E.R.O., Q/RUm 1/48.
24. E.R.O., D/DOp B8/1.
25. T. Bannister, 'Recollections of a Septuagenarian', *Thurrock Local History Society Journal,* No. 2, 1957.
26. *Ibid.*, No. 7, 1962. K. Bannister, 'Barges to Bulvan', I am indebted to Mr J. R. Hayston for these references.
27. E.R.O., Q/RUm 1/34.
28. E.R.O., D/DOp B59.
29. Charles Hadfield, *The Canals of South and South East England*, 1969 p.222.
30. E.R.O., D/DRa 01.
31. E.R.O., D/DRa 012.
32. E.R.O., D/DRa 03.
33. Hadfield, *South and South East England, op. cit.*, p. 226.
34. Professor A. W. Skempton kindly drew my attention to this letter.
35. E.R.O., D/DRa 04.
36. *Chelmsford Chronicle,* 30 October 1772.
37. E.R.O., Q/RUm 1/1.
38. E.R.O., Q/RUm 1/4.
39. E.R.O., D/Z 1/3.
40. 33 Geo III *c.*93.
41. E.R.O., D/DQs 135/2 and D/DRa 016.
42. J.H.C., 3 March 1794.
43. *Chelmsford Chronicle*, 15 December 1797.
44. John Rennie, Letter Books, Vol. 2 f.113 (ICE Library).
45. *Chelmsford Chronicle*, 8 February 1799.
46. 9 & 10 Will III *c.*19.
47. 5 Geo I *c.*31.
48. 13 Geo II *c.*30.
49. A. F. J. Brown, 'Colchester in the Eighteenth Century', *East Anglian Studies*, 1968.
50. 23 Geo II *c.*19.
51. 21 Geo III *c.* 30.
52. 51 Geo III *c.* 43.

53. E.R.O., Q/RUm 2/38.
54. E.R.O., Q/RUm 1/85.
55. *Colne Navigation Improvement*. Booklet published by *Essex Standard* Office, 1847. Copy in P.R.O., MT 19/24.

Notes to Chapter IV

1. Quoted in C. G. Grimwood and S. A. Kay, *History of Sudbury*, 1952.
2. J.H.C., xiv 474. Documentary evidence of the extent of Little and Dodd's rights has not been found.
3. 4 Anne *c*.15.
4. *Procs Inst Civil Engineers*, IV, 1845, comments by William Cubitt on a paper on 'The Exeter Canal'.
5. I am indebted to Colin Arthey of Sudbury for much of the information contained in this chapter.
6. 21 Geo III *c*.75.
7. E.R.O., T/A 286, Order Book of Stour Navigation Commissioners, 1781–1914.
8. Stour Navigation Minute Book, 1782–1817.
9. Colin Arthey, *The Stour Navigation*, unpublished thesis.
10. E.R.O., Q/RUm 1/49.
11. Letter by Francis de Visme quoting a conversation with William Cubitt, 1836. (I am indebted to Colin Arthey for this note).
12. Stour Navigation Commissioners Order Book, 1 November 1850.
13. E.R.O., T/A 200. Stour Navigation Minute Books, 1861–1892: 27 August 1862.
14. *Ibid.*, 8 April 1864.
15. *Ibid.*, 29 April 1864.
16. *Ibid.*, 18 December 1867.
17. *Ibid.*, 4 February 1873.
18. *Ibid.*, various dates.
19. *Ibid.*, 8 August 1879. Price delivered at Hull £190. This was a hand-operated appliance and was replaced by a steam powered one in 1880.
20. *Ibid.*, 21 October 1881.
21. *Ibid.*, 12 May 1882.
22. *Ibid.*, 2 August 1892 and 25 October 1892.
23. Rev A. G. H. Hollingsworth, *History of Stowmarket*, 1844.
24. 30 Geo III *c*.57.
25. Norfolk and Norwich Record Office, Stowmarket Navigation Minute Book.
26. John Rennie, Letter Books, Vol. 1 f.26 (ICE Library).
27. *Ibid.*, f.29.
28. *Ibid.*, f.40.
29. 33 Geo III *c*.20.
30. Following later improvements the dimensions were increased to 55ft by 14ft.
31. *Essex Herald*, 12 January 1819.
32. P.R.O., RAIL 326/1.

33. 9 & 10 Vict *c*.106.
34. B.M. State Paper Room, Reports of Commissioners, 1847, Vol. xxxi p10.
35. N.N.R.O., Stowmarket Navigation Minute Book.
36. *Ibid.*, 16 May 1922.
37. *Ibid.*, 16 March 1934.
38. 20 Geo II *c*.14.
39. B.M. Add MSS 19197 f.148b.
40. B.M. Add MSS 19185 f.226.
41. N.N.R.O., MS 362.
42. 30 Geo II *c*.47.
43. N.N.R.O., River Blyth Navigation Minute Book 1757–1839 B1.
44. B.M. Add MSS 19185 f.227.
45. Contemporary Report quoted in Roy Clark, *Black Sailed Traders*, 1961, p114.
46. *Ibid.*, p.114.
47. N.N.R.O., Blyth Navigation Minute Book, B1.
48. P.R.O. Map MPE 953.
49. Clark, *Black Sailed Traders, op. cit.*, p.129.

Notes to Chapter V

1. Blomefield, *History of Norfolk*, 1775, Vol. III p. 47.
2. I am indebted to Charles Hadfield for the information on the Aire & Calder traffic.
3. 22 Chas II *c*.16.
4. P.R.O., MT 19/123/629.
5. P.R.O., BT 41/109.
6. *Royal Commission on Canals and Waterways*, Vol. IV 1907.
7. 9 Will III *c*.5.
8. 9 Geo I *c*.10.
9. 20 Geo II *c*.40.
10. 23 Geo II *c*.6.
11. 12 Geo III *c*.14.
12. John Rennie, *Reports*, Vol. 10 f.16 (ICE Library).
13. House of Lords Record Office, Norwich & Lowestoft Navigation Bill, Minutes of Evidence, 1826.
14. H.L.R.O., Norwich & Lowestoft Navigation Bill, Minutes of Evidence, 1827.
15. *British Almanac*, 1829, p. 224.
16. 8 Geo IV *c*.42.
17. *British Almanac*, 1832, p.233.
18. *Norfolk Chronicle*, 5 October 1833.
19. J.H.C., 5 May 1848.
20. *The Star*, December 1954.
21. *Norfolk Chronicle*, 24 October 1908.
22. *Norwich Mercury*, 26 June 1773.
23. *Ibid.*, 27 September 1777.
24. *Essex Herald*, 1 June 1819.
25. J.H.C., 12 February 1773.

26. 13 Geo III *c*.37.
27. Percy Millican, *History of Horstead & Stanninghall*, 1937.
28. N.N. R.O., 59 X 2.
29. An example is to be seen in the Bridewell Museum, Norwich.
30. *Norwich Mercury*, 18 August 1810.
31. Millican, *Horstead, op. cit.*
32. 52 Geo III *c*.69.
33. *Norwich Mercury*, 16 April 1825.
34. *Ibid.*, 9 April 1825.
35. Jean Lindsay, *The Canals of Scotland*, 1968, p. 75.
36. H.L.R.O., Norwich & Lowestoft Navigation Bill, Minutes of Evidence, 9 May 1827.
37. *Ibid.*
38. *Norwich Mercury*, 18 June 1826.
39. *Ibid.*, 3 September 1826.
40. Robert Malster, *Wherries and Waterways*, 1971, p. 45.
41. 29 & 30 Vic *c*.121.
42. N.N.R.O., MS 4441.
43. *Ibid.*
44. Companies Registration Office, File No. 67465.

Notes to Chapter VI

1. For a detailed study of this river see Dorothy Summers, *The Great Ouse*, 1973, on which most of this section is based. I am most grateful to Miss Summers for permission to make use of her extensive researches.
2. This account broadly follows Gordon Fowler's papers 'Fenland Waterways, Past & Present' in *Proc. Cambridge Antiquarian Soc.*, xxxiii, 1933, and xxxiv, 1934. A map published by the Royal Geographical Society in 1946, revised 1970, gives a good pictorial representation. The river from Littleport through Welney is shown on Badeslade's map, 1725. See also H.C. Darby, *The Draining of the Fens*, 1956, and A. K. Astbury, *The Black Fens*, 1958.
3. See *supra*.
4. From the Pipe Roll; quoted in Beresford St Joseph, *Medieval England; an aerial survey*, 1958.
5. 43 Eliz I *c*.2.
6. T. S. Willan, *Bedford Historical Record Soc*, xxiv, 1946; also Dorothy Richards; *History of the Navigation Bedford to St Ives*, 1969 (Gt Ouse Restoration Soc journal, *The Lock Gate*) and Summers, *op. cit.* Based on the Francklin papers in Bedford C.R.O.
7. For a full account see Darby, *op. cit.* The various Acts etc are printed in S. Wells, *History of the Bedford Level*, 1830.
8. Dugdale and Badeslade are among those providing evidence on this.
9. Via the New Bedford River.
10. Summers, *op. cit.*
11. J. K. Wilson & A. H. Faulkner, *Fenland Barge Traffic*, 1972.
12. *Fenland Notes & Queries*, 1269.

13. *Ibid.*
14. See R. Russell, *Waterside Pubs*, 1974, pp. 20–41.
15. Summers, *op. cit.*
16. 30 Geo III, *c.*83.
17. Wm. White, *History, Gazeteer & Directory of Norfolk*, 1845.
18. See Darby, *op. cit.*, for a comprehensive list of pamphlets published on this issue.
19. For the Grand Junction Canal *see* Charles Hadfield, *The Canals of the East Midlands*, 2nd ed., 1970. This also includes a history of the Newport Pagnell Canal.
20. Summers, *op. cit.*, and A. H. Faulkner, *The Grand Junction Canal*, 1972.
21. Report to the Lords Commissioners of the Admiralty, by Capt James Vetch, R.E., and Capt John Washington, R.N. (Welland & Nene River Division).
22. 7 & 8 Geo IV *c.*47.
23. South Level Commissioners Minute Book 1 (Gt Ouse River Division).
24. Summers, *op. cit.*
25. Papers relating to the Simpson case are in Huntingdonshire R.O. and Great Ouse House, Cambridge.
26. *Royal Commission on Canals & Waterways*, Vol. V, 1909.
27. Information from A. V. Jackson.
28. Summers, *op. cit.*
29. Trading figures for King's Lynn are listed in Summers, *op. cit.*

Notes to Chapter VII

1. Herts C.R.O., 61728.
2. Bedford C.R.O., AD 1146.
3. Bedford C.R.O., HA 1222.
4. Bedford C.R.O., HA 1224.
5. J.H.C., Vol. xxvii.
6. 30 Geo II *c.* 62.
7. Herts C.R.O., 28900.
8. See *The Lock Gate*, No. 7, April 1963. Nos. 3–6 of this journal contain a pioneering history of the Ivel Navigation by M. C. Ewans.
9. Herts C.R.O., 61146.
10. Herts C.R.O., DE 5014.
11. *A Treatise on Inland Navigation* . . . London, 1785. Saffron Walden Museum.
12. *Torrington Diaries*, ed. Andrews, 1934.
13. Bedford C.R.O., L28/37.
14. Herts C.R.O., 61152.
15. Herts C.R.O., 61156.
16. Herts C.R.O., 61159.
17. Herts C.R.O., 61163.
18. *Thames Navigation—Observations upon the evidence . . . for a Bill for making a Navigable Canal . . . to be called the Hants & Berks Canal.* Maidenhead, 1825.

19. Herts C.R.O., 61165.
20. *The Lock Gate*, No. 4, July 1962.
21. Herts C.R.O., 61166, printed report of meeting.
22. Bedford C.R.O., HV 57/25.
23. See *River Cam: Environment & Conservation*, Dept of Architecture & Planning, Guildhall, Cambridge, 1973.
24. Some of these are referred to in Summers, *op. cit.*
25. Much of this would have been carried in sailing vessels, as on the Great Ouse, before the construction of Denver Sluice.
26. For the 1605 survey, *see* W. Dugdale, *History of Imbanking & Drayning*, (2nd ed. 1772). The 1618 surveys are reported in S. Wells, *op. cit.*
27. Cooper, *Annals of Cambridge*, Vol. III.
28. Ibid, Vol. IV.
29. 1 Anne *c.* 2.
30. Cooper, *op. cit.*
31. Cambridgeshire C.R.O., Q/S9/ 1–3.
32. BM, Add 35679.
33. *Cambridge Chronicle & Journal*, 14 Dec 1793.
34. Cooper, *op. cit.*
35. Wilson & Faulkner, *op. cit.*
36. Soon after this, the cut round the island at Jesus Green was filled in; see Malcolm Heron, *Ferry Path*, Cokaygne Press, 1974.
37. F.N.Q., 1269.
38. Wonba Smythe, *The Waterman of the River Cam*, republished Cokaygne Press, 1972.
39. Royal Commission on Historical Monuments, *NE Cambs.*, 1972.
40. Cambridgeshire C.R.O., Q/S9/1–3.
41. *Ibid.*
42. Report of H. Dunn, County Architect & Surveyor, 1906 (Cambridge Ref. Library).
(figures for 1898: tonnage 5,284; other income £556; profit £140
for 1905: tonnage 6,704; other income £611; profit £209).
43. Journal of Inspector of Canal Boats (Camb CRO) and Wilson & Faulkner, *op. cit.*
44. £1 a lock for a powered boat over 40ft.
45. See article on the *Viscountess Bury* by A. H. Leach in the Brochure of the Inland Waterways Assn National Rally of Boats at Ely, 1973.
46. R.C.H.M., *NE Cambs, op. cit.*
47. Fowler, *Proc CAS, op. cit.*
48. For the Car Dyke, *see* OS map of Roman Britain, 1956, Cyril Fox, *The Archaeology of the Cambridge Region*, 1923, and *N.E. Cambs, op. cit.*
49. Lewis, Slatcher & Jarvis, 'Flashlocks on English Waterways', *Industrial Archaeology*, Vol. 6 No. 3, 1969.
50. *Ibid.*

51. Swaffham Internal Drainage Board Minutes, quoted in *N.E. Cambs, op. cit.*
52. *Rot. Hund.* II (1818).
53. See Records of the Bedford Level in Cambs C.R.O.
54. *N.E. Cambs, op. cit,* and C. C. Taylor, *The Cambridgeshire Landscape,* 1973.
55. Taylor, *op. cit.*
56. Fox, *op. cit.*
57. *N.E. Cambs, op. cit,* and Wilson & Faulkner, *op. cit.*
58. Information from A. V. Jackson.
59. *N.E. Cambs, op. cit.*
60. H. Dunn's Report of 1906, *op. cit.*
61. Wilson & Faulkner, *op. cit.*
62. Information from A. V. Jackson.
63. *N.E. Cambs* and Wilson & Faulkner, *op. cit.*
64. A. K. Astbury, *The Black Fens, op. cit.*
65. Information from A. H. Faulkner.
66. H. Dunn's Report, *op. cit.*
67. Gordon Fowler, *op. cit.*
68. Cal S.P.D., 1635–6.
69. 11 Will III, *c.* 22.
70. West Suffolk RO, E2/17/1, Cullum MS.
71. *Ibid.*
72. *Ibid.*
73. West Suffolk RO, E2/17/7.
74. West Suffolk RO, 317/1.
75. West Suffolk RO, E2/17/1.
76. 57 Geo III *c.* 71.
77. West Suffolk RO, E2/17/1.
78. Lark Navigation Toll Book, West Suffolk RO, E2/17/4.
79. For the railway history of Bury see D. I. Gordon, *Regional History of the Railways of Great Britain,* Vol. 5 (Eastern Counties), 1968.
80. See the prospectus in West Suffolk RO.
81. According to G. R. Burnell's Report of 1863, navigation was virtually suspended (Summers, *op. cit.*).
82. *Royal Commission on Canals & Waterways,* Vol. 5 Pt. 2, 1909.
83. *Ibid.*
84. Dugdale, *op. cit.*
85. Fowler, *op. cit.,* and Astbury, *op. cit.*
86. *Ancient & Present State of the Navigation.*
87. Given in T. S. Willan, *River Navigation in England 1660–1750,* Appendix II, 1936.
88. 22 Car II.
89. S. Wells, *op. cit.* The condition of the river would have deteriorated after the construction of Denver Sluice; there was also a sandstorm in 1668 which choked the channel.
90. For descriptions of remains, see note 78, *supra.*
91. 30 Geo III *c.* 166.
92. see note 78, *supra,* and note 99, *infra.*

93. Wm White, *op. cit.*
94. Thetford Corporation Minutes.
95. Gordon, *op. cit.*
96. Wm White, *op. cit.*
97. The detailed story of this crisis is in the Thetford Corporation Minutes. The money was needed to pay off a mortgage on the Red Lion.
98. *Ibid.*
99. R. H. Clark, 'The Staunches & Navigation of the Little Ouse River', *Trans. Newcomen Soc.*, 1957, vol XXX. The staunches were operated by a large spoked wheel, raising and lowering a guillotine gate, the operator perching on a ladder and treading the spokes. There were also small doors to regulate the flow. Clark gives details as follows:
   Thetford Staunch, built by J. W. Gathergood, for £781 in 1835
   Thetford Middle, built by Burrell & Son, for £? in 1827
   Turfpool, built by J. W. Gathergood, for £781 in 1834
   Croxton, built by Burrell & Son, for £800 in 1830
   Santon Staunch, built by J. W. Gathergood, for £? in 1831
   Brandon Staunch, built by Beeton, for £? in 1837
   Sheepwash Staunch, built by Burrell & Son, for £800 in 1830
100. Thetford Corporation Minutes.
101. Bradshaw's *Canals and Navigable Rivers*, 1904.
102. A touching instance of local support was a gift in 1908 from the Handicraft Exhibition of £30 to repair the second staunch and outfall (Thetford Record of Gifts).
103. P. H. Reaney, *The Place Names of Cambridgeshire and the Isle of Ely*, 1943, and E. Ekwall, *English River Names*, 1928.
104. Dugdale, *op. cit.*
105. S. Wells, *op. cit.*
106. William White, *op. cit.*
107. Cambridge Canal Boat Inspection Register (Cambridgeshire C.R.O.).
108. Information from A. H. Faulkner. I am also grateful to Mrs Margaret Wilson, of Ferry Farm, Oxborough, for allowing me to make use of her research on the Wissey, some of which was published in *The Easterling*, Vol. 2, No. 2, 1975.
109. 24 Geo II *c.* 19.
110. J.H.C., 1751.
111. Nar Commissioners' Minute Book (King's Lynn Town Hall).
112. J.H.C., 1770.
113. 10 Geo III *c.*27. See also J. Priestley, *Historical Account of the Navigable Rivers, Canals etc.*, 1831.
114. Nar Commissioners' Minute Book.
115. Lewis, Slatcher & Jarvis, 'Flashlocks: An Addendum', *Industrial Archaeology*, Vol. 7, No. 2, 1973.
116. Norfolk and Norwich R.O.
117. William White, *op. cit.*
118. Gordon, *op. cit.*

119. Information from A. H. Faulkner.

Notes to Chapter VIII

1. See J. M. Steane, *The Northamptonshire Landscape*, 1974.
2. Anon., *Some Considerations of the River Nine, running from Northampton to Peterborow, and so to the Sea; showing the Feasibility and conveniency of making it Navigable*, printed 1653 (Cambridge University Library).
3. Nene Valley Drainage & Navigation; Statement of Facts by the Clerk, 17 February, 1881 (Welland & Nene River Division).
4. Western Division Minute Book 1 (W.N.R.D.).
5. *Ibid.*
6. *Ibid.*
7. *Northampton Mercury*, 17 October 1760.
8. *Ibid*, 31 March 1760.
9. Western Division Minute Book 2 (W.N.R.D.).
10. *Ibid.*
11. *Ibid.*
12. See Charles Hadfield, *The Canals of the East Midlands*, 2nd ed., 1970, and A. H. Faulkner, *The Grand Junction Canal*, 1972.
13. Western Division Minute Book 1.
14. Eastern Division Minute Book D (W.N.R.D.).
15. Eastern Division Minute Book B (W.N.R.D.).
16. Western Division Minute Book 3 (W.N.R.D.).
17. Western Division Minute Book 4 (W.N.R.D.).
18. Western Division Minute Book 5 (W.N.R.D.).
19. Eastern Division Minute Book D (W.N.R.D.).
20. In addition to Hartshorne's report, and a further statement from him on the navigation of the river, the published booklet included a report from John Beasley and Dr Charles Lloyd's comments on the effect of flooding on health. (Northampton, 1848; W.N.R.D.).
21. 15 & 16 Vict *c*.127.
22. *Fenland Notes & Queries*, 1001.
23. *Report of Langley Edwards for Amending the Outfall of the Nene*, 1771, Welland & Nene River Division Archives.
24. N. Walker & T. Craddock, *History of Wisbech & the Fens*, 1849.
25. *Ibid. See also* S. Smiles, *Lives of the Engineers*, Vol. 2, 1861.
26. Nene Outfall Commissioners' Minutes 1827–59 (W.N.R.D.).
27. *Ibid.*
28. Walker & Craddock, *op. cit.*
29. *Ibid.*
30. The history of Sutton Bridge is well described in the Lincoln Industrial Archaeology Group's publication, *An Industrial Archaeology & History of Sutton Bridge*, by N. R. Wright, 1970.
31. F. J. Gardiner; *History of Wisbech & Neighbourhood*, 1898.
32. Slater's *Directory* of 1849.
33. Gardiner, *op. cit.*
34. 15 & 16 Vict *c*.128.
35. *Cambridge Independent Press*, 6 March 1852.

36. Nene Valley Drainage & Navigation Improvement Committee Minutes (W.N.R.D.). The 'Statement of Facts' by the Clerk, 1881 (*op. cit.*) gives the figures as £5,425 to Atkinson and £4,250 to the Western Commissioners.

37. *Wisbech Advertiser,* various issues from Sept 1857–Dec 1859. Also three reports by John Fowler, 1857, 1858 and 1861 (W.N.R.D.), and Nene Drainage & Navigation Minute Book 2, 1857 (W.N.R.D.).

38. 'Statement of Facts', *op. cit.*

39. 25 & 26 Vict *c*.164.

40. See note 30, *supra.*

41. Second District Minute Books and Surveyor's Reports (W.N.R.D.).

42. 'A Brief Record' of some of the work of the River Nene Catchment Board, George Dallas, 1951.

43. Information from Messrs Whitworth.

44. Port of Wisbech Authority.

45. For an account of Vermuyden's work see L. H. Harris, *Vermuyden and the Fens,* 1953.

46. See H. C. Darby, *The Draining of the Fens,* 1956, and K. Astbury, *The Black Fens,* 1958.

47. 27 Geo II *c*.12.

48. Published Doncaster 1868. The small volume contains two other accounts of the voyage, by Thomas Roberts and George Farrington, who accompanied Lord Orford. Orford, a remarkable eighteenth century eccentric, was Robert Walpole's grandson and Horace Walpole's nephew.

49. Cambridgeshire C.R.O., R.59.31.4.6(d).

50. 50 Geo III *c*.125.

51. Cambridgeshire C.R.O., R.59.31.36.5(a).

52. V.C.H. *Cambridge and Isle of Ely.* 1953.

53. *Ibid.*

54. 7 & 8 Vic *c*.106.

55. See R. G. Clark, 'St Germans Sluice and Pumping Station', J.I.C.E., ii, 377.

56. These are still in operation (1977).

57. Board of Trade *Returns,* 1888.

58. Board of Trade *Returns,* 1905.

59. Royal Commission on Canals and Waterways, *Report,* Vol. 5, 1909.

60. Information from Messrs Ted Appleyard, Lou Doubleday and Vic Jackson.

61. B.M.Add MSS 356.85 ff.291–2.

62. *Stamford Mercury,* 15, 30 October 1792.

63. B.M. Add MSS 856.85. f.309.

64. J.H.C., 24 February 1794.

65. J.H.C., 27 February 1794.

66. Wisbech Canal Co, Annual General Assembly Minute Book 1 (Wisbech Museum).

67. *Ibid.*
68. *Chelmsford Chronicle,* 8 February 1799.
69. Assembly Minute Book, *op. cit.*
70. Assembly Minute Book 2.
71. *Ibid.*
72. *Ibid.*, and Walker & Craddock, *op. cit.*
73. E. J. S. Gadsden *et al., The Wisbech & Upwell Tramway,* 1966.
74. The last train ran on 20 May 1966 and the track has been taken up.
75. Assembly Minute Book 4.
76. Draft Bill, petitions and other documents in Wisbech Museum Library.
77. Assembly Minute Book 4.
78. Companies Registration File Canal 75, Companies House. Letter from D. F. Jackson to Registrar of Joint Stock Companies 21 Jan 1930.
79. V.C.H., *Cambridge & Isle of Ely,* Vol. iv.

Notes to Chapter IX

1. *History of Imbanking & Drayning,* 1772 ed.
2. Ingulph, quoted by H. C. Darby, *The Medieval Fenland,* 1940.
3. Alan Rogers, *The Making of Stamford,* 1965.
4. *Ibid.*
5. J.H.C., xi.
6. I am grateful for permission to use an unpublished paper by J. M. Palmer, 'The Stamford Canal: a 17th century Navigation', delivered to a conference organized by the Council for British Archaeology in 1959.
7. Wheeler, *History of the Draining of the Fens of S. Lincolnshire,* 1868.
8. See Charles Hadfield, *The Canals of the East Midlands,* 2nd ed., 1970.
9. Spalding Gentlemen's Society collection.
10. *Lincolnshire in 1836,* pub. J. Saunders.
11. N. C. Birch, *Stamford: an Industrial History,* Lincs Industrial Archaeology Group, 1972.
12. Information from Charles Hadfield.
13. Measurements by Reginald Thompson.
14. See Wheeler, *op. cit,* and 2nd ed.
15. *Ibid.*
16. The Spalding Gentlemen's Society has an impression.
17. In S.G.S. Museum, Spalding.
18. Hawkes MS, S.G.S. Museum.
19. In S.G.S. Museum.
20. N. Wright, *Spalding; an Industrial History,* Lincs Industrial Archaeology Group, 1973.
21. 34 Geo III *c.* 102.
22. *Lincolnshire in 1836.*
23. *Lincolnshire Chronicle & General Advertiser,* 4 January 1839.
24. N. Wright, *op. cit.*
25. Board of Trade *Returns.*

26. N. Wright, *op. cit.*
27. 'Reports relating to the River Welland and the Drainage of Deeping Fen' (Welland & Nene River Div).
28. *Ibid.*
29. *Ibid.*
30. *Ibid.*
31. *The Fenland Past & Present.*
32. 'Conservancy of Rivers (E. Midlands District)' I.C.E., 1882.
33. *British Trade Journal*, 1 March 1889.
34. Welland Catchment Board Minute Book (W.N.R.D.).
35. *Ibid.*
36. Welland River Board Minute Book (W.N.R.D.).
37. Dugdale, *op. cit.*
38. J. D. Birkbeck, *History of Bourne*, 1970.
39. *Ibid.*
40. Hawkes MS., S.G.S. Museum.
41. River Glen Report, John Kingston & Alfred Harrison, 1883 (W.N.R.D.).
42. N. Wright, *op. cit.*
43. Information from L. A. Edwards.
44. Slater's *Directory for Lincolnshire*, 1857.
45. S. Wells, *op. cit.*

Notes to Chapter X

1. V.C.H. *Lincoln*, Vol. 2, p. 383.
2. Joseph Priestley, *Historical Account of the Navigable Rivers, Canals, etc.*, 1831.
3. V.C.H. *Lincoln*, Vol. 2, p. 383.
4. 22 & 23 Chas II *c.* 25.
5. Sir William Stukeley, *Diaries and Letters*, Vol. 2, p. 275 (Surtees Society, Vol. 76).
6. T. S. Willan, *River Navigation in England, 1600–1750*, 1936, p. 124.
7. J. Scribo, *The Present Bad State of the Witham between . . . Lincoln and . . . Boston*, 1733.
8. V.C.H. *Lincoln*, Vol. 2, p. 384.
9. J. Grundy *et al.*, *Report concerning the ruinous condition of the River Witham with a scheme for its improvement*, 1761.
10. 2 Geo III *c.*32.
11. P.R.O., RAIL 885, Witham Minute Book, 3 November 1762.
12. *Ibid.*, 18 January 1763.
13. *Ibid.*, 1 April 1763.
14. *Ibid.*, 4 October 1766.
15. *Ibid.*, 16 December 1813.
16. *Ibid.*, 14 December 1780.
17. *Ibid.*, 27 April 1781.
18. W. Jessop, *Report on the means of making a compleat Navigable Communication between the Witham and the Fosdike at Lincoln*, 1791.
19. John Rennie, *Letter Books*, Vol. 2, f.237 (I.C.E. Library).
20. *Ibid.*, Vol. 2, f.428.

21. *Ibid.*, Vol. 2, f.437.
22. 48 Geo III *c*.108.
23. John Rennie, *Letter Books*, Vol. 6, 20 June 1816 (I.C.E. Library).
24. 52 Geo III *c*.108.
25. 7 Geo IV *c*.2.
26. 10 Geo IV *c*.123.
27. L. T. C. Rolt, *Isambard Kingdom Brunel*, 1957.
28. Charles Hadfield, *The Canals of the East Midlands*, 2nd ed., 1970, p.33.
29. Charles Hadfield & Gordon Biddle, *The Canals of North West England*, 1970, p. 279.
30. Charles Hadfield, *The Canals of Yorkshire and North East England*, 1972, p. 42.
31. *Ibid.*, p. 289.
32. See Chapter XI, p. ?.
33. John Rennie, *Letter Books*, Vol. 7 f.345 (I.C.E. Library).
34. Information from Peter White.
35. *Royal Commission on Canals and Waterways*, 1908, Ans. 24482.
36. *Railway Magazine*, March 1936, p. 226 and information from N. C. Birch.
37. British Transport Historical Records, G.N.R. 1/305/8.
38. Charles Hadfield kindly supplied this information from Canal Control Committee sources.
39. East Anglian Waterways Association *Newsletter*, 1971.
40. Frank Sharman, *'New Bolingbroke. A Nineteenth Century Canal Town?' Journal* of the Railway & Canal Historical Society, Vol. xx p. 57 (Nov 1974).
41. Witham Minute Book, 4 July 1786.
42. Lincs Archives Office, SMITH 9/2/9.
43. 32 Geo III *c*.107.
44. The source for most of the material in this section is to be found in the Horncastle Navigation Minute Books. Lincs Archives, T.L.E. 1/1/1–5.
45. Eastburn's invitation was sponsored by Jessop. Charles Hadfield tells me he was a pupil of Smeaton.
46. John Rennie, *Letter Books*, Vol. 2 f.129 (I.C.E. Library).
47. J.H.C., 22 May 1800.
48. *Ibid.*, 26 May 1800.
49. 39 & 40 Geo III *c*.109.
50. *Doncaster, Nottingham, and Lincoln Gazette*, 24 September 1802.
51. Lincs Archives Office, T.L.E. 1/1/10 Barge Book, 26 August 1868.
52. *Ibid.*, various dates.
53. Selden Society, *Public Works in Mediaeval Law*, Vol. 1 p. 295, 1915.
54. 32 Geo III *c*.106.
55. Sleaford Navigation Minute Book. In the keeping of Mr T. E. Dagwell of Sleaford.
56. *Stamford Mercury*, 18 and 25 April 1794.
57. *Ibid.*, 25 April 1794.
58. *Ibid.*, 2 May 1794.

59. I am indebted to Mrs Graham of Plaston, East Transvaal, South Africa, for this information.
60. Sleaford Navigation Minute Book.
61. Sleaford Navigation Account Book (with Mr T. E. Dagwell).
62. Hadfield, *East Midlands, op. cit.*, p. 64.
63. Transcript of case entered in Minute Book.
64. Sleaford Navigation Minute Book, 13 September 1841.
65. *Ibid.*, 14 May 1881.

Notes to Chapter XI

1. Sir William Dugdale, *History of Imbanking etc.*, 1662.
2. Patent Rolls, 15 Charles I, 24 February 1635.
3. I am indebted to Messrs Davey and Stubbs, solicitors, Brigg, for permission to examine the Ancholme papers in their possession.
4. Lincs Local History Society (IA Group), *History of the Ancholme Navigation*. Except in quotations the Ordnance Survey spelling 'Bishopbridge' has been adopted.
5. 7 Geo III *c*.98.
6. Ancholme Navigation Minute Book, 7 April 1778.
7. *Ibid.*, 2 July 1781.
8. *Ibid.*, 3 October 1792.
9. 42 Geo III *c*.116.
10. *Hull Advertiser*, 4 December 1802.
11. 6 Geo IV *c*.165.
12. Sir John Rennie's *Letter Books*, Vol. 3 f.158 (I.C.E. Library).
13. *Ibid.*, Vol. 7 f.114 (I.C.E. Library).
14. Ancholme Navigation Minute Book, 9 September 1823.
15. *Ibid.*, 16 April 1841, Sir John Rennie's *Letter Books*, Vol. 5 f.88 & Vol. 13 f.331 (I.C.E. Library).
16. *Hull Advertiser*, 20 June 1823.
17. P.R.O., BT 14/307.
18. *Hull and Lincs Times*, 25 May 1935.
19. Ancholme Papers.
20. *Stamford Mercury*, 13 July 1792.
21. No copy of Jessop's report has been traced.
22. 33 Geo III *c*.114.
23. Foljambe MSS, Nottinghamshire R.O.
24. Quoted in Joseph Crow's report, 1807.
25. Lincoln City Library, Local Pamphlets Vol. 15. LG 800.
26. 7 Geo IV *c*.44.
27. Charles Hadfield, *The Canals of South and South East England*, 1969, p. 85.
28. Lincoln City Library, LG 800/14.
29. Louth Navigation Minute Book, 18 February 1760 (Lincolnshire Archives Office).
30. *Ibid.*, 23 February 1760.
31. *Ibid.*, March 1760.
32. *Ibid.*, March 1760.
33. *Ibid.*, 28 August 1760.

34. *Ibid.*, 20 July 1761.

35. 3 Geo III *c*.39.

36. The information relating to the Chaplin lease is based on a printed pamphlet entitled, 'Louth Navigation. Printed Statement of Facts relative to an agreement entered into by the Commissioners and the late Charles Chaplin in the year 1777 for a lease of the Tolls arising from the said Navigation and under which agreement George Chaplin and Francis Chaplin Esqs now hold the said Tolls as drawn and submitted by Mr L Parker, Attorney at Law, by the direction of a Committee of the inhabitants of Louth to John Bell Esq, Barrister at Law, for his opinion also a copy of Mr Bell's opinion. Louth 1823'. A copy of this pamphlet is in the uncatalogued Louth Navigation papers in the Lincolnshire Archives Office.

37. 9 Geo IV *c*.30.

38. 10 & 11 Vict *c*.113.

39. 10 & 11 Vict *c*.148.

40. British Transport Historical Records (P.R.O.), GN1/319/16.

41. B.T.H.R. (P.R.O.)., *Ibid.*

42. *Report* to the Commissioners, 1828 (printed 1832), Lincoln County Library BANKS 20/11.

43. *Doncaster, Nottingham, & Lincs Gazette,* 29 April 1803.

44. *Ibid.*, 25 December 1807.

45. Personal information.

46. Lincs Archives Office, uncatalogued Louth Navigation Papers.

47. *Louth and North Lincs Advertiser,* 12 April 1924.

APPENDICES

APPENDIX I

Summary of Facts about the Canals and Navigations of Eastern England

A. *Rivers Successfully Made Navigable*

River	Date of Act under which Work was begun	Date Wholly Opened	Approx Cost at Opening (£)	Terminal Points	Length
Ancholme	1287 (1) (Patent) 1767	—	—	Bishopbridge — Ferriby Sluice	19 miles
Ant, *see* North Walsham & Dilham Canal Blyth (Halesworth) Navigation	1757	1761	3,822	Halesworth— Southwold	9 miles
Bourne Eau	1781	—	—	Bourne—Tongue End, junct with Glen	3½ miles
Brandon, *see* Ouse, Little Bure (Aylsham) Navigation	1773	1779	6,551	Aylsham— Coltishall	9 miles (2)
Cam	1702 (3)	—	—	King's Mill, Cambridge—Pope's Corner, Gt Ouse	14 3/8 miles
Chelmer & Blackwater Navigation	1793	1797	50,000	Chelmsford— Heybridge Basin	14 miles
Colne	1623 (4)	—	Not Known	Colchester to the sea	11 miles
Gipping, *see* Ipswich & Stowmarket Glen	—	—	—	Tongue End— R Welland	11½ miles
Great Ouse, *see* Ouse Horncastle Navigation (Bain)	1792	1802	45,000	Horncastle— R.Witham	12 miles (8)
Ipswich & Stowmarket	1790	1793	35,300	Ipswich— Stowmarket	17 miles

(1) The river was made navigable under a Patent of 1287. The 1767 Act authorized improvement
(2) The Bure continues as a natural navigable river for another 31 miles to its junction with the river Yare. The river also connects with a number of navigable dikes and broads, and with the river Thurne. These are all under the authority of the Great Yarmouth Port and Haven Commissioners
(3) The Act was for making the Cam 'more navigable'. It had been navigable to Cambridge since the Middle Ages

* Many of the bodies listed in this column throughout Appendix I do not own the waterways, but are responsible for their administration (eg Anglian Water Authority).

Greatest Number of Locks	Size of Boats Taken	Date of Disuse for Commercial Traffic	Date of Abandonment	Whether bought by Railway and Present Ownership *
2	69 ft x 16 ft	Open	Open	No. Anglian Water Authority
4	50 ft x 12 ft	1911	1934	No. A.W.A.
2	14 ft 6 in beam	1860s	1962	A.W.A.
5	54 ft x 12 ft 8 in	1912	1928	No. Gt Yarmouth Port and Haven Commissioners
4	100 ft x 14 ft	1951	Open	Cambridge—Bottisham lock, Cam Conservancy; Bottisham lock—Gt Ouse A.W.A.
13	60 ft x 16 ft	1972	Open	No. The Company of the Proprietors of Chelmer & Blackwater Navigation Co Ltd
1	(5)	Open	Open	No. Colchester Corporation
1 (6)	14 ft 6 in beam (7)	Mid-1920s	Open	A.W.A.
1 1	72 ft x 14 ft 6 in	1878	1884	No
5	52 ft 6 in x 13 ft 6 in	1922	1932	No. Leased for a time. A.W.A.

(4) The river was always navigable. The Act of 1623 authorized improvements
(5) Small coastal motor vessels can reach the Hythe but have to lie aground at low water. Max length 195 ft overall, 9 ft draught at neaps and 11 ft 6 in at springs. No restriction on beam
(6) A tidal gate, only operative when the water on each side makes a level
(7) Length of craft is restricted to about 30 ft, owing to the difficulty of turning in the higher reaches
(8) Including one mile of the Tattershall Canal (qv), which was absorbed by the Horncastle Navigation

River	Date of Act under which Work was begun	Date Wholly Opened	Approx Cost at Opening (£)	Terminal Points	Length
Lark	1700	c1720		Eastgate, Bury St Edmunds—junct with Gt Ouse	24 miles
Lee	Always Navigable	—	—	Hertford—R Thames	27¾ miles
Little Ouse, *see* Ouse					
Nar	1751	1759	2,600	West Acre—King's Lynn	15 miles
Nene	1724 (4)	1761		Northampton—The Wash	91½ miles
Norwich & Lowestoft	1827	1833	c 150,000	Norwich—Lowestoft	6 7/8 miles (5)
Old Nene	1753			Mere Mouth—Outwell	26 1/8 miles
Ouse Great	1617 (patent)	1689		Bedford—The Wash	74¾ miles (via New Bedford) 85¾ miles (via Old West)
Ouse, Little	1669/70	c1677		Thetford—Gt Ouse	22½ miles
Roding	1737	1764	Not known	Ilford bridge—River Thames	1¾ miles
Sleaford Navigation (Slea and Kyme Eau)	1792	1794	16,000	Sleaford—River Witham	12¼ miles
Stort	1766	1769	Not known	Bishop's Stortford—River Lee	13¾ miles

(1)   Including 2 on the Bow Back Rivers and 2 on the Limehouse Cut
(2)   The Lee's locks have been reconstructed several times: they are now 85 ft x 19 ft
(3)   The number of staunches between Narborough and West Acre is uncertain
(4)   An Act was obtained in 1713 but no work done under it. The river from Peterborough to Thrapston was opened under the 1724 Act, and from Thrapston to Northampton under the Act of 1756
(5)   This includes the Haddiscoe Cut (2 3/8 miles) which leaves the River Yare at Reedham, and 4½ miles from Oulton Dike through Oulton Broad to the sea at Lowestoft. The rest of the navigation is included under the Yare or the Waveney

Greatest Number of Locks	Size of Boats Taken	Date of Disuse for Commercial Traffic	Date of Abandonment	Whether bought by Railway and Present Ownership
25 (inc 14 staunches	88ft x 14ft 6in (Isleham lock only)	c1895 Bury–Icklingham. 1920s remainder	Open from Gt Ouse–Jude's Ferry	A.W.A.
24 (1)	88ft x 19ft (2)	Open	Open	No. British Waterways Board
1 (and c.12 staunches) (3)	11ft 2in beam	1884 (to Narborough); 1938 lowest reach		A.W.A. (below floodgates, King's Lynn Conservancy)
44 (inc 10 staunches)	78ft x 13ft	1969 (N'hampton Wellingborough)	Open	A.W.A.
1	85ft x 20ft		Open	Yes. Great Eastern Rly. (6)
1	46ft x 11ft 6in	1971	Open	Middle Level Commissioners
21 (including 3 staunches)	(7)	See text	Open (see text)	A.W.A.
8 staunches	12ft 6in beam	By 1914	Open to Brandon Staunch	A.W.A.
1	Length unlimited width 17ft	Open	Open	No. Barking & Ilford Navigation Co (1961) Ltd
7	72ft x 14ft 6in	1878 (8)	1881 (9)	No. A.W.A.
15	78ft x 13ft	Open	Open	No. British Waterways Board

(6) The present authority for Oulton Broad is Waveney District Council and for Mutford or Oulton lock and Lowestoft harbour the British Transport Docks Board
(7) Great Barford–Brownshill Staunch, Earith, 100ft. Unlimited below Earith, although the maximum length through the lock at Denver is 70ft. Beam: Great Barford–Earith, 10ft 6in; Earith–Denver, 12ft 6in; Denver–The Wash, 17ft 6in
(8) The lower 6½ miles remained navigable until the 1940s
(9) Under the Sleaford Navigation (Abandonment) Act, 1878

River	Date of Act under which Work was begun	Date Wholly Opened	Approx Cost at Opening (£)	Terminal Points	Length
Stour	1705	c1709	6,500	Sudbury— Manningtree	25 miles
Waveney	1670 (2)	—	Not known	Bungay— R Yare	25 miles
Well Creek				Outwell— Salter's Lode	5 3/8 miles
Welland	1571	c1670 (3)	5 000	Stamford— The Wash	36 miles
Wissey	None			Oxborough Hithe— Gt Ouse (4)	12 miles
Witham	Always Navigable	—	—	Lincoln—Boston	33 miles
Yare	Always Navigable	—	—	Norwich— Yarmouth	31 miles (6)

(1)   Traffic continued up to Dedham until c1930
(2)   From Beccles to Bungay
(3)   This refers to the opening of the 'Stamford Canal' from Stamford to Market Deeping

Greatest Number of Locks	Size of Boats Taken	Date of Disuse for Commercial Traffic	Date of Abandonment	Whether bought by Railway and Present Ownership
15	47ft x 10ft 9in (Locks 95ft to take two lighters)	1916 (1)	1937	No. A.W.A.
3	70ft x 16ft above Beccles	Open to Beccles	Closed to Bungay in 1934	No. Gt Yarmouth Port and Haven Commissioners
1	46ft x 11ft 6in	1969	Open	M.L.C.
14	110ft long below Spalding; 35ft above: 30ft beam to Market Deeping	1863 to Stamford c1935 to Spalding	Open to Folly River Outfall (22½ miles)	A.W.A. (above Fosdyke bridge)
none	Fenland lighters	1943	Open	A.W.A.
3 plus 4 on the Witham Navigable Drains (5)	78ft x 15ft 2in	Open	Open	Leased to Great Northern in 19th Century. British Waterways Board
None	Not limited by locks	Open	Open	No. Gt Yarmouth Port and Haven Commissioners

(4)   Stoke Ferry is usually regarded as the head of navigation, but it is possible for light craft to navigate to Oxborough Hithe

(5)   For the Witham Navigable Drains, see under Section C

(6)   There are in addition several navigable branches

B. *Rivers with Uncompleted Navigation Works*

River	Date of Act under which Work was Begun	Money Spent £	Terminal Points Authorized	Length on which Work was Done
Ivel	1757	c20,000	Tempsford—Burnt Mill, Hitchin and to Black Horse Mill, Bygrave and to Shefford	Tempsford—Biggleswade (1758) extended to Shefford (1823)

C. *Canals, the Main Lines of which were completed as Authorized*

Canal	Date of Act under which Work was Begun	Date Wholly Opened	Approx Cost at Opening £	Terminal Points	Branches Built	Length
Bottisham Lode				R Cam—Lode	—	2½ miles
Burwell Lode				Pout Hall (Reach Lode)—Burwell		3¼ miles
Cottenham Lode				Cottenham—Old West River		2 miles
Counter Wash Drain				Welches Dam—Mepal		3 miles
Fossdyke	Roman			Torksey (R Trent)—Lincoln		11 miles
Lakenheath Lode				Lakenheath—Little Ouse		3¼ miles
Louth	1763	1770	27,500	Tetney Haven—Louth		11¾ miles
Mardyke	None			Purfleet—Bulphan Fen	Nav drains	c5 miles
Mundon	None	1832		R Blackwater—White House Farm, Mundon		1¼ miles

Greatest Number of Locks	Size of Boats taken taken	Date of Disuse for Commercial Traffic	Date of Abandonment	Later Events
11	110ft x 12ft	c1870	1876	Now administered by A.W.A.

Greatest Number of Locks	Size of Boats Taken	Date of Disuse for Commercial Traffic	Date of Abandonment	Whether bought by Railway and Present Ownership
1 staunch	12ft beam	c1900		A.W.A.
—	50ft x 13ft 6in	1963	Open	A.W.A.
—	Fenland lighters	1890s		A.W.A.
—	Fenland lighters		Open	A.W.A.
1	78ft x 15ft 2in	Open	Open	Leased by rly, 19th cent. British Waterways Board
1 staunch	Fenland lighters	1910s	Partly filled in	A.W.A.
8	72ft x 15ft 1in	1924	1924	Leased in 19th cent A.W.A.
—	NK (1)	c1870		No. No authority
1 tide-lock	NK	c1880		No. No authority

(1)   Known as 'dumpy' barges

Canal	Date of Act under which Work was Begun	Date Wholly Opened	Approx Cost at Opening £	Terminal Points	Length
Middle Level Navigations					
Bevills Leam	1630	1631		Angle Corner— Mere Mouth	5 miles
Black Ham Drain & Yaxley Lode				Mere Mouth— Yaxley	3 5/8 miles
Farcet River				King's Dyke— Yaxley	3 3/8 miles
Forty Foot River	1649	1651		Wells Bridge (Old Nene)— Welches Dam (Old Bedford)	10 7/8 miles
King's Dyke				Stanground Sluice —Whittlesey	4¼ miles
Middle Level Drain	1844	1848		Three Holes—Well Creek Aqueduct	2 miles
New Dyke (1)				Nightingale's Corner—Home Station	3¼ miles
Popham's Eau		1605		Popham's Eau End (Old Nene) —Three Holes	2¼ miles
Ramsey High Lode				Saunder's Bridge— Ramsey	1 1/8 miles
Sixteen Foot River	1649	1651		Three Holes— Forty Foot River	9 5/8 miles
Twenty Foot River	1649	1651		Angle Corner— Twenty Foot End (Old Nene)	10 3/8 miles
Whittlesey Dyke				Whittlesey—Floods Ferry (Old Nene)	6 1/8 miles

(1)   This has two branches: Monks Lode, 2½ miles, and Raveley Drain, 3 miles. The latter leads to the Woodwalton Fen Nature Reserve

reatest umber f Locks	Size of Boats Taken	Date of Disuse for Commercial Traffic	Date of Abandonment	Whether bought by Railway and Present Ownership
	46ft x 11ft 6in	1971	Open	M.L.C.
	as above	1971	Open	M.L.C.
	as above	1971	Closed	M.L.C.
	47ft x 10ft 9in	1971	Open	M.L.C. to Horseways lock A.W.A., Horseways—Old Bedford
	46ft x 11ft 6in	1971	Open	M.L.C.
	47ft x 10ft 9in	1971	Open	M.L.C.
	46ft x 11ft 6in	1971	Open	M.L.C.
	as above	1971	Open	M.L.C.
	as above	1971	Open	M.L.C.
	as above	1971	Open	M.L.C.
	as above	1971	Open	M.L.C.
	as above	1971	Open	M.L.C.

Canal	Date of Act under which Work was Begun	Date Wholly Opened	Approx Cost at Opening £	Terminal Points	Branches Built	Length
New Bedford River (Hundred Foot)	1649	1651		Earith—tail of Denver Sluice		20¼ miles
North Walsham & Dilham	1812	1826	29,300	Antingham Ponds—junct R Ant		8¾ miles (1)
Old Bedford River	1630	1637		Welches Dam—Old Bedford tidal sluice		12¼ miles
Reach Lode				R Cam—Reach	Burwell and Wicken Lodes	3 miles
Soham Lode	—	c1790		Gt Ouse—Soham		4 3/8 miles
Swaffham Bulbeck Lode				Swaffham Bulbeck—River Cam		3 3/8 miles
Tattershall (Gibson's) (3)	None	1787	(4)	R Witham—Tattershall		1 mile
Thorney River				Thorney—River Nene		3½ miles
Waterbeach Lode				Waterbeach—River Cam		½ mile
Wicken Lode (5)				Reach Lode—Wicken		1½ miles
Wisbech Canal	1794	1796	16 500	Wisbech—Outwell		5¼ miles

(1) The North Walsham & Dilham continues as the River Ant for another 8 miles to its junction with the River Bure
(2) No formal abandonment
(3) The Tattershall Canal was absorbed by the Horncastle Navigation (q.v.), and then reconstructed

Greatest Number of Locks	Size of Boats Taken	Date of Disuse for Commercial Traffic	Date of Abandonment	Whether bought by Railway and Present Ownership
—	unlimited	see text	Open	A.W.A.
6	50ft x 12ft 4in	1934	— (2)	North Walsham Canal Co Ltd
1 tidal sluice	beam 15ft 6in	1971	Open	A.W.A.
1	50ft x 13ft 6in	c1939	Open	A.W.A.
1 staunch	Fenland lighters	c1890	Open	A.W.A.
1	99ft x 15ft 6in	1900s	Lower section open	A.W.A.
1	NK			
2	50ft x 12ft		1937	A.W.A.
—	Fenland lighters	1920s	Closed	—
	Fenland lighters (now light craft only)	1940s	Open	A.W.A.
2	50ft x 10ft 10in	1922	1926	Wisbech Corporation

(4) Sold to the Horncastle Navigation for £840
(5) A number of other short lodes and branches throughout the Fens were navigable at some time

Canal	Date of Act under which Work was Begun	Date Wholly Opened	Approx Cost at Opening £	Terminal Points	Length
Witham Navigable Drains:					
Cowbridge Drain	Not known	1568	Not known	Maud Foster Drain—Hobhole Drain	1½ miles
Maud Foster Drain	do	1568	do	Cowbridge Drain—River Witham	2½ miles
East Fen Catchwater Drain	do	1634	do	West Fen Catchwater Drain—Stickford Bridge	4½ miles
West Fen Catchwater Drain	do	1634	do	Stone Bridge Drain—Revesby Bridge	6½ miles
Hobhole Drain	1801	1801	do	North of Midville—The Haven tidal doors	13¾ miles
Stone Bridge Drain	1801	1801	do	Maud Foster Drain—Northlands	4 miles
Frith Bank Drain	Not known	1802 c1216 as a drain	do	Anton's Gowt Lock—West Fen Drain	2 miles
West Fen Drain	1801	1801	do	Frith Bank Drain—Hough Bridge	8 miles
Newham Drain	Not known	Not known	do	Anton's Gowt Lock—West Fen Drain	3½ miles
Medlam Drain	do	do	do	West Fen Drain—Revesby Bridge	6½ miles

There are other branch drains in this system which have been or are navigable.

(1) These are Cowbridge and East Fen locks, which form junctions between Maud Foster Drain and West Fen Drain and Cowbridge Drains respectively

Greatest Number of Locks	Size of Boats taken	Date of Disuse for Commercial Traffic	Date of Abandonment	Whether bought by Railway and Present Ownership
None	60ft x 11ft	Open	Open	No. Anglian Water Authority
2 (1)	do	do	do	do
None	do	do	do	do
1 (closed)	do	do	do in part	do
1 (closed)	do	do	do in part	do
None	do	do	do	do
1 (2)	do	do	do	do
None	do	do	do	do
None	do	do	do	do
None	do	do	do	do

(2) Anton's Gowt lock is controlled by the British Waterways Board

D. *Canals the Main Lines of which were not Completed*
None

E. *Canals Partly Built but not Opened*
Romford. Authorized in 1875. One lock chamber built and a short length of canal dug but not completed.

F. *Canals Authorized but not Begun*
1812 London & Cambridge Junction Canal between Bishop's Stortford and Cambridge.
1826 Alford Canal between Alford (Lincs) and the North Sea.

APPENDIX II

Principal Engineering Works

A. *Inclined Planes*
None.

B. *Lifts*
None.

C. *Tunnels over 500 yards*
None.

D. *Outstanding Aqueducts*
None

INDEX

353